BOUDICA

Boudica

Iron Age Warrior Queen

Richard Hingley and Christina Unwin

Hambledon and London

London and New York

Hambledon and London

102 Gloucester Avenue, London NW1 8HX

175 Fifth Avenue
New York, NY 10010
USA

First Published 2005

ISBN 1 85285 438 3

A description of this book is available from the
British Library and from the Library of Congress.

Typeset by Carnegie Publishing, Lancaster,
and printed in Great Britain by Cambridge University Press.

Distributed in the United States and Canada
exclusively by Palgrave Macmillan,
A division of St Martin's Press.

Contents

Illustrations

Text Illustrations

Acknowledgements

We very are grateful to the following individuals for their comments and kind assistance in the preparation of this book.

Professor Colin Haselgrove of the University of Durham and Dr J. D. Hill of the British Museum for comments on the Iron Age sections of the book; Dr Philip de Jersey of the Celtic Coin Index, Institute of Archaeology, University of Oxford for information and advice about the coins of the Iceni; Dr. John Davies, Chief Curator at Norfolk Museums for assistance regarding Iron Age Norfolk and the Norwich Boudica Gallery; Trevor Ashwin of Norfolk Archaeology and Environment for advice on Iron Age Norfolk; Dr Rosalind Niblett of St Albans City Council for information about Verulamium; Philip Crummy of the Colchester Archaeological Trust for the considerable assistance that he provided with information about Iron Age and Roman Colchester and his careful comments on the text; Dr Paul Sealey of Colchester Museums for advice about Roman Colchester and other issues related to the events of AD 60 to 61; Francis Grew of the Museum of London for advice on Roman London and the Museum of London Boudica display; Professor Edith Hall of Durham University for media extracts about Boudica and several lively discussion of the subject; Theresa Calver for information on the stained glass window from Colchester Town Hall; Dr Roger Tomlin and R. D. Grasby for advice on the redrawing of Julius Classicanus's tomb; Alex Thorne, Iceni Brewery, Terry Deary and Martin Brown for help with the illustrations; Dr Valentina Vulpe and Dr Robin Skeates for translating Ubaldini's medieval Italian; Dr Ardle MacMahon for advice on published sources; Ruth Hingley for her comments on the text; University of Durham Library and the Sackler Library, Oxford for access to books and Professor Barry Cunliffe of the University of Oxford Institute of Archaeology and Professor Peter Wells of the University of Minnesota for the original idea for this book.

Special thanks are due to our editors, Martin Sheppard and Tony Morris, for their interest in the topic and meticulous attention to the editing and production of this book.

To the memory of Peter and Jean Unwin

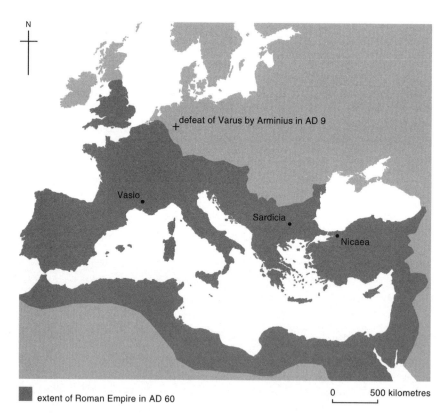

1. A map of the Roman Empire in AD 60, showing places outside Britain connected with the story of Boudica.

Introduction

Just about everyone who learns the history of England is taught a version of the story of Boudica. She is one of those rare individuals from the past who have become folk heroes and play an important role in many of the popular accounts of the history of England and of Britain.[1] In this select group are a variety of historical and legendary characters including Julius Caesar, King Arthur, Alfred the Great, Robin Hood and Winston Churchill. Boudica has long been popular in Britain and appears regularly in school history books and televisual accounts of the British past. She is familiar to us, yet at the same time a shadowy figure. Although she lived in the ancient past and is recorded by our history, we really know very little about her, despite the fact that she has been studied for almost five centuries. Boudica's story is sufficiently dramatic that it has excited, enthused and, sometimes, revolted generations of people.

Information about her is to be found in books and articles, popular television dramas, plays, galleries in museums, festivals and novels together with many webpages on the internet – a web-search in June 2004 located an astonishing 89,400 web pages with references to 'Boadicea' or 'Boudica'. In the past, Boudica was the subject of an equally wide variety of representations, including works of art (paintings, engravings and sculptures), poems, books, political works and plays. All these draw in some way upon the historical and archaeological knowledge that we possess, yet they represent her in widely differing ways.

In brief, Boudica was a woman who appears to have been the wife of the king (or leader) of one of the British tribes (or peoples), the Iceni. She led a rebellion against the Roman government seventeen years after the initial invasion of Britain by the Romans. We know that she lived through the first sixteen years of the Roman occupation of Britain and that she died resisting Roman rule, with the aid of her own tribe and others, probably in AD 60 to 61. Boudica did this through direct action that led to the destruction of several towns and thousands of deaths. She was eventually defeated by the Roman army and died, either from ill health or by suicide. She is one of a number of native leaders who, according to Roman literary sources, led opposition, revolts or rebellions against Roman rule in the early years of the empire.[2] These included Viriatus in Iberia,[3] Vercingetorix in Gaul,[4] Civilis and Arminius (Herman) in Germany,[5] and Caratacus in Britain.[6]

Boudica's life as a member of the aristocracy of an Iron Age tribe when Rome dominated Britain during the first century AD, the information for the rebellion that she led against Rome and a review of her story through to the internet age are all included. We shall explore the knowledge that we have for Boudica, derived from the classical writers who wrote about her. The detail provided by the two classical authors does not mean, however, that we actually know very much about her. The Roman accounts were written by wealthy and powerful men who lived at the Mediterranean core of the Roman Empire and who had certainly never met her nor even visited Britain. They also wrote some time after the end of the events that they described. For these two writers, the tale of Boudica was useful because it provided a moral story for their intended audiences in Rome and the Mediterranean. The only other source that we have for her is the archaeological material that has been collected during the past few hundred years which serves to support some of the classical writing.

All knowledge of Boudica seems to have been lost during the decline and fall of Roman power over Britain during the late fourth to sixth centuries and the next surviving written references to her do not appear until the early sixteenth century. With the rediscovery of the classical sources during the Renaissance, the views that were expressed by the classical authors appealed to the later writers who took up her story. Writers and artists, with different aims and ambitions, made moral observations about their own societies by developing the story of Boudica. From the sixteenth century onwards writers and artists portrayed Boadicea in a wide variety of ways. She became a popular figure in history books and plays.

Boudica has been given a variety of other names over the past few

Falkirk

Anglesey

Wall
Mancetter
Metchley
Coventry
Grandford
Stonea
Witcham
Gravel
Ashill
Caistor-by-Norwich
Thetford
Rendham
Camulodunum
Verulamium
Londinium

100   0   100 kilometres

land over 200 metres OD

2. A map of Britain, showing places connected with the story of Boudica.

hundred years, in particular 'Boudicca' and 'Boadicea', but Boudica appears to be the correct form of the spelling of her name. Research on Celtic languages in Europe has indicated that Boudica's name means 'victory'. Boadicea remains, however, a better-known version of her name. The first part of the book, 'Boudica', explores the evidence for the 'real' character; while the second part, 'Boadicea', reviews the stories woven around her from the sixteenth century to the twenty-first.[7] People interpreted her in the context of their own times and explored their concerns and interests through the example she provided.

PART ONE

Boudica

1

Iron Age and Roman Britain

The Ancient Britons were by no means savages before the conquest, and they had already made great strides in civilization, e.g. they buried each other in long round wheelbarrows (agriculture) and burnt each other alive (religion) under the guidance of even older Britons called Druids or Eisteddfods ...

The Roman conquest was, however, a *Good Thing*, since the Britons were only natives at that time.

W. C. Sellar and R. J. Yeatman *1066 and All That* 1930, 10–11.

Sellar and Yeatman's book, *1066 and All That*, was a parody of school teaching and contemporary attitudes to British history. Yet their observations about the way that people thought about the pre-Roman period and the conquest of Britain by the Romans still echo the way that some people understand these times. Television programmes and popular books sometimes still suggest that Iron Age populations in Britain were effectively primitive barbarians and that the Roman Empire brought them the gifts of peace and civilisation. These ideas stem from the classical authors who wrote about Britain, presenting us with a one-sided argument – for we do not have a contemporary British account of life before and during the conquest. The ancient Britons left no written records. When we do hear their views, as is the case with the speeches that are given to Boudica by the Roman authors, they are written from a Roman perspective.

The immediately pre-Roman period in Britain is known as the Iron Age,[1] so-called because it was the first period in Britain when iron was in regular use. Despite the fact that this metal is not common in the archaeological record until the third century BC at the earliest, the Iron Age is usually thought to have commenced in the eighth century BC. As such, the name 'Iron Age' appears to be inappropriate, but it is well

established. The Iron Age is usually supposed to have come to an end
when the Romans invaded Britain. The invasion of AD 43 resulted in
large areas of the south and east being brought into the empire. Other
parts of Britain were conquered during the second half of the first
century AD. The Iron Age therefore lasted rather longer in some areas
than in others. For instance, in the territory of the Iceni it effectively
lasted until AD 60 to 61, when the tribe was defeated and the territory
annexed by Rome.

From the mid first millennium BC onwards, there was an increasingly
complex series of developments within Britain.[2] Iron Age society was
characterised by communities who lived in settlements of varying sizes.[3]
Throughout much of the south of Britain it was usual for these settlements to be enclosed by some form of boundary – an earthen bank and
ditch, a timber-built palisade or a stone wall. They contained houses of
round or oval plan, the typical types of domestic housing for many Iron
Age communities (figure 3). Modern reconstructions demonstrate that
they would have been warm and comfortable.

The communities that lived in these settlements had a well-developed
agricultural economy, derived from over three thousand years of experience. It was based upon mixed arable and pastoral farming.[4] People
used hand-made pottery and were largely self-sufficient. Finds of
weaponry and jewellery indicate that some people had access to objects
that showed their status to other members of the community. In addition, the weaponry suggests that society was dominated by a warrior
aristocracy.[5] It is likely that influence and power in some Iron Age societies was partly derived from success in warfare and that people
represented this power through the ownership of elaborate weapons.
Other objects were also used to indicate status. We shall see that one of
the Roman authors mentioned that Boudica wore a golden necklace,
possibly a torc, or an object similar to the recently discovered gold necklace from the Winchester treasure.[6] It is indeed likely that Boudica
would have worn such an object, for torcs were associated with religious
and political authority in at least some Iron Age societies.[7] Torcs were
penannular metal bands that were worn around the neck. Over one
hundred gold torcs have been found in Iron Age hoards in Britain,[8] a
major example being that from the territory of the Iceni close to Snettisham. Some objects that were used to demonstrate status and power

3. An Iron Age roundhouse from West Stow in Suffolk, with a cut-away section to show the construction and interior. (*Drawn by Christina Unwin. Reconstructed from the plan in West 1989, figure 19*).

4. The Iron Age hillfort at Maiden Castle in Dorset. (*Crown copyright. NMR*)

came from the Continent and from Ireland, while others were copied from such items. This shows that people travelled between the Continent and Britain and that objects passed into and across Britain. Many communities, however, were probably settled and stayed in one place with no particular need to travel long distances.

The hillforts of Wessex and the Welsh Marches are perhaps the most famous of the Iron Age settlements in Britain.[9] These hillforts were significant places within the landscape during the period from 600 BC to around the end of the first millennium BC, some developing into major centres (figure 4). They were defended hilltop settlements that may have acted as stores for the surplus of a community and were, perhaps, places to which people came in times of trouble. Hillforts are not common, however, in every area of Britain. In particular, they were not common across eastern Britain and they were rare in the territory of the Iceni.

The existence of weapons and hillforts indicate that people did not always live peaceful lives. We do not know, however, how usual it was for communities to be in conflict during the Iron Age. The Roman writers suggest that war was common in 'barbarian' society, but it is likely that the conditions that led to warfare amongst these people were in part a result of the Roman expansion into their territory. The enlargement of the Roman Empire across western Europe resulted in great instability; prior to these times people in Britain may have lived for much of the time in comparative peace.

We do not know very much about the nature of Iron Age warfare. The weapons suggest that hand-to-hand fighting was usual. Julius Caesar, who invaded Britain in 55 BC and again in 54 BC, wrote that the ancient British used chariots in war, and other classical authors also refer to chariots.[10] They were probably common in Iron Age Britain; examples have been found buried with the dead in the Yorkshire Wolds, although some regard these as carts rather than war chariots.[11] Carts were probably a common form of transport from around 200 to 100 BC in certain areas of Britain.[12] The careful excavation of one new example in 2001 by the British Museum, and a life-sized well-researched reconstruction of the vehicle, indicate that some of these Yorkshire carts or chariots were light and manoeuvrable with good suspension, and that they might well have been used in battle. War chariots were still in use in the territory of

the Iceni during the middle of the first century AD, as they are mentioned
in the context of Boudica's rebellion, indicating that this style of warfare
continued to be used in East Anglia at this time.[13] War chariots probably ceased to be fashionable elsewhere in Britain, not having an obvious
function within the Roman province, where warfare was not permitted.
The dramatic idea that Boudica's chariot had scythes fitted to the outside of the wheels has no historical basis;[14] ancient British chariots were
light affairs that served to take significant people to the battlefields and
away again.

Both of the classical authors, Tacitus and Dio, who wrote about
Boudica suggested that women were often chosen as leaders in Britain.
From their accounts it appears that women may also often have led their
people into battle. We know of one other female leader, Cartimandua,[15]
who was the head of a people called the Brigantes and who ruled over
an extensive territory in northern England. She dominated this area for
some time after the initial conquest of the south and east with the support of the Roman government. We do not know, however, how usual
female leaders were during the Iron Age. Tacitus and Dio may have been
exaggerating the actual situation in order to make a particular point. We
shall see that the Roman men who wrote the histories found the idea of
female rulers outrageous but at the same time exciting. They may have
been seeking to emphasise the barbarity of the Britons by stressing
female involvement in politics and warfare.

From around 150 BC the south east of Britain, including the areas that
are now Kent, Essex and Hertfordshire, underwent a series of changes
that mark a radical break from earlier centuries.[16] These events are used
by archaeologists to divide the period that they name the 'middle' Iron
Age from the 'late' Iron Age. Objects from societies on the Continent,
probably obtained by people within south-eastern Britain through trade,
become increasingly common from this time. During the later first century BC Roman power and influence eventually assumed a key role in
Britain as the empire spread into north-western Europe (figure 5). As a
result, from around 20 BC, south-eastern England was increasingly influenced by the culture of the people of the area that is now northern
France.[17] It is often argued that this culture was 'Romanised' because it
was characterised by the importation of objects from the Mediterranean
and the Continent, and also by the adoption of new ways of living.

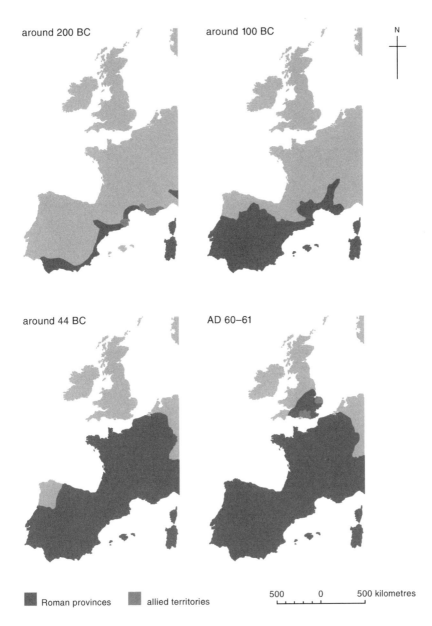

around 200 BC

around 100 BC

N

around 44 BC

AD 60–61

Roman provinces   allied territories

500   0   500 kilometres

5. Roman imperial expansion. (*After Millett 1990, figure 1*)

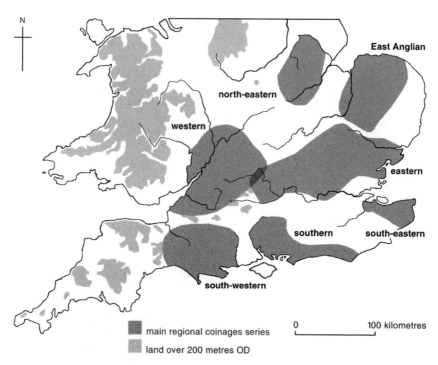

6. Late Iron Age coinages. (*After Millett 1990, figure 3*)

When archaeologists talk about 'Romanised' culture, they mean objects influenced by styles that existed in the Mediterranean and the Roman Empire in general.

British society in the immediately pre-Roman period appears to have featured a range of small political groups, known to archaeologists as 'tribes'. Boudica was the wife of a leader of one of these tribes. We have information about these tribal groupings from the writings of classical authors and also from the evidence of the coins produced by these groups. Julius Caesar's account is a particularly important source of information. He described the groups that he encountered during his two invasions of the south east in 55 and 54 BC within his broader account of the campaigns that he conducted in Gaul (*De Bello Gallico*). We also have detailed accounts of the tribes of southern Britain in the early first century AD from the classical authors who wrote about the successful invasion of Claudius. Virtually none of the names of the tribal groups mentioned by Caesar appear to be the same in the later texts, with the exception of the people of Kent (Cantium), the Trinovantes of the area that is Essex today and perhaps, as we shall see, the Iceni.[18] From Caesar's account, and from those of later classical writers, we also have the names of a number of the men and women who ruled these tribes.

During the final few centuries BC, various tribes produced regional coinages (figure 6). Coins were first introduced into Britain from continental societies that had been producing them for some time.[19] Modern society uses coinage as a very basic element in our everyday lives. It is easy to view Iron Age coins in a similar way. Coins would, however, have been totally new to the people of Iron Age Britain. Some coins were of gold and silver and would have been very valuable, probably too precious to have been of use as currency. They may rather have formed a type of bullion – a metal reserve out of which impressive metal artefacts were made.[20] The relationships that were forged through the exchange of coinage included treaties, tribute, ransom, dowries for important marriages and the payment of mercenary soldiers. Coins may also have been passed around between people in order to enable wealth to be exchanged, but it is unlikely that they were used to buy and sell directly. During the later Iron Age some tribal groups started to produce coins in bronze and it is thought that these may sometimes have been used directly for exchange and trade due to their far inferior value. This is uncertain, however, as we really do not know that people were involved in market exchange at this time. Powerful individuals within a tribe may have given coins to their followers to encourage their loyalty and also as an indication of the community to which they belonged – in other words, as tokens of their tribal identity. In the case of the Iceni, Iron Age coins are hard to interpret and cannot often even be given an accurate date.

A few of the coins series actually show variants on the names of the individuals given in the Roman historical sources and also more rarely the names of tribes. Occasionally these individuals are given the title *rex* ('king') on the coin, suggesting that certain people were developing a knowledge of Latin. The use of the term *rex* may indicate that the tribal leader had a special relationship with Rome,[21] for certain important tribal leaders in late Iron Age Britain had special alliances that tied them to Rome.[22] Although it is impossible to establish a complete political history from the coins, this has long been a popular activity of archaeologists and coin specialists. The information from the coins allows us to produce a speculative map to show the number and extent of Iron Age tribal groups (figure 7), including the Trinovantes and the Iceni, peoples who rebelled in AD 60 to 61 under Boudica. This suggests that over a wide area people felt a common identity at this time and that there was some form of centralised political leadership exercised by the male or female 'kings'. Many of the hillforts of southern Britain appear to have gone out of use by the latter part of the Iron Age. During this period, sites called *oppida* characterised the top of the settlement hierarchy across much of the south and east.[23] The term is derived from the Latin word *oppidum* meaning 'town'. One of best understood of these sites is centred on the area that constitutes modern-day Colchester (pre-Roman name, Camulodunon).[24] Another example was at Verlamion, close to St Albans in Hertfordshire.

These *oppida* were not fully 'towns' in the Roman or in the modern sense, being characterised by a dispersed pattern of settlement. For instance, at Camulodunon we know of several distinct areas of occupation inside an extensive but discontinuous series of dykes – banks and ditches (figure 8). The site also appears to have a high-status settlement at Gosbecks and a variety of rich burials, particularly at Stanway and

7. The Iron Age tribes of Britain. (*After Cunliffe 1991, figure 8.1*)

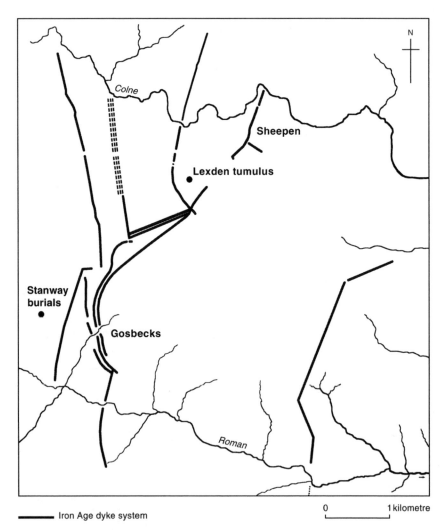

Colne

Sheepen

Lexden tumulus

Stanway
burials

Gosbecks

Roman

N

▬▬▬ Iron Age dyke system

0   1 kilometre

8. Late Iron Age Camulodunon. Some of the dykes were actually built in early
Roman times. (*After Crummy 1997, plan on p. 14*)

Lexden.[25] Although *oppida* in general represented a highly variable class of site, they appear to have shared a number of characteristics.[26] Often, as at Camulodunon, *oppida* had discontinuous dyke systems, while there is usually evidence for high-status occupation indicated by large quantities of continental imports connected with eating and drinking, including amphorae, other pottery and glassware. Verlamion was broadly comparable to Camulodunon, having a number of areas of occupation and activity as well as wealthy burials, to either side of a marshy zone alongside the River Ver.[27]

Where we have evidence for houses on these sites, it appears that the standard roundhouse of the British Iron Age was no longer common. Instead, a variety of timber-built rectangular buildings had become typical of houses on *oppida* and other settlements in the south east during the later Iron Age. These houses may have been influenced by architectural traditions within continental societies that had been incorporated within the Roman Empire. Forms of everyday items also changed in these areas. There was a strong tradition of hand-made pottery across much of Britain in the early and middle Iron Age;[28] in the late Iron Age many of the communities of the south and east adopted the continental tradition of making pottery on a potter's wheel.

The rich burials of the late Iron Age elite clearly illustrate the new ways of living being introduced into the south east of Britain.[29] The objects that were placed with the dead as grave goods are often complete and remain impressive indicators of the social changes that were taking place. A very rich burial at Welwyn (Hertfordshire), placed in a grave pit, probably dates to the third quarter of the first century BC.[30] The body of the dead person was cremated and accompanied by five amphorae from Italy, which would have held well over one hundred litres of wine. There were also a strainer for removing dregs from the wine, a silver drinking cup of Italian manufacture, mixing bowls, and thirty pottery vessels, presumably intended for feasting. The amphorae found in burials of this type and on settlement sites and *oppida* in general indicate that aristocratic members of the tribes in pre-Roman times had access to wine and olive oil imported from the Mediterranean. Imported pottery and metalwork suggest that these important people ate and drank in new ways using items that were derived from continental societies that formed part of the Roman Empire. The items of jewellery indicate that they had adopted new fashions of dress similar to those of people on the Continent.

Towards the end of the Iron Age it is likely that one of these tribal groups expanded to take control over many of the others. Cunobelinus, perhaps king of the tribe called the Catuvellauni, is described as 'king of the Britons' (*Britannorum rex*) by the Roman author Suetonius.[31] It has been proposed recently that Cunobelinus was one of the rulers who had a particularly close relationship with Rome and symbolised his power on the coinage that he produced by drawing upon images derived from imperial Rome.[32] His coins differ from many earlier examples in showing the head of the king in a way that is derived directly from Roman coins with their images of the emperor. In these terms, the coins of Cunobelinus are more Romanised than those of many of his predecessors; he effectively copied Roman symbolism to indicate his own status and power. By this time Rome had extended its power over the whole of the Mediterranean and was expanding across western Europe. The British ruler was effectively shown in Roman guise in order to symbolise his connection with Rome and power within Britain. Cunobelinus's tribal capital appears to have been at Camulodunon. Although he was dead by the time of the invasion of AD 43, Camulodunon was, as we shall see, the main target of the initial Roman invasion of Britain. Perhaps his close relationship with Rome was not renewed by his successors and this may have provided one reason for the Roman invasion in AD 43.

Recent work on the details of the character of regional coin distribution and the nature of the settlement record suggests that this picture of centralised tribes in the pre-Roman period is rather too simple.[33] The fact that, at the most, three of the tribes that were mentioned by Caesar survived into the first century AD may be significant in showing that the late Iron Age political system in Britain was highly unstable. Perhaps tribal groups developed and declined over the course of the late first century BC and early first century AD. In reality, in some areas of Britain, *oppida* and high-status settlements were quite common;[34] a variety of such sites can be identified in each of the tribal territories. In addition, there are far too many individual coin styles to represent the Iron Age groups recorded by the Roman authors. This suggests that there were more tribal groupings, many of which we are unaware of because their names did not survive within the political geography of Roman Britain.

It is likely that tribes in later Iron Age Britain were less centralised than has often been supposed, and that political hierarchies were more flexible and networks of power less extensive than past interpretations have suggested. There may have been a variety of small sub-tribal groups, each with its own leader and aristocratic elite. At certain times these may have come together to form a broader tribal grouping under a single tribal leader, for instance when threatened with invasion by Rome.[35] Cunobelinus may have had overall, though not complete, control over a number of these tribes. This would explain why his tribal capital, Camulodunon, appears to been located within the territory of another tribe, the Trinovantes, after the Roman conquest. Perhaps Cunobelinus dominated the Trinovantes and his coinage was distributed as a way of tying the aristocracies of other tribes to him across an extensive territory.

Archaeological evidence from the late Iron Age in south-eastern Britain indicates that the aristocracies of these relatively decentralised tribes were obtaining increasing numbers of goods from contacts with the expanding Roman Empire. Their burials suggest the adoption of Roman-style practices of eating, drinking, dressing and appearance, while the *oppida* may indicate the introduction of certain features of Mediterranean-style living.[36]

Another topic of relevance to the story of Boudica is that of the druids. The classical authors tell us that the druids formed a type of religious and philosophical group in Roman Gaul and Britain.[37] We know from the writings of Julius Caesar that druids were an important part of ancient British society in the middle of the first century BC. Accounts from later Roman authors indicate that they survived well into the first century AD,[38] although the Romans carried out a campaign to destroy them. It is often suggested that the Roman government objected strongly to the druids because of their practice of human sacrifice, but it is more likely that this objection arose because these people acted as a focus for acts of resistance. It has also been thought that the druids have a link to the story of Boudica due to the fact that her rebellion broke out around the time when a Roman army was attacking the stronghold of the druids on Anglesey.[39] It has even been suggested that

one motive for the events of AD 60 to 61 may have been the Romans'
suppression of the druids, which would suggest that the rebellion was
actually a religious war.[40] Despite this, the two classical authors who
wrote about Boudica do not mention the druids in connection with
either her life or the rebellion.

The Romans viewed Britain as a primitive and barbaric place.[41] Authors
from the Mediterranean, including Pytheas and Caesar, had visited
Britain and written about it during the first millennium BC.[42] These
authors wrote accounts of an area that they did not know in detail, viewing Britain as a remote and isolated island, populated by uncivilised
peoples with peculiar ways. Julius Caesar wrote that:

> By far the most civilised are those living in Kent (a purely maritime dis-
> trict) ... Most of the tribes of the interior do not grow corn but live on milk
> and meat and wear skins.[43]

Other accounts of the lives and culture of the ancient Britons present
equally dismissive views.

Later classical authors, writing between the time of Caesar and that of
Tacitus, portrayed Britain in a different but cognate way. In accounts of
this date Britain was described as an island that was ripe to be incorporated into the expanding Roman Empire.[44] The location of Britain was
of considerable significance to classical authors: 'Ocean' represented a
divine spirit to the Roman mind.[45] It had long been felt that there was
a need to define a boundary to the territory of the Romans. Campaigning beyond it was a particularly challenging activity; at the same time
the conquest of Britain was also the conquest of Ocean.[46] This special
significance partly accounts for their interest in the island and its eventual conquest. When he successfully invaded the island in AD 43, the
Emperor Claudius was conquering not just new territory but also effectively the spirit of the ocean itself.

Despite the dismissive accounts of Iron Age society in these Roman
literary sources, the archaeological evidence tells us that the people of
Britain were not primitive barbarians at this time but had their own
civilisation.[47] We know that communities all over Britain had agricultural economies and lived in impressive settlements.[48] Even before the
conquest of AD 43, this civilisation drew upon the culture of people who

lived in continental Europe, already part of the empire. The growing interest of the native British aristocracy in Roman ways of life probably assisted the conquest of Britain by the Roman army and administration.[49] Some of the native leaders accepted Roman rule without much opposition; others may have provided direct assistance to the Roman army during its invasion.

The Roman conquest began in AD 43 with the arrival of a vast Roman army. The initial phase of the invasion was masterminded by the Emperor Claudius, whose army of around 40,000 men crossed the Channel and fought several minor battles. Claudius arrived shortly before a decisive battle at Camulodunon, transporting war-elephants by ship from the eastern part of the empire. The victorious Roman army then continued northwards and eastwards, conquering large areas and incorporating territory into the new province over a period of years. This was achieved by defeating opposition and establishing forts and roads to help to control the country.[50] The forts varied in size, according to the nature of the army unit that was housed within them. After Claudius's triumphal arrival at the *oppidum* of Camulodunon, a fortress was established to dominate the settlement.[51] The name of the *oppidum* was now Romanised to 'Camulodunum'.[52] This fortress was the base of the Twentieth Legion (figures 9 and 10) – legions were the elite infantry units that formed the basis of the Roman army. The remains of six skulls were found in the ditch of this fortress, two of them showed possible sword cuts, and it has been suggested that they may represent native victims of the Roman army,[53] although this is not conclusive.

Some of the tribes of Britain came swiftly under the direct control of the empire as their native leaders capitulated or were defeated by the Roman army. Some individuals resisted with particularly determination. One was Caratacus. He appears to have been one of the sons of Cunobelinus and fought a continuous campaign against the Romans between AD 43 and 51, when he was captured and taken to Rome.[54] He was pardoned by the Emperor Claudius after a speech that established the myth of Caratacus as a brave and noble barbarian.[55]

Several other tribes were left under the direct control of friendly native kings and queens (figure 11). In reality, the close proximity of the Roman army to these tribes meant that they were effectively incorporated into

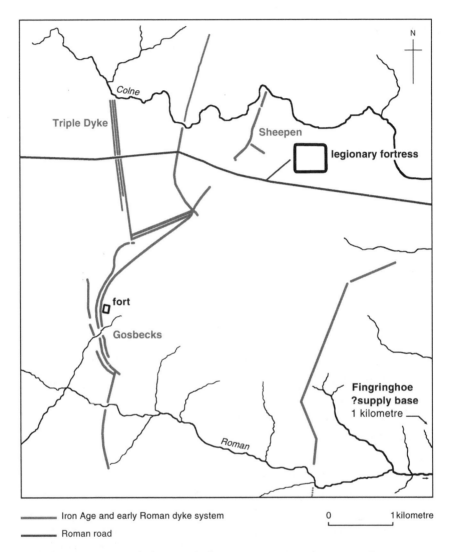

Triple Dyke

Colne

Sheepen

legionary fortress

N

fort

Gosbecks

Fingringhoe
?supply base
1 kilometre

Roman

Iron Age and early Roman dyke system

Roman road

0   1 kilometre

9. Early Roman Camulodunum. (*After Crummy 1997, plan on p. 34*)

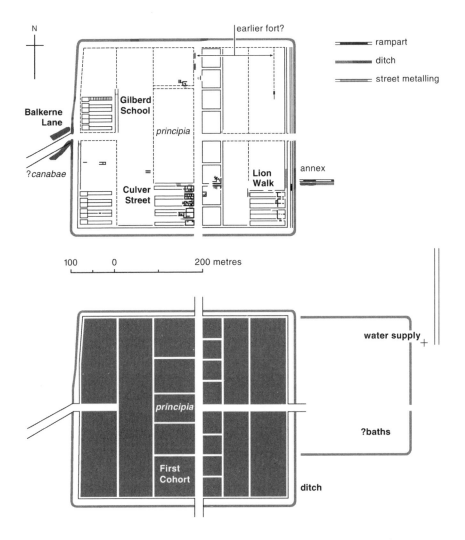

10. The fortress at Camulodunum. (*After Crummy 1999, figures 2 and 3*)

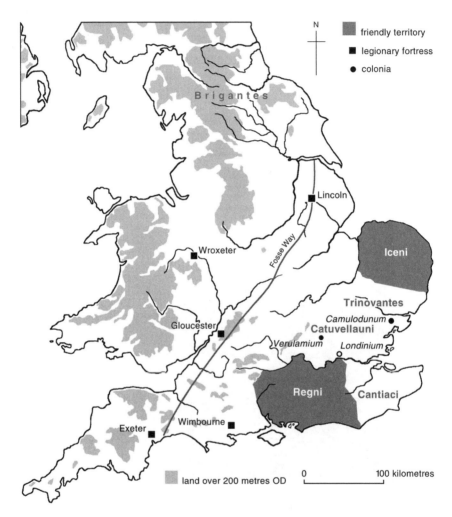

11. Early Roman Britain and the rulers friendly to the Romans. (*After Cunliffe 1988, figure 61*)

the empire while being nominally free. Rome usually absorbed friendly kingdoms into its empire on the death of their leaders. Two of the three cooperative rulers that we know about in Britain were a woman, Carti-mandua of the Brigantes, and a man, Prasutagus of the Iceni.[56] The third friendly king was Cogidubnus (or possibly Togidubnus), possibly the builder of a palatial villa at Fishbourne (Sussex) and the ruler of a tribe called the Regni.[57]

Southern Britain was gradually conquered during the first and early second centuries and the tribes of these friendly rulers were assimilated by the Romans into the province of Britannia. The Roman army ensured that newly conquered territory was settled before moving on to the north and west once peaceful conditions had been established. At Colchester the fortress was abandoned around AD 49 to 50 and a colony – a town for retired soldiers – established. This was called *Colonia Victricensis*, effectively 'Colony of the Victorious', providing urban amenities for retired legionaries, each of whom received an allocation of land.[58] The colony at Colchester was a town populated primarily by Roman citizens, who had come into Britain as legionary soldiers, and their dependants.[59] The establishment of a colony would have required the removal of lands from the existing owners. It has been estimated that, if three thousand veteran soldiers were settled, then this would have resulted in the removal of around 37,750 hectares (90,500 acres) of land from native use at Colchester. This is equivalent to an area around the colony with a radius of five and a half miles (nine kilo-metres).[60] According to the Roman author Tacitus, the establishment and development of this colony was one of the major reasons for the revolt of AD 60 to 61.

The removal of native property around the colony evidently did not directly affect all of the wealthy natives. The pre-Roman settlement at Gosbecks, within Camulodunon, was still in use during the conquest period. A Roman fort was built here and a temple with an associated theatre was added later. The rich native burial site at Stanway, close to Gosbecks, also continued to be used after the Roman conquest until around AD 60. The evidence from Gosbecks and Stanway suggests that at least part of the aristocracy of the tribal community at Camulodunon was left in place by the Roman administration when the fortress and later colony were established.[61] Perhaps in this case the new Roman

settlers were careful to cooperate with the native aristocracy of the tribe
and left them in possession of their land. The fortress and succeeding
colony were planted into the native landscape alongside the pre-Roman
oppidum, leaving the native centre at Gosbecks alone but presumably
dispossessing others.

Victorian descriptions of Roman Britain often show the Roman
towns as settlements of incoming Romans surrounded by primitive
native peoples who continued to live in their Iron Age settlements
during the period of Roman rule. At Colchester we have such a colony
of Roman citizens. The real situation in the Roman province was, however, very different. Colchester was the only colony established by Rome
during the first forty years of the new Roman province. At the same
time a variety of other towns were developed.[62] These towns were vital
to the government of the province but they were usually built, unlike
Colchester, with the full involvement of the native elite. The government of a province was entrusted to two Roman officials. The provincial
governor was responsible for the army and the government of the
province, while the procurator was in charge of taxation. Both had
major roles in the rebellion of Boudica. The Romans were not able to
send enough junior administrators to carry out all of the functions of
government across all of the provinces that made up the Roman Empire.
In order to establish a new province, it was necessary for the Roman
administration to create local self-government.

The Romans usually attempted to establish a new civilian system of
self-government within the provinces, with the traditional tribal elite
taking control of the new local units called *civitates* (cities or city
states).[63] These appear to have been developed from the pre-Roman
tribes and usually adopted pre-exiting names; the records of the names
of the *civitates* actually constitute the source for the names of many of
the Iron Age tribes of Britain. It is likely, however, that there would have
been many changes in the organisation and boundaries of the individual tribes during their reconstitution into *civitates.* Most of the *civitates*
appear to have been developed with a single town, or *civitas* capital,
which acted as the basis of local government within the province. *Civitas* capitals often developed close to the previous tribal centre – the
oppidum. A very clear example of such a development is provided by
archaeological evidence for the site of Verulamium (St Albans), which

fell within the *civitas* of the Catuvellauni. This town grew in the middle of the first century AD on the site of the *oppidum* of Verlamion.

Verulamium was generally similar in form to the colony at Colchester. Its significance is indicated by the fact that, when the Romans built the main road that linked London and the midlands, Watling Street, it was routed through the town.[64] In due course it grew into an extensive settlement, with a regular street system and a variety of public buildings.[65] At Colchester the town was built over the abandoned legionary fortress and reused much of the pre-existing structure. It was also, as we have seen, imposed onto the pre-existing native settlement. At Verulamium the development of the town provides a direct contrast to the colony, appearing to evolve as the result of the development in Roman form of a pre-existing settlement.[66] The town at Verulamium developed as a native centre of government, created by the local aristocracy, but with new ideas about architecture and urban planning that they derived from Rome.

The *civitas* system was probably established as the Roman army moved forward into the province. It is often viewed as the vital building-block of Roman imperialism. The *civitas* was governed and controlled by the native elite but with the assistance and support of the Roman administration. It was also the centre for the taxation of the *civitas*. The money from this tax was paid to the Roman state and used to support the Roman army and central administration. The development of Verulamium by AD 60 may well suggest that at least one of the *civitates* within the province was acting as a centre of local self-government by the time of Boudica's rebellion. Some of the friendly kingdoms, although not formally a part of the province, may also have had towns that were comparable with Verulamium. At Chichester (Sussex), Winchester (Hampshire) and Silchester (Berkshire) *civitas* capitals started to develop within the territory that is likely to have belonged to Cogidubnus.[67] After this early beginning, the *civitates* acted as successful centres of local government throughout the history of the Roman province and many grew into impressive towns.

We, therefore, have an impression of the character of Roman Britain in AD 60. The army had moved further north and west, having conquered and apparently settled the south and east. Within these southern and eastern areas, civil government was being put in place, based on the developing network of *civitas* capitals. In the military areas, control of territory was still in the hands of the army, although in due course *civitates* were established in these areas as the army moved further into the north and west. All the areas of the Roman province were linked together by roads, which assisted the army to move soldiers and supplies and were increasingly useful for the traders who moved between towns.

To turn to the Iceni themselves, in his account of the invasions of 55 and 54 BC, Julius Caesar mentions a tribe living to the north of the Thames called the Cenimagni. It is thought possible that these were the people who were later to be known as the Iceni, although this is not certain. Several of the tribes of late Iron Age Britain have names that can be translated, but the meaning of the name 'Iceni' is unclear.[68] It is likely that the name used by Caesar may even have meant 'Iceni magni', the 'great', 'strong' or perhaps 'extensive' Iceni,[69] referring to the fact that they were a powerful people or that they occupied or controlled an extensive area. The general lack of correspondence between the names used by Caesar and the later references to British tribal groupings leaves a degree of uncertainty about the pre-conquest existence of the tribe. The Iceni, however, appear to have been one of the late Iron Age tribes not directly incorporated into the Roman province during the invasion of AD 43. The first that we hear of them, except for Caesar's possible reference, is in around AD 47 to 48.[70] At this time, the Roman author Tacitus tells us that the tribe rose up in revolt.[71] They appear to have been provoked into action as a result of the attempt of the Roman governor, Ostorius Scapula, to disarm suspect Britons and to establish a forward line of control, probably at the rivers Trent and Severn. Tacitus tells us that before this time they had come into alliance with the Romans without battle.[72] These events suggest very strongly that the Iceni were defined as a friendly kingdom during the initial invasion of Britain and remained so for a generation. We know that the Iceni were ruled by Prasutagus in AD 60 to 61, which indicates that they were not absorbed into the empire after their initial uprising. In turn this suggests either that the ruling aristocracy was not involved in the revolt of AD 47 to 48, or that Prasutagus was placed in control of the tribe after the revolt.

Despite the scarcity of references to the tribe in the historical sources, we do have a wealth of archaeological information for the Iron Age from this area.[73] This includes evidence derived from excavation and individual finds of archaeological objects, especially of the coins. The best evidence that we have for the location and extent of the tribal territory of the Iceni is provided by the Iron Age coinages that they are thought to have issued (figures 12 and 13). The distribution of types of coins that have been related to the tribe covers all of the modern county of Norfolk and parts of Suffolk, Cambridgeshire,[74] Essex and East Leicestershire,[75] including the area of the central Fenlands around March.[76] As many as 15,000 silver Iron Age coins are usually attributed to the Iceni.[77] There appear to be at least sixty-five different coin types and, in addition to the silver examples, some gold coins have been found. The earliest of the gold coins, which may have been issued by around 65 BC,[78] have been found both singly and in hoards. Some coins have legends (including ANTED, ECEN and ECE) that have been taken to represent either the abbreviated names of tribal leaders, or subdivisions within the tribal group. As we have seen, the Roman literary sources do not record the names of the tribal leader of the Iceni prior to AD 60 to 61, so we are not certain that these words represent the names of tribal leaders.[79] It is quite possible that the tribe had a number of sub-groups. The coinage evidence may indicate that the Fenlands only became part of the territory of the Iceni during the first century AD,[80] or that this area remained a boundary zone between two tribes.[81]

Archaeological investigation in this area indicates that people lived within a variety of types of settlement, many of which appear to have been unenclosed by boundary structures.[82] These settlements consisted of scatters of roundhouses with associated storage pits and enclosures; a large number of these may have represented farmsteads rather than more extensive developments. Many of these settlements are ill-defined in that they do not have substantial enclosing ditches or enclosures around the individual houses (figure 14). In these ways they contrast with many of the more monumentally defined settlements to the south and west.[83]

Hillforts are generally rare in the territory of the Iceni, in contrast to areas in southern England,[84] although some examples of defended enclosures are known, for instance, in north-west Norfolk. These are often not in hilltop locations, and relatively little is known about many

12. A selection of coins of the Iceni. The example at the top left is a gold stater, the other coins are silver units. Scale twice actual size. (*By permission of the Celtic Coin Index, Institute of Archaeology, University of Oxford*)

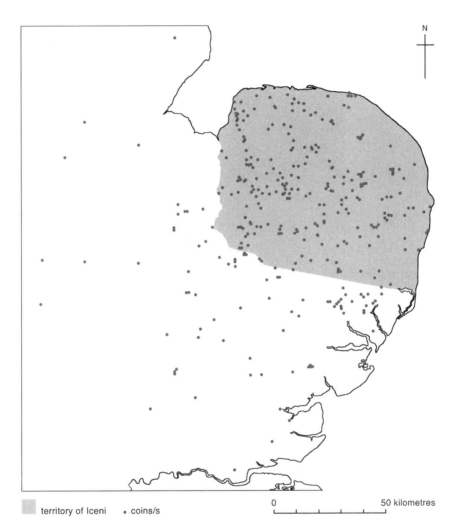

territory of Iceni　　•　coins/s

0　　　　　　　　　　　50 kilometres

13. Distribution of the coins of the Iceni. (*From information supplied by Philip de Jersey*)

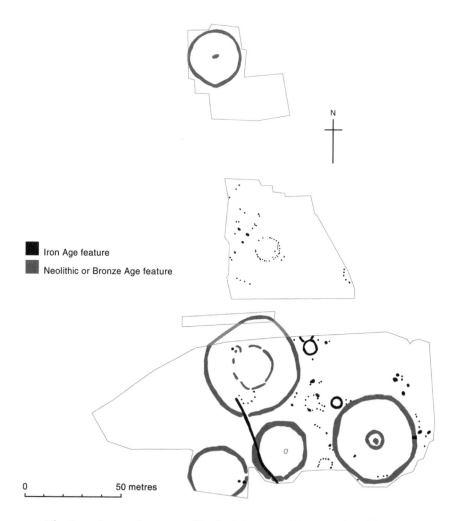

N

Iron Age feature

Neolithic or Bronze Age feature

0   50 metres

14. The Iron Age settlement at Harford Farm, Caistor St Edmund. The Iron Age structures were built within the space between the earlier ritual monuments. (*After Ashwin and Bates 2000, figure 75*)

of them.[85] Only a few sites have been excavated. Stonea Camp (Cambridgeshire), which lies on the south east of an 'island' in the Fens, appears to have been first constructed during the second century BC (figure 15). During the limited excavation at the camp, very little evidence was found for internal occupation; the ditches contained dismembered human bones that may indicate a ritual use for the enclosure.[86] Perhaps people were being killed at the camp and their bodies deposited at the site, or perhaps the dead were brought to the site. We have seen that the Roman authors often associated religion in the Iron Age with human sacrifice; perhaps Stonea was one of the places in which these sacrifices occurred. The fort was modified at a later date and produced some Roman finds which have been taken to suggest that it played a role in the Icenian revolt of AD 47 to 48,[87] although there is no definitive evidence for this.

Other evidence for the events of AD 47 to 48 is scarce. Roman military sites are very rare in the territory of the Iceni. An important recent discovery, however, has been made about five and a half miles (nine kilometres) to the north west of Stonea Camp.[88] The significant Roman site at Grandford has been known for some time, but aerial photographs taken in July 1999 provided vital new information about the site. This Roman settlement straddles the 'Fen Causeway', a Roman road that runs east to west across the Fens. The road probably originated at the legionary fortress at Longthorpe (near Peterborough). Small-scale excavations undertaken during the 1960s produced evidence demonstrating that there was occupation throughout much of the Roman period, but the new aerial photographs have located two distinct and overlapping Roman forts.[89] The larger fort is around 140 by 100 metres (459 by 328 feet) in extent and may have formed the base for an auxiliary unit of around five hundred men. The earlier of these two forts may well date to the period just after the revolt of AD 47 to 48, and it is possible that the Fen Causeway and the fort at Grandford were constructed in the aftermath of this insurrection.[90] A second probable fort site has also been located at Eldernell, four and a half miles (seven kilometres) to the west of Grandford.[91] The construction of these two forts and the road may have been part of the Roman effort to settle the area after the initial rebellion. This suggests that the second fort at Grandford is likely to date to the period immediately after the rebellion of AD 60 to 61.

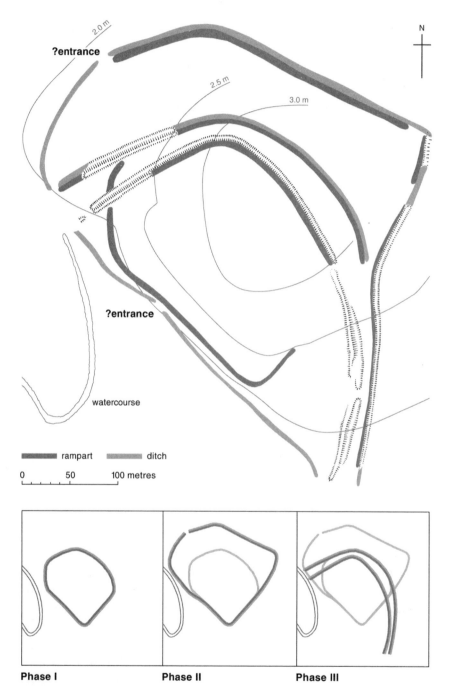

15. The Iron Age fort at Stonea Camp in Cambridgeshire, showing three possible phases in its early development. (*After Jackson and Potter 1996, figure 4*)

Hoards of metalwork and coinage have been commonly discovered in the territory of the Iceni. One coin hoard that was found in 1993–95 in south-west Norfolk contained coins belonging to the tribe and may date from the time of the revolt of AD 47 to 48;[92] it consisted of about eighty silver coins. There is no other clear evidence for this rebellion.

During the first century BC and the early first century AD the Iceni appear to have been living differently to the other tribes of south-eastern Britain.[93] It has been suggested that, in contrast to much of the south and east, where the late Iron Age witnessed the development of *oppida* and where there were rich graves and imported objects, the Iceni were conservative.[94] Imported objects in pre-conquest contexts are relatively rare and, although a coin tradition did develop in this period, the evidence suggests that the tribal aristocracy did not adopt Roman ways of drinking, feasting and dressing. In fact, traditional hand-made pottery appears to have remained common across much of the territory into the early first century AD and possibly in some cases until AD 60 to 61,[95] although wheel-made forms were adopted at some settlements.[96] There is only limited evidence to indicate that sites similar to the *oppida* of south-eastern Britain may have existed in the territory of the Iceni.[97] Some possible examples have been suggested (figure 16), at Thetford, Saham Toney,[98] Stonea and Chatteris,[99] and Caistor-by-Norwich (also called Caistor St Edmund), the latter of which later became the site of the *civitas* capital of the Iceni.[100] These sites have produced extensive archaeological information and collections of Iron Age coins, although none has yet produced convincing evidence that it was directly comparable to Camulodunon and Verlamion. At these East Anglian sites a number of hoards containing coins and metalwork have been found.

A remarkable archaeological discovery at Fison Way, Thetford (figure 17), in Norfolk, has been considered to represent the 'palace' of Boudica by some,[101] and the location for the tribal meeting that led to the rebellion of AD 60 to 61 by others.[102] It is, in fact, one of a number of comparable enclosures in the area.[103] In its final form, at the time of the revolt, it consisted of an area of about 220 by 175 metres (722 by 574 feet), the perimeter of which was defined by a substantial enclosure of no less than nine concentric wooden fences. Inside were large and imposing circular wooden buildings. Evidence may indicate that Iron Age coins

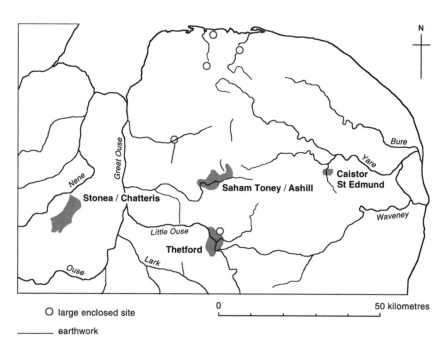

16. Possible tribal centres among the Iceni. (*After Davies 1996, figure 10, with additions by the authors*)

17. The late Iron Age site of Fison Way, Thetford, in Norfolk. (*Drawn by Sue White. By permission of Norfolk Archaeology and Environment*)

were produced here and an unusual number of brooches were found. [104]
Whilst Roman imports, amphorae and imported pottery were few, they
were rather more common than on many other sites in the region. [105]
Some items from the site may have represented offerings to the gods,
including pieces of Roman military equipment. [106] It is likely that Fison
Way represented a sacred centre for a tribal group, but we cannot tie any
historical events directly to it. [107]

Scholars have argued that it is possible to recognise one tribal leader,
Prasutagus, from the coin evidence (figure 18). The Roman writer Tacitus mentioned Prasutagus, the husband of Boudica, in relation to
events leading up to the revolt of AD 60 to 61. [108] We do not know how
long he had been ruling by this time. Prasutagus was, however,
described by Tacitus as having had a 'life of long and renowned pros-
perity'. [109] This has been taken to indicate that he ruled from at least the
time of the earlier revolt of AD 47 to 48, and possibly from the time of
the Roman invasion itself. [110] Some of the later coins that were produced
in this area have a Latin phrase on the obverse that has been taken to
read SUBRIIPRASTO, encircling a human head. [111] It has been suggested
that this phrase represents SUB RI(CON) PRASUTAGUS, 'under king
Prasutagus', with another legend on the reverse relating to the mon-
eyer. [112] Although Tacitus's writing contains the only reference that we
have to Prasutagus, these coins may provide further evidence for him.
In contrast to the previous coins of the Iceni, they display a new Roman-
ness, including a Roman style head on the obverse, with the unusually
long Latin legend. [113]

The linking of these coins to Prasutagus has recently been questioned.
Two recent coin finds have led to the rereading of the earlier legend
on the reverse of these coins as SUB-ESVPRASTO rather than SUB-
RIIPRASTO. This suggests that the coins show the name of an
individual called Esuprastus, a previously unknown king. [114] This name
could still in theory relate to the historical king Prasutagus. As the only
source for him and his rule is Tacitus in the *Annals*, it is possible that
the name of the king was not correctly received by Tacitus or was erro-
neously transcribed by those who copied the *Annals* at a later date. [115]
Nevertheless, it is equally likely that there was another king, called
Esuprastus, who was issuing coins in what is today East Anglia in the
middle of the first century AD, using a Roman coin style. [116] The idea that

18. Three silver coins struck for 'Esuprastus'. Scale twice actual size. (*By permission of the Celtic Coin Index, Institute of Archaeology, University of Oxford*)

the Iceni may have had multiple kings recalls the complexity of late Iron Age tribal organisation in Britain. Perhaps there were effectively several kings in this area and Prasutagus was the one who had the closest relationship with Rome and, perhaps, also some control over the others. Julius Caesar's 'Cenimagni' might have been the name of the tribe that had the most control in the area during the mid 50s BC. It is equally possible that the Iceni ceased to produce their own coinage when they became a friendly kingdom of Rome in AD 43.[117] In other words, none of the Icenian coinage was necessarily produced after the initial Roman conquest of Britain, although people evidently continued to hoard it after this date.[118]

The case of the supposed coinage of Prasutagus demonstrates the tendency people have to manipulate the archaeological evidence to fit preconceived ideas. There is a strong desire to find evidence that will fit in with the stories told by the classical writers, with the result that archaeological information has been effectively misinterpreted. This is but one of several cases.

The status of Prasutagus as a friendly king strongly suggests that he was a pro-Roman ruler. He may well have provided support for the invasion of AD 43 and perhaps have helped the Romans during the revolt of AD 47 to 48. If he had not, it is unlikely that the Iceni would have been allowed to remain free from Roman control until AD 60 to 61. It has also been suggested that he may have been a citizen of Rome.[119] Roman citizenship was often awarded to friendly kings, although Tacitus does not mention this in the case of Prasutagus. If Prasutagus was a Roman citizen, Boudica is also likely to have shared his status.[120] For most ancient historians the defining feature of Roman identity has been common citizenship.[121] To be fully Roman required an individual to be a citizen of Rome. Roman identity was not a matter of a person's ethnicity, nation, linguistic or descent group but one that was achieved or awarded.[122]

During the early expansion of the Roman Empire, in the Republican period, Roman citizenship was extended to groups of allies, making them effectively Roman.[123] This enabled the aristocracies of widely-spread peoples to be incorporated into the imperial system. The creation of Roman citizens was continued by Augustus and later Roman emperors and it is possible that Prasutagus was awarded this status by

Claudius in AD 43. In Britain at this time the number of Roman citizens was probably strictly limited, demonstrating the potential significance of Prasutagus as a political figure among the Iceni. Roman administrators and legionary soldiers, such as those living in the colony, would have been citizens, but the vast majority of the population was not. Prasutagus may even have used a traditional form of Roman will in his attempt to try to ensure that his territory remained in the hands of his family when he died. [124]

Although imported objects remained relatively uncommon in the territory of the Iceni during the first century AD, in contrast to some areas of the south east, a few sites are now producing evidence for such imports. [125] A king of the status and apparent wealth of Prasutagus must surely have had access to the types of imported objects that were acquired by the late Iron Age and early Roman aristocrats of south-eastern England. Indeed, he is likely to have received gifts from the Roman administration throughout the 40s and 50s in exchange for his support. He probably resided within an Icenian version of the *oppida* at Camulodunon and Verlamion, but if so the site has yet to be found.

2

The Classical Sources

Much of our knowledge of Boudica is derived from three classical texts that have survived until today. Tacitus records her name as 'Boudicca', while another author, Dio, wrote in Greek and called her 'Boudouika', which can be translated as 'Boudouica'. The two versions of her name, Boudicca and Boudica, are common in recent accounts of the rebellion of AD 60 to 61 and these have replaced the popular version of the name (Boadicea) in most academic accounts of the events in Roman Britain. The study of the 'Celtic languages' suggests that Tacitus's spelling was incorrect and that her name should have one 'c'.[1] Tacitus's misspelling with an extra 'c' was copied when the 'u' was replaced with an 'a' and the second 'c' by an 'e' in the medieval period; this is how the name 'Boadicea' came about.[2] The name Boudica meant precisely 'Victoria';[3] it is interesting that an ancient British leader who fought such a determined battle against the Romans was given such a name at birth.

There are difficulties in using the classical writings as the basis for an understanding of the events of AD 60 to 61. These can be illustrated by the problems that we have sorting out the date of the actual revolt that Boudica led. If we are uncertain of the date of the rebellion, other aspects of the events are even less clear. Past scholarly accounts of the life and actions of Boudica have sometimes used the Roman writings in an uncritical way. Even modern writers have effectively take all three Roman historical sources and combined the elements that they perceive as useful into an internally consistent account of Boudica's life and actions.[4] For instance, in one scholarly account, although much of the description of the events is taken from Tacitus's work in the *Annals*, Dio's dramatic description of the appearance of Boudica is used and described as 'the most dramatic picture of a Celtic heroine in classical literature'.[5] In another standard account of the events of AD 60 to 61,[6] Tacitus was again used to provide a definitive account of the history of the conflict, to which information taken from other historical and archaeological sources is added to supplement the detail. For example, some of the description of the final battle in Dio's account is felt to be helpful and is adopted.[7] Another recent account also used elements of all three historical sources to build a story.[8]

Although it is impossible to ignore the classical writings, any direct reliance on these sources is problematic. The Roman Empire produced a variety of authors who wrote histories of Rome. These literary works gave accounts of the development of the city and its empire – the rise of Rome to dominance over much of the known world. In Roman society history was a branch of literature. Writers at this time told interesting stories rather than necessarily attempting to recount an accurate description of historical events.[9] Written accounts were produced to communicate with other members of the Roman aristocracy,[10] people who often shared the same ideas and interests as the authors. These accounts, written by male Roman aristocrats for members of their own class, show the interests and concerns of such a group.[11]

The writings of classical authors may provide a vital source of information about the events of Boudica's rebellion, but care is necessary when using these to provide any form of historical framework for the events in Britain at this time. They are not straight-forward historical accounts and, perhaps, tell us more about the attitudes of classical authors to powerful women in non-Roman societies than they do about the events of the rebellion.[12] Classical authors often put wholly fictitious speeches into the mouths of the principal characters, whether they are Romans or 'barbarians'. Boudica is no exception and we shall see that she was given a number of speeches by the two classical authors who wrote about her. These speeches were invented and aimed to communicate ideas that would be of interest and concern to aristocratic male Romans. The attitude of the Romans to the Britons was dictated by their view of the Mediterranean as the centre of the world. Britons were seen as peripheral barbarians, whether noble or otherwise; sometimes they could be civilised thorough the actions of Rome,[13] but it was considered that they were naturally inferior and should dutifully accept their subservient status.

Two classical writers provide accounts of the life and actions of Boudica – Tacitus and Cassius Dio. The Roman aristocracy included peoples who originated within provinces that had been conquered by Rome and who had effectively taken on a Roman identity. Neither Tacitus nor Dio came from the city of Rome itself. Tacitus was, by common consent, the greatest Roman historian, yet the information that we have about his life is limited, derived from his own writings and those of a number of other classical writers. We know neither the correct form of his name nor the date or place of his birth. His full name was either Publius Cornelius Tacitus or Gaius Cornelius Tacitus.[14] It is likely that he was born around AD 56 to 57,[15] a few years before the revolt of Boudica. Tacitus's place of birth was probably Gallia Narbonensis (Provence in southern France), possibly at the town of Vasio. He originated in one of the provinces of the Roman Empire rather than from the city of Rome or even from Italy. He held a variety of posts in the Roman administration and army, and in AD 77 he married the daughter of Julius Agricola, the newly appointed governor of the province of Britain. Tacitus's writings include a number of verbal attacks upon the Roman Empire that are assigned to native leaders.[16] Tacitus wrote in this way because his objective was to criticise the autocratic rule of the early Roman emperors; he is extremely sceptical about power and about the motives and character of those who exercised it. A minute proportion of these writings is concerned with Boudica, but he wrote about her in two works: the *Agricola* (*De vita Agricolae*), completed probably in AD 98;[17] and the *Annals*, composed around 115–17. The *Agricola* is a biography of Tacitus's father-in-law, while the *Annals* is an account of the Roman Empire from AD 14 to 68. It is likely that Tacitus died around AD 117.

Both of Tacitus's accounts were written some time after the rebellion had been crushed. He was, nevertheless, writing within living memory of the events. His close relationship with his father-in-law, Agricola, suggests that some of his knowledge of historical events in Britain at this time may have been passed down directly to him.[18] Agricola had served as a military officer in Britain at the time of the revolt and may even have witnessed some of the events. As Agricola was on the spot, he could have provided an eyewitness account of the events that was used by Tacitus in his writings.[19]

The earliest surviving account is that in the *Agricola*.[20] Tacitus's brief comments serve to indicate the potential fragility of the account of

Boudica in the *Annals*. This is because they indicate some important differences in Tacitus's description of the same historical events.[21] In the *Agricola* Tacitus describes how the Britons rose under Boudica while the governor Suetonius Paulinus was attacking the island of 'Mona' (Anglesey). Suetonius Paulinus was a provincial governor, an appointment of the emperor. He was the most senior Roman administrator in the province and he had been involved in campaigns in Wales for some time.

Tacitus tells us that:

> Suetonius Paulinus enjoyed two years of success, conquering tribes and establishing strong forts. Emboldened thereby to attack the island of Anglesey, which was feeding the native resistance, he exposed himself to a stab in the back. For the Britons, freed from their repressions by the absence of the dreaded legate, began to discuss the woes of slavery, to compare their wrongs and sharpen their sting in the telling. 'We gain nothing by submission except heavier burdens for willing shoulders. Once each tribe had one king, now two are clamped on us – the legate to wreak his fury on our lives, the procurator on our property'.[22]

The 'legate' was Suetonius Paulinus, while the procurator was the Roman official who was appointed to take charge of taxing the province. The procurator at this time was Catus Decianus. Tacitus continues:

> 'We subjects are damned in either case, whether our masters quarrel or agree. Their gangs of centurions or slaves, as the case may be, mingle violence and insult. Nothing is any longer safe from their greed and lust. In war it is the braver who takes the spoil; as things stand with us, it is mostly cowards and shirkers that rob our homes, kidnap our children and conscript our men. Any cause is good enough for us to die for – any but our country's. But what a mere handful our invaders are, if we reckon up our own numbers. The Germans, reckoning so, threw off the yoke, and they had only a river, not the Ocean, to shield them. We have country, wives and parents to fight for; the Romans have nothing but greed and self-indulgence.'[23]

'The Germans' refers to the way that a Germanic army under Arminius, popularly known as Herman, had defeated a Roman army in AD 9.[24] This event forced Augustus to revise his plans to conquer extensive areas beyond the Rhine. Tacitus continues:

> 'Back they will go, as the deified Julius went back, if only we can rival the

valour of our fathers. We must not be scared by the loss of one battle or even two; success may foster the sprit of offence, but it is suffering that gives the power to endure. The gods are at last showing mercy to us Britons in keeping the Roman general away, with his army exiled in another island. For ourselves we have already taken the most difficult step – we have begun to plot. And in an enterprise like this there is more danger in being caught plotting than in taking the plunge.'[25]

Tacitus considers the supposed grievances of the Britons in a way that suggests that resentment against Rome was widespread. It is significant, however, that many of the arguments that Britons voice against the Romans in this quotation are stock examples. Roman historians place a number of comparable grievances into the mouths of native peoples who were in conflict with Rome in a variety of contexts.[26] We might well wonder how Tacitus, or Agricola if he provided Tacitus with information, could have been aware of the nature of these British grievances. Presumably Britons would not have talked openly to a Roman officer such as Agricola. It is probable that Tacitus is merely putting formulaic complaints about Roman rule into the mouths of the provincials.

Tacitus continues by discussing Boudica and the rebellion:

Goaded by such mutual encouragements, the whole island rose under the leadership of Boudicca, a lady of royal descent – for Britons make no distinction of sex in their leaders.[27]

It is not clear how often female warrior leaders featured within Iron Age society in Britain, but they may well have been fairly common and both of the other accounts of Boudica mention comparable factors. The narrative continues:

They hunted down the Roman troops in their scattered posts, stormed the forts and assaulted the colony itself, in which they saw their slavery focused; nor did the angry victors deny themselves any form of savage cruelty. In fact, had not Paulinus, on hearing of the revolt, made speed to help, Britain would have been lost. As it was, he restored it to its old obedience by a single successful action.[28]

This account gives the bare bones of the information presented in the *Annals* but differs in detail. No mention is made in this brief description of the Iceni, the tribe under Boudica's command. In the *Agricola* the emphasis is placed on the idea that the whole of the island rose up against Rome. In fact, elsewhere in the same work the forces of Boudica are described as from the tribe of the Brigantes rather than the Iceni.[29] The mention of the overwhelming of forts suggests that Boudica attacked Roman military fortifications, a statement that we shall see that Tacitus appears to contradict in the *Annals*. This leads us to wonder to what extent we can trust the information about the rebellion in the two accounts of Tacitus.

Tacitus concludes by giving us some important information about the aftermath of the revolt.

> But many guilty rebels refused to lay down their arms out of a peculiar dread of the legate. Fine officer though he was, he seemed likely to abuse their unconditional surrender and punish with undue severity wrongs which he insisted on making personal. The government therefore replaced him by Petronius Turpilianus. They hoped that he would be more merciful and readier to forgive offences to which he was a stranger.[30]

This information has been used to explain the actions of the Roman government after the defeat of the rebellion.

The image of Boudica that is presented in the *Annals* is the one that has dominated accounts in the archaeological literature. One reason for its popularity is that this account is far fuller than that provided in the *Agricola*. In this work, Tacitus clearly states that a terrible disaster was suffered in Britain during the consulship of Caesennius Paetus and Petronius Turpilianus.[31] The consuls were the senior Roman magistrates and we can date their periods of office with accuracy. This reference has been taken to indicate that the rebellion broke out in AD 61; as the action apparently occurred over two years, the rebellion may well have taken place in AD 61 to 62.[32] Despite this, for various reasons, the majority of authorities argue that the rebellion started in AD 60.[33] As with many of the basic facts about the rebellion of Boudica, however, we cannot be certain of the dates of the various events.

Tacitus again describes how the provincial governor, Suetonius Paulinus, undertook an expedition against the island of Mona, which was thickly populated and had provided sanctuary for many. The Roman army conquered and placed a garrison over the island but in the meantime news arrived of a sudden uprising. Tacitus describes the nature of this in some detail.

> While Suetonius was thus occupied, he learnt of a sudden rebellion in the province. Prasutagus, king of the Iceni, after a life of long and renowned prosperity, had made the emperor co-heir with his own two daughters. Prasutagus hoped by this submissiveness to preserve his kingdom and household from attack. But it turned out otherwise.[34]

This is a particularly important statement because this is the only place in the classical literature where we are told that Prasutagus was king of the Iceni. The *Annals*, in fact, provides the only link between Boudica and the Iceni. As we have seen, elsewhere Tacitus describes Boudica as leading the Brigantes. Without Tacitus's account in the *Annals* we would believe Boudica to have been a Brigantian ruler and we would be totally unaware of Prasutagus.

It is also interesting that Tacitus suggests that Prasutagus had drawn up a Roman-style will, presumably in order to protect the interests of his family.[35] Such wills were part of a long tradition that had developed during the contact between Rome and friendly kings from the second century BC onwards. Often made when a king did not have a son to whom he wished to leave his territory, such a will can be taken as an indication that Prasutagus had adopted Roman ways, in this case channelling power through male hands.[36]

Tacitus then describes Roman barbarity.

> Kingdom and household alike were plundered like prizes of war, the one by Roman officers, the other by Roman slaves. As a beginning, his widow Boudicca was flogged and their daughters raped. The Icenian chiefs were deprived of their hereditary estates as if the Romans had been given the whole country. The king's own relatives were treated like slaves.[37]

Such an action against an aristocratic British household that had long been supportive of Rome would have been particularly shocking to Tacitus's wealthy and privileged audience in Rome.[38] The idea that slaves and soldiers should have carried out such actions against an aristocratic native family that had been friends of Rome would have outraged aristocratic Roman sensibilities.

Tacitus continues:

> And the humiliated Iceni feared still worse, now that they had been reduced

to provincial status. So they rebelled. With them rose the Trinobantes and others. Servitude had not broken them, and they had secretly plotted together to become free again. They particularly hated the Roman ex-soldiers who had recently established a settlement at Camulodunum. The settlers drove the Trinobantes from their homes and land, and called them prisoners and slaves. The troops encouraged the settlers' outrages, since their own way of behaving was the same – and they looked forward to similar licence for themselves. Moreover, the temple erected to the divine Claudius was a blatant stronghold of alien rule, and its observances were a pretext to make the natives appointed as its priests drain the whole country dry.[39]

In this account it appears clear that it was not all of the Britons who rose up to fight the Romans, but the Iceni, the Trinobantes (or Trinovantes) and unspecified others. Far greater detail is given for the reasons that drove both the Iceni and the Trinovantes to rebellion. The *Annals* present a rather more sympathetic version of the events of AD 60 to 61. It describes the provocations that the Britons had suffered, factors that are absent from Tacitus's account in the *Agricola*.

Tacitus then turns to the course of the revolt that began with the destruction of the colony at Colchester:

It seemed easy to destroy the settlement; for it had no walls. That was a matter which Roman commanders, thinking of amenities rather than needs, had neglected. At this juncture, for no visible reason, the statue of Victory at Camulodunum fell down – with its back turned as though it were fleeing the enemy. Delirious women chanted of destruction at hand. They cried that in the local senate house outlandish yells had been heard; the theatre had echoed with shrieks: at the mouth of the Thames a phantom settlement had been seen in ruins. A blood-red colour in the sea, too, and shapes like human corpses left by the ebb tide, were interpreted hopefully by the Britons – and with terror by the settlers.[40]

Tacitus writes of the temple of Claudius, a senate house and a theatre, and also suggests that the colony had no walls. Much effort has been expended by archaeologists in their attempts to locate these structures and Tacitus's account does appear to be accurate in stating that the settlement was undefended by perimeter earthworks. The statue of the Roman goddess Victory has not been found. The statue, if it was not a literary flourish by Tacitus, may have been erected to commemorate the

Roman invasion of Britain. Its collapse evidently provided an ill omen of troubled times ahead, but we cannot be certain that this was more than a legend that had built up around events.

We do learn that:

Suetonius, however, was far away. So they appealed for help to the imperial agent Catus Decianus. He sent them barely two hundred men, incompletely armed. There was also a small garrison on the spot. Reliance was placed on the temple's protection. Misled by secret pro-rebels, who hampered their plans, they dispensed with rampart or trench. They omitted also to evacuate old people and women and thus leave only fighting men behind. Their precautions were appropriate to a time of unbroken peace.

Then a native horde surrounded them. When all else had been ravaged or burnt, the garrison concentrated itself in the temple. After two days' siege, it fell by storm. The ninth Roman division, commanded by Quintus Petilius Cerialis Caesius Rufus, attempted to relieve the town, but was stopped by the victorious Britons and routed. Its entire infantry force was massacred, while the commander escaped to his camp with his cavalry and sheltered behind its defences. The imperial agent Catus Decianus, horrified by the catastrophe and by his unpopularity, withdrew to Gaul. It was his rapacity which had driven the province to war.[41]

This account suggests the total destruction of the colony and we shall see in the next chapter that the archaeological evidence supports Tacitus on this point. It also provides some details of the sequence of events that were connected with the sacking of the town which we do not have from any other source. He continues:

But Suetonius, undismayed, marched through disaffected territory to Londinium. This town did not rank as a Roman settlement, but was an important centre for businessmen and merchandise. At first, he hesitated whether to stand and fight there. Eventually, his numerical inferiority – and the price only too clearly paid by the divisional commander's rashness – decided him to sacrifice the single city of Londinium to save the province as a whole. Unmoved by lamentations and appeals, Suetonius gave the signal for departure. The inhabitants were allowed to accompany him. But those who stayed because they were women, or old, or attached to the place, were slaughtered by the enemy. Verulamium suffered the same fate.[42]

This information appears to provide conclusive evidence for the destruction of Londinium and archaeological evidence supports this. The archaeological evidence for the destruction of Verulamium is, however, less clear-cut.

We then learn that:

> The natives enjoyed plundering and thought of nothing else. Bypassing forts and garrisons, they made for where loot was richest and protection weakest. Roman and provincial deaths at the places mentioned are estimated at seventy thousand. For the British did not take or sell prisoners, or practise other war-time exchanges. They could not wait to cut throats, hang, burn, and crucify – as though avenging, in advance, the retribution that was on its way.[43]

In this section we have an apparent contradiction to the statement, in the *Agricola*, that forts were stormed. In addition, the justifiable grievances of the Britons are now overshadowed by the severity of their violence against the Roman and pro-Roman population of the town they destroyed. The sympathy of the Roman audience for the atrocious treatment of Boudica's family and people would be severely reduced by this evidence of native barbarity and lack of reason.[44] We do not know, however, whether this information is reliable. Perhaps Tacitus was exaggerating.

He then turns to the Roman response to these atrocities.

> Suetonius collected the fourteenth brigade (or legion) and detachments of the twentieth, together with the nearest available auxiliaries – amounting to nearly ten thousand armed men – and decided to attack without further delay. He chose a position in a defile with a wood behind him. There could be no enemy, he knew, except at his front, where there was open country without cover for ambushes. Suetonius drew up his regular troops in close order, with the light-armed auxiliaries at their flanks, and the cavalry massed on the wings. On the British side, cavalry and infantry bands seethed over a wide area in unprecedented numbers. Their confidence was such that they brought their wives with them to see the victory, installing them in carts stationed at the edge of the battlefield.[45]

Much discussion has occurred about the potential site of this battle, but Tacitus does not present enough information for it to be located with certainty. We then learn of how Boudica managed the final battle.

> Boudicca drove round all the tribes in a chariot with her daughters in front of her. 'We British are used to woman commanders in war', she cried. 'I am

descended from mighty men! But now I am not fighting for my kingdom and wealth. I am fighting as an ordinary person for my lost freedom, my bruised body, and my outraged daughters. Nowadays Roman rapicity does not even spare our bodies. Old people are killed, virgins raped. But the gods will grant us the vengeance we deserve! The Roman division which dared to fight is annihilated. The others cower in their camps, or watch for a chance to escape. They will never face even the din and roar of all our thousands, much less the shock of our onslaught. Consider how many of you are fighting – and why. Then you will win this battle, or perish. That is what I, a woman, plan to do! – let the men live in slavery if they will.'[46]

Again this presents a stock idea of the type of statement that a native war leader would make to his or her followers prior to an important battle. It is unlikely that Tacitus would have had a reliable account of what Boudica actually said and the statement is probably made up. It supports the comments in the *Agricola* by suggesting that the British were used to women leaders in times of war and also gives us a reference to Boudica riding in a chariot.

The Roman commander Suetonius Paulinus's statement, which Tacitus then provides, may, perhaps, be more accurate:

'Disregard the clamours and empty threats of the natives!' he said. 'In their ranks, there are more women than fighting men. Unwarlike, unarmed, when they see the arms and courage of the conquerors who have routed them so often, they will break immediately. Even when a force contains many divisions, few among them win the battles – what special glory for your small numbers to win the renown of a whole army. Just keep in close order. Throw your javelins, and then carry on: use shield-bosses to fell them, swords to kill them. Do not think of plunder. When you have won, you will have everything.'

The general's words were enthusiastically received: the old battle-experienced soldiers longed to hurl their javelins. So Suetonius confidently gave the signal for battle. At first the regular troops stood their ground. Keeping to the defile as a natural defence, they launched their javelins accurately at the approaching enemy. Then, in wedge formation, they burst forward. So did the auxiliary infantry. The cavalry, too, with lances extended, demolished all serious resistance. The remaining Britons fled with difficulty since their ring of wagons blocked the outlets. The Romans did not spare even the women. Baggage animals too, transfixed with weapons, added to the heaps of dead.[47]

Tacitus gives us this account of the defeat of Boudica's army. He continues:

> According to one report almost eighty thousand Britons fell. Our own casualties were about four hundred dead and a slightly larger number of wounded. Boudicca poisoned herself. Poenius Postumus, chief of staff of the second division which had not joined Suetonius, learning of the success of the other two formations, stabbed himself to death because he had cheated his formation of its share in the victory and broken regulations by disobeying his commander's orders.[48]

The figures that Tacitus presents for the number of British deaths are likely to be exaggerated, although there is no need to doubt that the Roman army overcame a much larger force of Britons.

Finally, Tacitus turns to the ways in which the Roman army cleared up any remaining resistance.

> The whole army was now united. Suetonius kept it under canvas to finish the war. The emperor raised its numbers by transferring from Germany two thousand regular troops, which brought the ninth division to full strength, also eight auxiliary infantry battalions and a thousand cavalry. These were stationed together in new winter quarters, and hostile or wavering tribes were ravaged with fire and sword. But the enemy's worst affliction was famine.[49]

So ended the rebellion of Boudica according to Tacitus's account in the *Annals*.

Cassius Dio, who came from Nicaea in Bithynia, a Roman province in north-west Turkey, lived from around AD 150 to 235. He also held important posts in the Roman administration and wrote a history of Rome in eighty books, twenty-six of which survive. By contrast with Tacitus, who wrote in Latin, Cassus Dio wrote in Greek. His account, which appears to have been written around the end of the second century, almost 150 years after the death of Boudica, is particularly important for the Roman history of Britain. It contains the only narrative that we possess of the invasion of Britain by Claudius in AD 43. That he wrote his account of the revolt of AD 60 to 61 at some considerable time after Boudica's death is often considered to limit its value.[50] It is likely, however, that he derived much of his information from earlier writers whose work has

subsequently been lost, and there is much material in his account of Boudica that is not included in the writings of Tacitus. This suggests that Dio
had access to accounts of the revolt that have not survived,[51] although it
is difficult for us to assess the accuracy of his writings. Dio relates that:

> a terrible disaster occurred in Britain. Two cities were sacked, eighty thou-
> sand of the Romans and of their allies perished, and the island was lost to
> Rome. Moreover, all this ruin was brought upon the Romans by a woman,
> a fact which in itself caused them the greatest shame.[52]

This figure of 80,000 differs slightly from Tacitus's information on
deaths in Camulodunum, Londinium and Verulamium. In addition, he
mentions two cities (πολεισ 'poleis') rather than three. Perhaps he did
not consider Londinium to have been a city at this time. As in the case
of Tacitus's account in the *Agricola*, Dio does not mention the Iceni or
the Trinovantes and gives the impression that the whole island was up
in arms. He also does not mention the abuses that Boudica and her
daughters are supposed to have suffered at the hands of the Romans.
Dio's portrayal of Boudica is less sympathetic than Tacitus's image in
the *Annals*.

Dio continues:

> Indeed, Heaven gave them indications of the catastrophe beforehand. For at
> night there was heard to issue from the senate-house foreign jargon mingled
> with laughter, and from the theatre outcries and lamentations, though no
> mortal man had uttered the words or the groans; houses were seen under the
> water in the river Thames, and the ocean between the island and Gaul once
> grew blood-red at flood-tide.[53]

This information is broadly comparable to that included in Tacitus's
Annals. Dio provides some significant information at this point that is
not included in Tacitus about loans that had been made to the Britons
by the Emperor Claudius and by Seneca, chief minister to both Claudius
and Nero. The recalling of these loans is seen as one reason for the
revolt.

> But the person who was chiefly instrumental in rousing the natives and per-
> suading them to fight the Romans, the person who was thought worthy to
> be their leader and who directed the conduct of the entire war, was Buduica
> [Βουδουικα] a Briton woman of the royal family and possessed of greater
> intelligence than often belongs to women. This woman assembled her army,

to the number of some 120,000, and then ascended a tribunal which had
been constructed of earth in the Roman fashion. In stature she was very tall,
in appearance most terrifying, in the glance of her eye most fierce, and her
voice was harsh; a great mass of the tawniest hair fell to her hips; around her
neck was a large golden necklace; and she wore a tunic of divers colours over
which a thick mantle was fastened with a brooch. This was her invariable
attire. She now grasped a spear to aid her in terrifying all beholders and
spoke . . . [54]

This is the only description of Boudica provided by the ancient sources
and it has been very important in the way that artists have represented
her since the sixteenth century.

Dio presents a lengthy and detailed speech that Boudica is supposed
to have made to her army. Although it is far longer than the speech in
Tacitus, it is again unlikely to contain accurate information. This brief
excerpt gives the flavour of the whole speech:

'You have learned by actual experience how different freedom is from slavery. Hence, although some among you may previously, through ignorance of
which was better, have been deceived by the alluring promises of the
Romans, yet now that you have tried both, you have learned how great a mis-
take you made in preferring an imported despotism to your ancestral mode
of life, and you have come to realise how much better is poverty with no
master than wealth with slavery. For what treatment is there of the most
shameful or grievous sort that we have not suffered ever since these men
made their appearance in Britain? Have we not been robbed entirely of most
of our possessions, and those the greatest, while for those that remain we pay
taxes? Besides pasturing and tilling for them all our other possessions, do we
not pay a yearly tribute for our very bodies? How much better it would be
to have been sold to masters once for all than, possessing empty titles of freedom, to have to ransom ourselves every year! How much better to have been
slain and to have perished than to go about with a tax on our heads! Yet why
do I mention death? For even dying is not free of cost with them; nay, you
know what fees we deposit even for our dead.' [55]

Statements are attributed to Boudica in this account that were to be significant for the way that her image was used in England in the sixteenth
century and later. She states that:

'although we inhabit so large an island, or rather a continent, one might say,
that is encircled by the sea, and although we possess a veritable world of our

own and are so separated by the ocean from all the rest of mankind that we
have been believed to dwell on a different earth and under a different sky,
and that some of the outside world, aye, even their wisest men, have not
hitherto known for a certainty even by what name we are called, we have,
notwithstanding all this, been despised and trampled underfoot by men who
know nothing else than how to secure gain. However, even at this late day,
though we have not done so before, let us, my countrymen and friends and
kinsmen, – for I consider you all kinsmen, seeing that you inhabit a single
island and are called by one common name, – let us, I say, do our duty while
we still remember what freedom is, that we may leave to our children not
only its appellation but also its reality. For, if we utterly forget the happy state
in which we were born and bred, what, pray, will they do, reared in
bondage?'[56]

We also learn that:

When she had finished speaking, she employed a species of divination, let-
ting a hare escape from the fold of her dress; and since it ran on what they
considered the auspicious side, the whole multitude shouted with pleasure,
and Buduica, raising her hand toward heaven, said: 'I thank thee, Andraste,
and call upon thee as woman speaking to woman; for I rule over no burden-
bearing Egyptians as did Nitocris, nor over trafficking Assyrians as did
Semiramis (for we have by now gained thus much learning from the
Romans!), much less over the Romans themselves as did Messalina once and
afterwards Agrippina and now Nero (who, though in name a man, is in fact
a woman, as is proved by his singing, lyre-playing and beautification of his
person) …'[57]

Boudica not only draws attention to a supposed British goddess
Andraste but also displays a detailed knowledge of societies in the
Mediterranean, of which she is in reality unlikely to have known very
much.[58] The hare is a common motif in later images of Boadicea from
the sixteenth century onwards. Her comments upon former powerful
women in Roman society and also upon the supposed effeminacy of
Nero are clearly directed at Dio's Roman audience and play on their
opinion that Boudica was stepping outside the proscribed limits of her
gender by her warlike actions.[59]

Dio continues:

Having finished an appeal to her people of this general tenor, Buduica led
her army against the Romans; for these chanced to be without a leader,

inasmuch as Paulinus, their commander, had gone on an expedition to Mona, an island near Britain. This enabled her to sack and plunder two Roman cities, and, as I have said, to wreak indescribable slaughter. Those who were taken captive by the Britons were subjected to every known form of outrage. The worst and most bestial atrocity committed by their captors was the following. They hung up naked the noblest and most distinguished women and then cut off their breasts and sewed them to their mouths, in order to make the victims appear to be eating them; afterwards they impaled the women on sharp skewers run lengthwise through the entire body. All this they did to the accompaniment of sacrifices, banquets and wanton behaviour, not only in all their other sacred places, but particularly in the grove of Andate. This was their name for Victory, and they regarded her with most exceptional reverence.[60]

We do not know how reliable this disturbing picture is, but again it plays on the perceived barbarity of the native Britons, a stock theme for a Roman aristocratic audience and one that also occurred within Tacitus's works. By these horrible atrocities it is effectively the sexuality of the women that is destroyed through the abuse that is carried out on their bodies.[61] Dio then tells us more of Suetonius Paulinus's actions:

Now it chanced that Paulinus had already brought Mona to terms, and so on learning of the disaster in Britain he at once set sail thither from Mona. However, he was not willing to risk a conflict with the barbarians immediately, as he feared their numbers and their desperation, but was inclined to postpone battle to a more convenient season. But as he grew short of food and the barbarians pressed relentlessly upon him, he was compelled, contrary to his judgement, to engage them.[62]

Dio presents a full account of the battle but one that does not tie in closely with Tacitus's description, which implies that he may have had access to an account of Boudica's rebellion that is now lost to us.

Buduica, at the head of an army of about 230,000 men, rode in a chariot herself and assigned the others to their several stations. Paulinus could not extend his line the whole length of hers, for, even if the men had been drawn up only one deep, they would not have reached far enough, so inferior were they in numbers; nor, on the other hand, did he dare join battle in a single compact force, for fear of being surrounded and cut to pieces. He therefore separated his army into three divisions, in order to fight at several points at one and the same time, and he made each of the divisions so strong that it could not easily be broken through. [63]

Dio gives a lengthy description of speeches that the Roman commander is supposed to have made to his soldiers in their three divisions before returning to the battle, He then continues:

> After addressing these and like words to them he raised the signal for battle. Thereupon the armies approached each other, the barbarians with much shouting mingled with menacing battle-songs, but the Romans silently and in order until they came within a javelin's throw of the enemy. Then, while their foes were still advancing against them at a walk, the Romans rushed forward at a signal and charged them at full speed, and when the clash came, easily broke through the opposing ranks; but, as they were surrounded by the great numbers of the enemy, they had to be fighting everywhere at once. Their struggle took many forms. Light-armed troops exchanged missiles with light-armed, heavy-armed were opposed to heavy-armed, cavalry clashed with cavalry, and against the chariots of the barbarians the Roman archers contended. The barbarians would assail the Romans with a rush of their chariots, knocking them helter-skelter, but, since they fought without breastplates, would themselves be repulsed by the arrows. Horseman would overthrow foot-soldier and foot-soldier strike down horseman; a group of Romans, forming in close order, would advance to meet the chariots, and others would be scattered by them; a band of Britons would come to close quarters with the archers and rout them, while others were content to dodge their shafts at a distance; and all this was going on not at one spot only, but in all three divisions at once. They contended for a long time, both parties being animated by the same zeal and daring. But finally, late in the day, the Romans prevailed; and they slew many in battle beside the wagons and the forest, and captured many alive. Nevertheless, not a few made their escape and were preparing to fight again. In the meantime, however, Buduica fell sick and died. The Britons mourned her deeply and gave her a costly burial; but, feeling that now at last they were really defeated, they scattered to their homes. So much for affairs in Britain. [64]

In this account we hear about the use of chariots by the Britons and are also presented with more details of the battle, although we do not know the degree of their accuracy. Boudica becomes ill and dies, rather than taking poison, another dramatic contrast with Tacitus's account in the *Annals*. We also hear that she was given a costly burial, which, during the seventeenth to nineteenth centuries, inspired a number of antiquaries to search for her remains.

These three accounts of the events provide a good deal of information. It is important to realise, however, that Tacitus and Dio were engaged in a form of story-telling which limits the archaeological value of their accounts. To the Roman aristocracy Britain was a distant and remarkable place and Roman writers made use of this idea in various ways in their accounts. The aims that lay behind them restricts the value of the information that they present to us.[65] Some of the ruling classes in Rome will have had knowledge of events in Britain, having served in senior positions within the army or the administration there, but there would have been no one to put forward a contrasting view to those that were developed by these writers. Tacitus used events in Britain to moralise about the state of the empire in more general terms. For instance, the comments that are put into the mouths of the Britons in the *Agricola* and the speech made by Boudica before the final battle in the *Annals* are intended for Tacitus's audience in Rome rather than representing an accurate historical account. They articulate an aristocratic Roman rhetoric of dissent.[66]

Roman writers explored issues that interested their audiences. In these terms, Boudica was highly relevant as an influential female native leader who led her people to war against Rome. Queens fascinated educated Roman men.[67] Roman writers, almost invariably male, effectively provided stereotypical views of these female leaders. They were not so much an assortment of individuals as a recognisable type, recurring from time to time and place to place. Male Roman writers wrote about powerful women, such as Boudica, in native societies using a stock formula. To understand why this might have been the case we need to consider Roman attitudes to kingship and gender.

Early in its history the city of Rome had been ruled by kings, but later the idea of kingship was generally feared, even after the first emperor, Augustus, effectively adopted monarchical rule. Although the expanding empire of Rome came into contact with many kings, the Roman aristocracy maintained a serious distrust of monarchy. The Roman aristocratic male mind was much concerned with the concept of the abuse of unfettered power.[68] While native kings are described in unflattering terms, the Roman fear of kingship emerges far more strongly in accounts of barbarian queens, such as Cleopatra VII of Egypt and the two recorded native queens of Britain. The fear of monarchical rule was associated with anxieties concerning issues of gender, as native queens were perceived as breaking with the acceptable gender roles of Roman society.[69] Roman women usually had limited power in a society ruled by men, although they could have wealth and influence.[70]

Britain was effectively a theatre for classical Roman views of women.[71] Two powerful female figures emerged during the first century AD to feed the Roman fascination – Cartimandua and Boudica. Cartimandua was queen of the Brigantes, who occupied northern Britain. She cooperated with the Romans and was permitted to keep her kingdom until AD 69. She appears to have had various problems with her tribe as a result of her pro-Roman views and Tacitus gives a vivid account of some of her actions in the *Annals* and *Histories*. He portrays her as treacherous, immoral and adulterous.[72] Boudica, in the *Annals*, is developed in contrast to Cartimandua, as moral, if ultimately misguided.[73] This suggests that we should be critical of the accounts that Tacitus provides for the life and actions of Boudica.

In the *Annals*, Tacitus describes Boudica as a high-ranking woman who was a mother acting to avenge herself, her wronged daughters and her people. In fact, she is not described as a queen at all, merely the wife of King Prasutagus, thereby avoiding Roman censure. Tacitus's portrayal of Boudica in the *Annals* is of a heroic figure. She revolts against Rome because of serious provocation from the Roman authorities, including the removal of the property of her husband Prasutagus and the raping of their two daughters. The treatment that Tacitus records as having been meted out to Boudica and her daughters was outrageous – it was completely at odds with their royal status, in addition to being carried out by their social inferiors – Roman slaves and junior officers.[74] To educated members of the Roman elite, such as Tacitus and his intended audience, the physical abuse of high-ranking members of a native society by slaves would have been particularly shocking. It is only with the atrocities committed by the ancient Britons on the inhabitants of the three towns and with the return of Suetonius Paulinus from the island of Mona that Rome regained both the military and moral upper hand over the Britons.[75]

The gender issues raised by Tacitus's account in the *Annals* are,

however, far wider than the role of Boudica herself.[76] It has been suggested that the struggle between Suetonius and the Britons was, at least
in part, developed as a dispute between masculine Roman order and
feminine native disorder.[77] We hear that the Britons brought their wives
to watch their expected victory over the Romans and, in fact, their presence at the scene of the final battle effectively increased the scale of the
rout that the Britons suffered at the hands of the Romans. In addition,
Suetonius is made to say that there were more women than there were
men in the British ranks.[78] Although Tacitus uses Boudica's gender in a
positive manner to emphasise her scandalous treatment by the Romans,
her gender also presented him with a problem.

Tacitus had already developed these aspects of Boudica in the *Agricola*. She is described as of the royal house but Tacitus says nothing
about Prasutagus, the flogging of Boudica or the rape of her daughters.
She is presented as a ruling queen – a grotesque character to the Roman
mind.[79] This image of unfettered female power contrasts directly with
Boudica's role in Tacitus's *Annals* as a provoked maternal figure. In
turn, Dio's account of Boudica has been characterised as 'inventions and
inversions' of Tacitus's writings.[80] It is closer to the image put forward
in the *Agricola* in that Dio does not mention the role of Prasutagus or
the removal of his property by the Romans. He also does not mention
the abuse of Boudica or her daughters, as recorded in the *Annals*. As
such, the provocation to which Boudica appears to have been subjected
is excluded from Dio's account. Instead he stresses the ignominy of the
Romans in being beaten in the initial engagements of the rebellion by a
force led by a woman.[81]

Overall, Boudica is pictured as a queen who led a revolt against Rome.
It has been suggested that Dio effectively portrays her as an iniquitous
and monstrous female who fought against the rightful power of Rome.[82]
Dio describes Boudica as psychologically and physically male: she has
the size, voice and weapons of a man.[83] In fact, as we have seen, in the
speech that she makes to the Britons at the start of the revolt, she claims
to be more of a man than her counterpart, the emperor Nero. His
effeminacy is stressed and it is significant that as a writer Dio had a fascination with the sexuality of several Roman emperors.[84] Dio effectively
uses Boudica to support an idea that he developed in his work – that, in
the reign of the Emperor Nero, gender transgressions were the order of

the day.[85] Boudica becomes a 'masculine female' in order to counter the effeminacy and corruption of the Roman emperor. Placed in the mouth of a barbarian woman, the criticisms of Nero and Rome are especially telling, as educated Romans judged non-Romans (barbarians) as inferior to Romans and women as inferior to men.[86] The emphasis that Dio places on the damage and chaos caused by the rebellion of the Britons – two cities sacked, many Romans and provincials killed, and the island alienated from Rome – demonstrates the power and perceived barbarity of Boudica and her followers. As such, Dio's Boudica is an inversion of the honourable, wounded mother figure of the *Annals*.[87]

Dio's description effectively portrays Boudica as a forceful and formidable warrior-queen, inspiring her portrayal by later writers as sexually attractive.[88] As we shall see, this idea of a forceful and glamorous female leader was a gift to later British poets, dramatists and artists.

One final account, probably of Boudica, was written by the sixth-century British author Gildas, who describes her actions in *The Ruin of Britain* (*De excidio et conquestu Britanniae*). He writes that:

> A treacherous lioness butchered the governors who had been left to give fuller voice and strength to the endeavours of Roman rule.[89]

This reference, which is probably to Boudica, may demonstrate that knowledge of her actions survived in Britain after the fall of the Western Roman Empire. The native historians Bede and Nennius also mention Boudica's revolt, but they do not mention Boudica herself.[90] Bede, who finished his *Ecclesiastical History* in AD 731, records how Britain was almost lost to the Romans during the reign of the Emperor Nero and that at this time 'two very noble cities were captured and destroyed'.[91] The knowledge that these authors had of the rebellion may have been derived from the writings of Tacitus and Dio surviving in monastic collections in Britain. After this time, all memory of Boudica was probably lost, as the classical literature itself was no longer available to scholars.[92]

3

The Archaeological Evidence

The terrible events of 60–61 are very much writ large both in the ancient literature, and in the ground today.

T. W. Potter 2002, 35.

As we have seen, the works of Roman literature that tell us about the events of AD 60 to 61 were written by high-ranking male authors for a Roman audience. Much of the 'evidence' that they provide needs to be evaluated critically. The archaeological evidence must be considered with equal care. For generations, people have been enthusiastically searching in the archaeological record for the historical events mentioned by Tacitus and Dio.

In the past, people have often tried to locate history through archaeological excavations; the search for the site of ancient Troy is a good example. The revolt of Boudica has similarly been used as a seductive chronological marker to work out the archaeological sequence of events in early Roman Britain.[1] Archaeologists working in London, Colchester and Verulamium, when excavating early Roman deposits, have noted layers of burning overlying destroyed buildings. They have identified this as the result of the destruction of these towns by the British rebels. Evidence for other dramatic acts of vandalism elsewhere in southern Britain, and other disparate pieces of archaeological material, have also been connected with Boudica and her followers. Burning, vandalism and connected activities on sites in the south and east of Britain and dating to the period of the middle of the first century AD are often automatically tied in with the rebellion, sometimes without a sufficiently detailed analysis. For example, it has been suggested that human skulls from the Walbrook stream in London may have come from victims of the massacre in Londinium of AD 60 to 61.[2] These particular remains, however, form part of a long tradition of the deposition of human skulls in the River Thames and the Walbrook. Dating indicates that they were put in these watercourses throughout the Iron Age and up until the second century AD.[3]

To demonstrate this point further, consider two examples of misidentification, one from the nineteenth century and another from the twentieth. When 'the famous discovery' was made of the remains of a 'priest of the temple of Colchester' in around 1826, it was argued that he was buried alive by Boudica's followers. We know of this discovery because the Rev. H. Jenkins wrote an early description of the site of Camulodunum, published in 1842 in the journal *Archaeologia*. He described the discovery of this body at the point where a Roman road ran across an 'old British road' on Lexden Hill (just to the west of the colony). Workmen widening a turnpike road found various relics, apparently including gold rings, but:

> The most extraordinary relique ... was the skeleton of a man with his head downward, and a patera beside him ... From the emblem of his office, and the mortal aversion with which the Britons regarded the priests of Claudius, we may imagine the skeleton to have been that of a priest, who in his attempt to escape during the insurrections, had been seized by the Britons and buried alive.[4]

The patera, a small bowl with a single straight flat handle, is a fairly common find from Roman sites, although it is rarely found with burials. The presence of a patera is certainly not easily identifiable as a badge of office for priests of Claudius and, without convincing evidence that the burial occurred in AD 60 to 61, it is highly unlikely that the individual was buried by the rebellious ancient Britons. In addition, the argument that he was buried alive is not convincing. In the past, some authors have been quite willing to accept attractive ideas, such as the capture and burial of this priest,[5] but the evidence does not stand up to close scrutiny.

The second example of misidentification involves the tombstone of a Roman auxiliary soldier called Longinus Sdapeze (figure 19). This was found in Lexden Road, Colchester in 1928,[6] quite close to the burial of the supposed priest. It is now on display in Colchester Museum. Longinus became famous within Roman archaeology because his tombstone, although damaged, is very well preserved. The stone presents us with

19. The tombstone of Longinus Sdapeze from Colchester. (*Copyright Colchester Museums*)

some fascinating information about this soldier, such as the fact that he served as a cavalry officer with a unit called the First Thracian Cavalry. He came from a place called Sardicia (the modern Sofia in Bulgaria) and died aged forty after fifteen years of service in the Roman army. The stone is a very fine example of a type that occurs on a number of military sites across Britain and Germany. It is carved with an image of Longinus on a horse, riding down and presumably killing a naked native Briton. It was found face down and damaged. Previous authors have suggested that, at the time of Boudica's revolt, native Britons may well have been enraged by the stone's overt portrayal of the power and dominance of Rome.[7] This would certainly account for the removal of the face of Longinus and the blow to the horse's nose, before the stone was tipped onto its face to obscure the figure entirely.

Unfortunately, this no longer appears to be a likely reconstruction of events. More recent archaeological work on the site of the stone's discovery in 1996 located some stone chippings from the same tombstone and also, more remarkably, the missing face of Longinus.[8] It is now thought that the damage may actually have occurred when the tombstone was discovered by the workmen who uncovered it. The importance of the stone was probably not realised until it was turned over, by which time the workmen may have started to break it up.[9] The damage to the stone may not have been connected in any way with the actions of Boudica or her followers.[10] The idea of the effective 'beheading' of Longinus and the destruction of his tomb by Boudica's forces no longer appears probable. It still remains a possibility that the rebels pushed down the stone, as its unworn state suggests that it was not left in the open and exposed to the weather for very long. In addition, the stone has been cracked across its base, which may indicate that it was pushed over by force.[11] In reality, however, we do not know how it came to fall upon its face and there may be no connection whatsoever with the events of AD 60 to 61.

These two examples – the burial with a patera and the tombstone of Longinus – demonstrate the value of detailed archaeological work. If the burial of the supposed priest of Claudius were to be excavated today, we have more detailed ways of assessing the date at which the body was buried. The idea that he was buried alive could also be investigated. Careful and thorough excavation can also result in important evidence being recovered, such as that for the face of Longinus. The work that led to this discovery effectively involved the excavation of the activities of the workmen in 1928. As a result, we have a fuller understanding of the context of the overturning of the tombstone.

A third example of possible misidentification is both more mundane and also more complex. A shop that stocked high-quality Roman pottery (samian ware) was excavated in Colchester, the so-called 'First Pottery Shop', during the 1920s.[12] Samian was a distinctive and high quality Roman pottery that was made in Gaul (modern-day France) and imported into Britain in large quantities for use by the army and civilians.[13] The shop's stock probably ran to several thousand vessels, mostly imported, intended for the dining tables of rich people who lived in and around the colony. The shop was burned to the ground just after the middle of the first century AD, leaving an assemblage of pots (figure 20) and also some molten glass vessels. Stacked samian bowls were found cemented together by molten glass that had dripped from above before the building collapsed.[14] For many years after its discovery the destruction of this shop was claimed as clear evidence for the burning of the town by Boudica's followers.[15] More recently, detailed work at the factories at which the samian pottery was produced, and the places where it was used and thrown away, has told us far more about the pottery and enabled it to be dated with more accuracy. Detailed analysis of the samian assemblage from this shop has indicated that it was distinctively earlier than other collections of samian from destruction deposits at Camulodunum, Verulamium and Londinium that do appear to be of Boudican date.[16] It would appear that this pottery shop was selling out of date samian to the population of Camlodunum in AD 60 to 61, as it is unlikely that it burned down independently of the actions of Boudica and at sometime beforehand.[17] Indeed, recent excavations close by have provided no evidence for an earlier fire.

Modern excavation and the detailed analysis of what is found can often provide a fuller understanding of the history of past events; those of AD 60 to 61 can sometimes be seen to be rather more complex than past accounts have suggested. Modern analysis of archaeological stratigraphy may enable us to locate Boudican destruction deposits on significant sites, but careful examination is required if errors are to be

20. Samian pottery from the destruction layer at Colchester. (*Copyright Colchester Archaeological Trust*)

avoided. Interpretations of the archaeological evidence must be cautious since, as these three examples show, it is very tempting for archaeologists to claim that their evidence has an association with Boudica. Where careful analysis has been undertaken, as on the samian assemblages from the three towns, some of the evidence presented in the historical accounts may be assessed in comparison with the information from archaeological research.

Since the 1980s archaeologists have effectively undermined much of the evidence that has previously been associated with Boudica's rebellion. That having been said, it would appear that, for at least two sites, the events of AD 60 to 61 have left a clear archaeological picture that links them with the historical evidence. Since early in the twentieth century archaeologists working in London have claimed evidence for the rebellion in the form of a thick layer of burning close to the base of the Roman layers in the city.[18] Similar evidence has been found in Colchester.[19] In each case this layer of burned material overlies the remains of the early Roman settlement. It varies in depth from a few centimetres to half a metre (an inch to a foot and a half) across the built-up areas. Building remains and material culture survive both beneath and within the deposit on both sites. Owing to the swift and catastrophic burning and general destruction of the settlements, the evidence gives us a snapshot of the development of two Roman towns in southern Britain less than twenty years after the Roman invasion. It also gives the archaeologist the opportunity to date sealed assemblages of material that were in use at the time of the revolt, particularly pottery.[20]

At Camulodunum and Londinium the results of the Boudican revolt may be compared, on a smaller scale, with those of the volcanic eruptions that smothered Pompeii and Herculaneum.[21] These two Roman cities, whose sites are close to modern Naples, were buried after the eruption of Mount Vesuvius in AD 79.[22] Over the past three hundred years, excavations at the sites have produced remarkable evidence both for buildings and for the daily lives of the inhabitants. The sacking of Camulodunum and Londinium had an almost equally dramatic impact, totally destroying the towns and dramatically reducing the local urban populations.

Verulamium presents a more complex problem. It has often been supposed that the evidence for this site indicates that it was totally destroyed at the same time as Camulodunum and Londinium.[23] Recently, however, it has been argued that the destruction of property at Verulamium was rather less thorough than at the other two towns as it is restricted only to a few areas.[24] Within the town it now appears that some of the burning that has been uncovered may have occurred in an unrelated fire around AD 80, long after Boudica's death.[25] This leads us to wonder if the Boudican destruction of the town would have been suggested at all if Tacitus had not mentioned it.

Boudica's rebellion presents the archaeologist with an opportunity. The resultant burned deposits sealed the buildings of the settlements and so have enabled archaeologists to study the evidence and to build up a picture of the early towns of the south east. The colony at Camulodunum, as we have seen, was an official town of Roman settlers. Tacitus tells us that it included a number of public buildings. By AD 60 Londinium appears to have been developed as a trading place for merchants. It was a planned settlement with ribbon developments, but few traces have yet been found of public buildings. Verulamium was a tribal town and was developing as a settlement with a range of public buildings. Excavations have been undertaken at all three sites and have produced evidence of their extent and the nature of the acts of destruction that were carried out. On all the sites only limited areas of the original settlements have been excavated, but we can build up a fairly coherent picture from the work so far.

Tacitus tells us that, after her problems with the Roman administration, Boudica led a rebellion in which her tribe was joined by the Trinovantes and others. Dio tells us that the army was around 120,000 strong at this time. We are told that the Trinovantes had been provoked into supporting the rebellion because they were outraged as the result of the establishment of a colony for retired soldiers at Colchester. These veterans were soldiers from the legions who had been settled in a Roman-style town. Tacitus tells us in the *Annals* that this colony was established as a settlement of ex-soldiers;[26] this seems to have been in around AD 49 to 50. The aim of the Roman administration was to protect the country against revolt and to familiarise the provincials with law-abiding government.

The colony was effectively designed as a showpiece of Roman culture and we know from Tacitus's narrative that it contained a major temple and a theatre. The temple to the divine emperor Claudius there seemed to the Britons, according to Tacitus, to be a 'a blatant stronghold of alien rule', while the establishment of the colony had dispossessed at least some of the native people of their land and resources. The senate house may have formed part of the forum and basilica complex, of a type that was standard in Roman towns. A theatre is mentioned by both Tacitus and Dio. It is possible that these two public buildings are described by these authors because they assumed that a colony would contain such buildings.[27]

Roman colonies were common throughout the Roman Empire. They often had a standard form with a grid system of paved roads and a focal forum and basilica complex that was the centre of local government by the local senate, or governing body, of the colony. A colony was a self-governing group of Roman citizens, effectively an extension of the city of Rome itself. Since the 1970s an important series of excavations have been carried out within the modern town of Colchester (figure 21). Although limited in extent, this has provided vital evidence about the earlier fortress and the later colony.[28] The colony was established when the pre-existing legionary fortress was abandoned and many of its buildings and streets were reused in the early phases of its development.[29] Many of the military buildings were adapted for civilian use, providing houses for the settlers. It has been suggested that the defensive ditches of the fortress were filled in because the area it contained was not large enough for the laying out of the public buildings and houses of the colony. Excavations at the Balkerne Lane site indicate that buildings burned in AD 60 to 61 were built over the filled in ditches and ramparts of the defences, which confirms Tacitus's claim that the colony was undefended when it was attacked by Boudica.[30] The headquarters building of the fortress may have acted as the new forum and basilica.[31]

The area beyond the fortress to the east, which had formed an annex, was given over, at least in part, to public buildings, including the temple of Claudius and perhaps the theatre.[32] The temple of Claudius indicates that Camulodunum operated as the centre of imperial worship before the revolt.[33] It is possible, for various reasons, that the building of the temple began prior to the death of Claudius in AD 54.[34] It was a monumental building, the podium of which survives today in the vaults

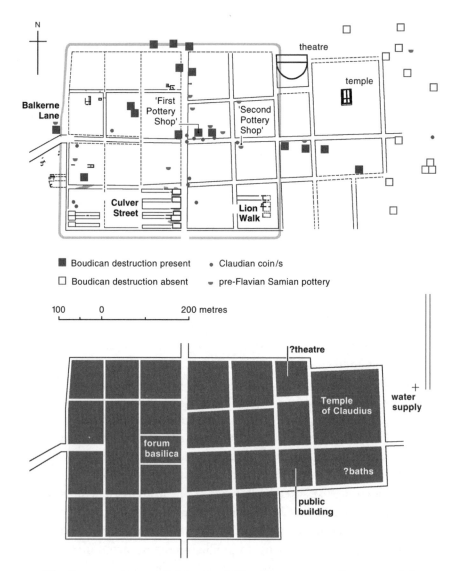

theatre

temple

Balkerne
Lane

'First
Pottery
Shop'

'Second
Pottery
Shop'

Culver
Street

Lion
Walk

■ Boudican destruction present   • Claudian coin/s

☐ Boudican destruction absent   ◡ pre-Flavian Samian pottery

100   0   200 metres

?theatre

water
supply

Temple
of Claudius

forum
basilica

?baths

public
building

21. The Roman colony at Colchester. (*After Crummy 1999, figures 2 and 3*)

of Colchester Castle. Most colonies also possessed a theatre, where plays and religious ceremonies were performed. The site of the theatre has been located close to the temple of Claudius;[35] it may have played a role in the way that the cult of the emperor functioned.

In addition to the veteran soldiers, the colony would have attracted tradesmen and merchants. Some may have travelled to the province to exploit new economic opportunities but others must have come from the native population of Britain. There is evidence that, prior to the revolt, small shops fronted the road leading to Londinium. Two pottery shops, for example, supplied samian pottery to the inhabitants of the colony. In AD 60 to 61, this colony was a prosperous and developing town of cosmopolitan inhabitants. The population of the town and surrounding territory may have numbered only around 4000 people,[36] possibly more. The evidence from excavations demonstrates that the colony was totally destroyed in AD 60 to 61.

The Britons attacked this colony, which was only defended, according to Tacitus, by two hundred lightly-armed men in addition to its own garrison. The town had no walls and was overwhelmed. The defenders made a final stand at the temple of Claudius where they took shelter; and, after a siege that lasted two days, were finally defeated. The Ninth Legion attempted to relieve the town but was routed with the loss of the entire infantry force, while their commander escaped with the cavalry.

None of these events, apart from the sack of the town itself, has left any specific traces that have been found by archaeologists. Evidence for the destruction of the colony has been located from the 1920s onwards.[37] Sheepen, the site of a late Iron Age and early Roman industrial complex and settlement, outside and to the north west of the colony, effectively ceased to be occupied around the time of the rebellion.[38] Some of the structures on this site showed signs of burning and much of the debris was 'decently' buried in pits after the rebellion.[39] Evidence was found for the production of Roman military equipment at this site, including various fragments of body armour, weapons and a remarkable 'bagful' of helmets, which had been dumped in a pit.[40] At the time of the excavation it was suggested that, when Sheepen was destroyed, metal-workers on the site were working in a desperate attempt to rearm the colonists.[41] This is an attractive picture, but it is now felt more likely that the military metalwork was scrap, brought to the site sometime after AD 43 for recycling, and that the deposits are not directly connected to the Boudican destruction.[42]

During the excavations of the colony itself, a distinctive layer of burned material was found to lie across the Roman deposits in a dated horizon that relates to the period of around AD 60 to 61 (see figure 21 for the location of deposits in which Boudican destruction was present).[43] There are thousands of other archaeological layers under the present town, but the destruction layer is so distinctive that it is easily recognisable.[44] It sometimes represents half of the total depth of the Roman period deposits and ranges from a few centimetres to half a metre in thickness.[45] It has been suggested that the tiled roofs and daub walls of the buildings would have prevented the fire from spreading easily from one property to another. As a result, it is likely that the rebels set light to the buildings one by one and fed the fire with care in order to destroy the colony thoroughly.[46]

Much of the deposit is made up of daub, red or black clay that was incorporated in the timber buildings of the colony. Most early towns in Britain had buildings that were built in similar ways, but the daub used to build house walls does not survive unless it was exposed to fire. The conflagration that engulfed the town fired the clay into a solid mass that has survived to be uncovered during archaeological excavations (figure 22). Fragments of painted plaster and tiles from roofs, together with pottery, are common; more personal items include two door keys that were found within the destruction deposit.[47]

Occasionally the lower parts of the walls of the buildings are preserved to a height of up to 0.6 metre (one foot ten inches), providing important information for the buildings of both the legionary fortress and the early phase of the colony.[48] In other places walls collapsed in large sections during the fire.[49] A surprising variety of building techniques were represented, but many of the buildings were modest structures and there are few mosaics or tessellated floors to indicate that people aspired to grander architecture.[50] At least one room in a building at Lion Walk was, however, decorated with painted wall plaster.[51]

Because the colony was burned so thoroughly, this destruction deposit is found over all the parts of the town that were occupied around AD 60. Later on the town was rebuilt and extended further eastwards, but burned deposits are not found in these areas. Some significant

22. The remains of a building in Colchester destroyed by fire in AD 60 or 61. (*Copyright Colchester Archaeological Trust*)

collections of pottery found in particular buildings may indicate shops or warehouses. At North Hill a building that appears to have been a store produced more than thirty identical mortaria. An easily recognisable form of pottery that was introduced to Britain by the Romans, a mortarium was an open bowl with grits set into its inside face so that foodstuffs could be ground down. Another room produced over eighty flagons and in the next room were found twenty amphorae, large two-handled jars, mostly from Spain and originally containing olive oil. [52] The pots had all been smashed, possibly by the rebellious Britons. This building also contained large quantities of carbonised grain. [53] On the High Street were the two shops that sold samian, one of which was burned along with much of its stock of pottery and glassware, including over six hundred vessels of samian pottery. [54]

The burning of the colony also preserved the remains of other food-stuffs, presenting information on the diet of the colony's inhabitants. Several sites have produced carbonised grain, often predominantly wheat. [55] In Culver Street a deposit mostly of barley had started to germinate before it was burned. It is likely that this was part of the malting process of ale production. If so, this is the earliest convincing example of ale-making in Britain. [56] Some evidence was found for more exotic food-stuffs, as at Lion Walk, where there was a deposit of twenty-three dates (figure 23) which must have been imported from the Mediterranean, and a single plum. [57] Figs were found in one of the pottery shops, as were lentils, horse beans (a variety of broad bean) and the spice coriander.

Other finds also tell us something of the lives of the people. One remarkable find in Lion Walk was a pair of textile mattresses that had been tucked into the corner of a room and preserved because of the conflagration. [58] At Sheepen a leaded bronze dice-shaker was found with two dice. Lamps, moulds and a glass cameo of a sea nymph have been found on other sites together with some coins. Mixed up with the occasional complete find are a whole range of broken objects, including pottery and brooches. Very few finds of any real material value to their owners have been found, which may indicate that the site was cleared of valuable possessions by the occupants before the fire, or that it was thoroughly cleared of anything of worth after the destruction. [59] Tacitus's account suggests that few of the occupants managed to escape, but he may have overdramatised the scale of the slaughter for effect. It is possible that the valuable objects were removed by the rebels after the burning of the colony, but it is also evident that there was a later clearing up operation before or during the rebuilding of the colony. In places the mixed nature of the burned deposit shows that it was disturbed as part of the works that were carried out to rebuild the town.[60] Tiles with burn marks have been found reused in the foundations of later buildings.[61] Pits that were dug into the destruction layer and backfilled with burned material may indicate other attempts to look for valuable objects.[62] There are three groups of Roman coins that may have been buried during the revolt. All consist of relatively low numbers of brass or copper coins.

The tombstone of Longinus in the cemetery to the west of the colony may have been pushed over onto its carved face during the revolt, although it now appears that it may have been damaged much more recently. This stone was found just over three metres (ten feet) from the edge of a Roman road which it originally faced.[63] Another tombstone possibly pushed over by Boudica's rebels was that of Marcus Favonius Facilis (figure 24), an officer in the Twentieth Legion. This was also broken at the base and found face down in the ground.[64] Both tombstones were relatively unweathered and this suggests that they may have been buried in AD 60 to 61. Tacitus's account suggests that there were many deaths among the inhabitants of the colony, but few bodies have been found. At the Telephone Exchange site the charred and disarticulated remains of an adult lay on the veranda of a building fronting a street.[65] The fact that human remains from the colony are rare may suggest either that the scale of the conflagration was sufficient to incinerate completely the remains of the victims, or that the bodies were removed after the fire.

There is another possible reason for the absence of human bodies in the burned remains. Dio describes how the victims of the conflict were slaughtered, accompanied by 'sacrifices, banquets and wanton behaviour'. This occurred in all of 'their sacred places', but also, in particular 'in the grove of Andate', who appears to have been the Britons' goddess of victory. If Dio's account was based on an accurate record, this may suggest that many victims were removed alive and sacrificed as offerings to the gods in special places. In France, pre-Roman shrines occasionally produce masses of human bones, suggesting human sacrifice on a large scale, although it is equally likely that they represent a form of communal burial tradition.[66] Human remains are sometimes

0   5 centimetres

23. Charred dates from the destruction layer of AD 60 or 61 in Colchester. (*Copyright Colchester Archaeological Trust*)

24. The tombstone of Marcus Favonius Facilis from Colchester. (*Copyright Colchester Museums*)

found on pre-Roman sacred sites in Britain, although there is no evidence for the sacrificing of large numbers of people.[67] It has been argued that the references to human sacrifices in accounts such as that of Dio actually result from the fact that authors from the Mediterranean tended to overemphasise the barbaric nature of the native peoples of Britain and the Continent. Perhaps they did this in order to emphasise the contrast between the native peoples of the periphery of the empire and those whom they perceived as the civilised people of Rome and the Mediterranean.[68] Dio may certainly have been exaggerating the actions of the Britons. If the victims of the sacking of Camulodunum, Londinium and Verulamium were taken away to suffer a grisly death at sacred sites, such places have yet to be located.

Two objects that may represent looting by Boudica's followers are possibly from a single equestrian statue of the Emperor Claudius that had been hacked to pieces. A life-sized hollow bronze head thought to represent Claudius was found in the River Alde at Rendham in Suffolk in 1907 (figure 25).[69] It is now on display in the Roman Britain gallery of the British Museum, while a copy is on display in Colchester Museum. A jagged line around the neck demonstrates that it was wrenched from the body of the statue,[70] while a slight backward tilt of the neck suggests that it may once have been part of a statue that portrayed the emperor on horseback.[71] Part of the leg of a bronze horse has been found at Ashill in Norfolk, thirty-seven miles (sixty kilometres) from Colchester. The fragment was found by a metal-detector user in 1979 and is now on display in Norwich Museum and Art Gallery. It represents the hock of a horse from a hollow bronze statue; both ends of the piece are ragged, suggesting that the original object was roughly chopped up.[72] Metalurgical analysis of the Ashill fragment and of the head from Rendham indicates that both pieces have a similar low lead content and may come from the same statue.[73] The leg fragment was found in the southern part of a ditched enclosure (figure 26) that was partly excavated in the nineteenth century; it is not clear whether this represents a settlement or ritual enclosure, or even a Roman fort.[74]

If this statue was indeed of Claudius it may even have been looted from a public building at Camulodunum or elsewhere,[75] broken up on site and parts removed for deposition on sacred sites in various locations in southern Britain. The head would have made a splendid trophy that

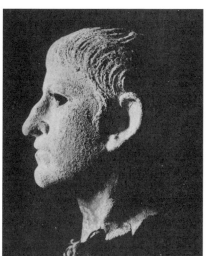

25. The head of a life-size bronze statue of the Emperor Claudius, found in the River Alde. (*From Macdonald 1927, plates II and III*)

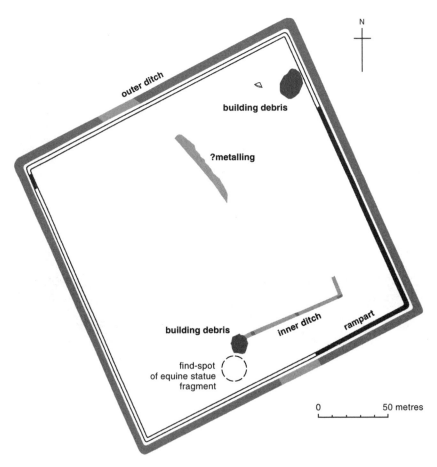

N

outer ditch

building debris

?metalling

building debris

inner ditch

rampart

find-spot
of equine statue
fragment

0   50 metres

26. The enclosure at Ashill in Norfolk. (*After Lawson 1986, figure 2*)

could have been carried on a pole to have mud and rubbish thrown at it by a jeering and triumphant Britons.[76] It may have been thrown into the river because of fears of reprisals during the repression of the rebellion;[77] but there is an alternative interpretation. The places where the statue fragments were found may actually provide us with some indication of the location of two of the sacred sites that were mentioned by Dio. During the Iron Age it was a common practice to deposit metal objects in rivers and bogs[78] and perhaps the find from the River Alde indicates a sacred place associated with a river. The enclosure at Ashill produced a variety of additional unusual finds and may, along with the site at Fison Way (Thetford), represent an important tribal sanctuary. Perhaps, if Dio's accounts of human sacrifices are to be believed, the remains of some of the people lie close by these two places.

Tacitus tells us that London, although it not did rank as a Roman settlement, was an important centre for businessmen and merchandise at the time it was attacked by Boudica's followers. He also states that the settlement was evacuated before it was burned by the rebels, but records that some of the people who stayed behind – because they were women, old, or attached to the place – were slaughtered.

The early history of London is unclear. In contrast to Camulodunum and Verulamium, no trace of substantial pre-Roman occupation has been found. Settlements have been located at a few sites, for instance to the south of the River Thames at Southwark, but these sites appear to be farms of a type that was typical across southern Britain. No evidence for an *oppidum* has been found.[79] The Thames at London was far wider at this time than it is today; detailed analysis suggests that the river featured extensive tidal channels and mud flats (figure 27). At high tide it is likely that the river was around one thousand metres (3280 feet) wide in places.[80] It would have been a major barrier to communication. The islands and the two low hills on the north side of the river presented an obvious location for the establishment of a river crossing.[81] The earliest causeway across these mudflats may have built around AD 50–52, or perhaps slightly earlier, exploiting the island in the middle of the river.[82] Alternatively a ferry may have operated at this early stage in the development of London, with the first bridge being constructed at a later date. The crossing of the Thames at this point is likely to have been

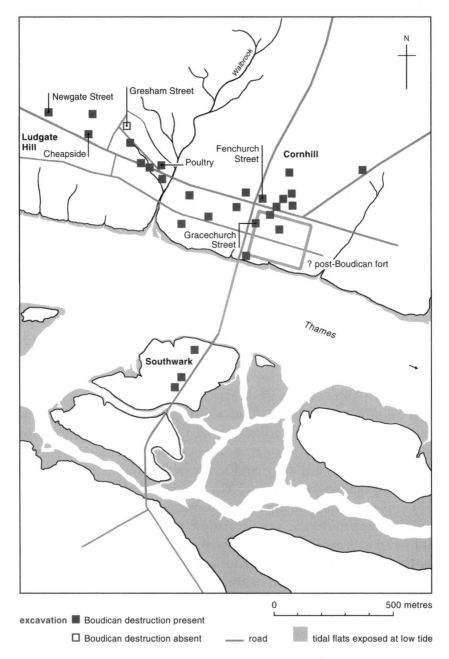

N

Walbrook

Newgate Street   Gresham Street

Ludgate Hill

Cheapside

Poultry

Fenchurch Street   **Cornhill**

Gracechurch Street

? post-Boudican fort

Thames

Southwark

0   500 metres

excavation ■ Boudican destruction present

☐ Boudican destruction absent   —— road   tidal flats exposed at low tide

27. Early Roman London. (*After Drummond-Murray and Thompson 2002, figure 40. Based on information provided by the Museum of London Archaeology Service*)

the reason that the initial settlement at London began to develop,[83] coming to represent the hub of the new Roman road network in Britain.

It appears that a small settlement began to develop by AD 47, expanding into to a larger area by AD 60. It has been suggested that there may have been an early Roman fort at London and, while no definite evidence has been found to support this, some ditches, possibly dug by the Roman military, have been located.[84] The heart of the settlement was located just to the north of the site of London Bridge today, on the southern side of Cornhill. It appears to have had a fairly orderly layout, with buildings set parallel to or at a right angle to the river, arranged along various roads.[85] Recent excavation at 1 Poultry, alongside the Roman-period stream (today the Walbrook) has indicated that the first road was probably laid out by AD 47,[86] dated by the dendro-chronological analysis of the wooden drain which ran under it. Dendrochronology is an archaeological technique that dates wood by counting tree rings in the timber and cross-matching other recorded fragments in order to calculate the year in which the tree was felled. This method of dating has been particularly useful in London, as wood is often preserved in the waterlogged conditions that are found during archaeological excavations in the city.[87] This date of around AD 47 may indicate the initial foundation of the settlement and it is possible that the earliest occupation covered an area between Poultry and Cornhill. Many of the houses at Poultry, however, were built around AD 58 to 59, suggesting that settlement was spreading swiftly in this direction from the early core of London around Cornhill. By AD 50 settlement had also spread to the area south of the Thames, modern Southwark.[88]

By AD 60 London appears to have spread westwards from the Walbrook stream towards Ludgate Hill. By this time the settlement was a large and lively frontier town, possibly covering around fifteen hectares (thirty-seven acres) with a cosmopolitan population that was derived from various parts of the empire. Recent archaeological excavation has produced important evidence about the early development of the town. For example, work at 1 Poultry has uncovered rich evidence for settlement that predated AD 60 to 61.[89] The initial road on this site was well made from rammed gravel laid on a raised bed of sand and clay and silt; it was wide enough for two carts to pass each other and was flanked by timber drains. By AD 60 a side road had been constructed and earth-and-timber buildings occupied most of the road frontage, with sheds and outhouses in the land to the rear (figure 28). Evidence for light industry and manufacturing was also found. Excavation at Cheapside has located a nine-metre (29 feet six inches) wide road, one of the first features on the site, and an adjacent building constructed of timber that was felled in AD 53, with a rebuilding phase six years later.[90]

Most of the buildings of this developing settlement were rectangular in plan and had wattle and daub walls, earthen floors and roofs of thatch or wooden shingles, while the buildings at Southwark had tile roofs.[91] Fragments of green and red painted plaster indicate that rooms in some houses were decorated, but only in the case of three out of the thirty-five buildings of this date that have been studied.[92] Purbeck marble was a popular form of building material from the Isle of Purbeck used to decorate public buildings and private houses in the early Roman period. A tile and concrete floor was found in one of the buildings to the west of the Walbrook. It also produced an impressive collection of imported pottery and was probably the house of an important person in the community.[93] On the periphery of the settlement at Newgate Street evidence has been found for timber-built roundhouses constructed in the native tradition.[94] During more recent excavations eleven similar buildings have been found in a slightly more central location at 10 Gresham Street. These appear to predate AD 60 and were associated with the production of native-style glass beads.[95] Roundhouses were the standard form of pre-Roman building across much of southern Britain. The examples from early Roman London are very important because they suggest that the population of the town at this time included native people in addition to settlers originating from outside Britain, as settlers are unlikely to have built round buildings.

There is little evidence for impressive classical public buildings such as the temple of Claudius, although such structures were built later in the history of Roman London. A simple street grid had been laid out and a gravelled area near to the centre may have been the site of an early market.[96] The occupants of at least part of the town had piped water, indicated by a wooden water-main apparently dating to before AD 60.[97] These features suggest that the growing town may have had its own town council running affairs and organising the developing infrastructure of the settlement.

28. A reconstruction of early Roman occupation at 1 Poultry, London. (*Drawn by Judith Dobie. From Rowsome 2000, p. 19*)

Evidence for industrial activity includes a kiln that was being used to produce pottery for use by the occupants of London, and there is also evidence for the production of bronze, iron and glass objects.[98] There were immigrant craftsmen with new skills: for example, a potter, Caius Albucius, from the area that is now western Switzerland.[99] Industrial remains from the settlement indicate that a cutter of glass intaglio seal-stones and glass-blowers were present in the town at this time. These individuals are likely to have been immigrants, as their skills were new to Britain. It has been suggested that the London of AD 60 was a city still recognisable today – lively, cosmopolitan and with a flourishing financial sector.[100] The growing town was also limited in extent, however, and the population may not have been above a few thousand; so we should be careful in drawing simple parallels between Roman Londinium and the modern City of London.[101]

As at Colchester, quantities of burned grain were found in the Boudican destruction layers. Grain from the site at 160–62 Fenchurch Street contained non-native einkorn, a variety not cultivated in Britain today. The presence among lentils of bitter vetch, which had been growing as weeds among the crop when it was harvested, suggests that it was probably imported from the Mediterranean.[102] Beetles called granary weevils were found at 1 Poultry and these probably initially also came to London among consignments of corn from abroad, as they are not known in Britain prior to the Roman invasion.[103] Burned lentils from Southwark also demonstrates that food was imported from the Mediterranean.[104] Fine pottery and amphorae containers for olive oil and wine also indicates that Londinium was involved in a considerable trading network with the Continent.[105] The fact that Tacitus mentions traders may suggest that a port had been developed on the Thames by this time, although no traces have yet been found of wharves of this date.[106]

The extensive burned deposits found on sites of this date in London have assisted the archaeologists to establish the extent of the settlement. Destruction is again indicated by a readily identifiable horizon of burned debris associated with or sealing artefacts that date to the period AD 55–60.[107] This burned layer is similar in nature to the one from Colchester and is typically 30–60 centimetres thick. Excavations suggest that few buildings survived the fire.[108] Recent excavation at Southwark indicates that settlement here was also burned at this time.[109] The native-style roundhouses found in Newgate Street appear to have been destroyed,[110] but the initial results of the excavation of those at 10 Gresham Street suggest that these were not burned.[111] This may indicate that the destruction of the town was selective.

Some possessions have been located within and beneath the burned layer, including the collection of grain discussed above, coins and pottery.[112] During recent excavation at 1 Poultry a vivid picture of events at this time has emerged.[113] The destruction deposit overlay the ruins of the early buildings, some with burned timbers still in place. To the north side of the main road a shop sold household goods, including samian pottery. A deposit of charred spices was also found, including mustard, dill and fennel, with some coriander and black cumin; all of these were used in Roman cooking. Some small spoons were lying nearby, perhaps for measuring the spices.[114]

Objects have been found in London that may represent war booty. On display at the Museum of London are three bronze arms from three independent statues. The most recent example was found at 30 Gresham Street in 2001.[115] Broken off from the statue below the elbow, the arm was found in the filling of a large pond that became choked with rubbish around AD 70.[116] This particular statue was gilded with gold leaf that would originally have shone brilliantly. The hand is finely detailed and it has been suggested that it may have belonged to a statue of Nero destroyed during the rebellion.[117] There is an alternative and, perhaps, more likely explanation. The statue may have been destroyed after Nero's death in AD 68 when his memory was damned by the Roman senate.[118] In any case, the arm may have been placed in the pond as a votive offering to the gods, or the action of placing it in a rubbish-filled pond may have been an additional way of dishonouring a dead and discredited emperor.[119] The fact that it was not deposited until around AD 70 presumably indicates that it did not represent the spoils of war, unless someone kept it hidden for ten years after the rebellion before throwing it away.

The two other arms in the Museum of London display were found in a Roman well in Great Tower Street in 1844 and in Gracechurch Street in 1867 respectively. These are probably not connected with Boudica's rebellion and the date at which they were deposited is unclear.

According to Tacitus, a third town – Verulamium – suffered the same fate, although he does not tell us much about the town, only that it was a *municipium*, [120] a town with a chartered constitution that enabled certain of its officials to become Roman citizens. It appears that the initial development of Verulamium was at the initiative of the local elite. These people seem to have formed a special relationship with Rome during the conquest period and, with Roman support, established the wealthy early Roman-period town. It has been argued that the Romans were so impressed with the early development of the town that they made it a *municipium*. [121] Towns in the Roman Empire were sometimes granted this honour as a special privilege and a town with this title was a community of people who had a special relationship with Rome that was carefully defined in a charter issued by the emperor. This would have given the community at Verulamium a status within the province second only to that of the colony at Camulodunum. Tacitus's reference to Verulamium as a *municipium* is, however, the only evidence that we have for the fact that the community had been granted this status, again indicating the limitations of our literary sources for the events of Boudica's revolt. It has recently been argued that Tacitus's attribution of the status of *municipium* to Verulamium was actually a literary flourish. This device enabled him to include in the acts of Boudica the destruction of the colony at Camulodunum, the provincial capital at London and the only *municipium* in Britain – Verulamium. [122] Archaeologists believe that London became the provincial capital some time after the Boudican revolt; Tacitus was writing forty years after the rebellion and was anticipating London's elevation to this role. In general, there is some doubt, therefore, whether the developing town at Verulamium had the status of *municipium* at the time of the revolt. It may in fact have been granted this status subsequently.

In the past, it was thought that a Roman fort was established at Verulamium during the early conquest period as part of the official settlement process within the province. Artefacts associated with Roman soldiers have been found in the settlement and, while the evidence for a fort no longer appears to be convincing, these objects may provide evidence for the presence of Roman soldiers within the expanding settlement. [123] Archaeologists now believe that the Roman town developed directly from the pre-Roman *oppidum* (figure 29). In fact, the

Roman military equipment may actually have belonged to members of the local native aristocracy, recruited into the Roman army early in the history of the province. Roman military equipment from a rich native burial at Folly Lane, just to the north east of Verulamium, dated to around the mid 50s, may indicate that a wealthy local man served as a cavalry officer in an auxiliary unit of the Roman army.[124] He would have been dead by the time of Boudica's revolt, but this suggests that some of the occupants of the town might actually have been serving with the Roman army before AD 60. This would explain why Roman military equipment has been found within the early phases of the town,[125] as it appears that tribal leaders at Verulamium cooperated with Rome during the invasion period.

During the early period, Verulamium was focused around a late Iron Age enclosure (the 'central enclosure') that lay just to the north of the river crossing (figure 30). Around the time of the Roman invasion a causeway was established across the river close to this enclosure,[126] providing an interesting parallel to the roughly contemporary developments at Londinium. It has been argued that the burned deposits at Verulamium give us a clear indication of the extent and nature of the growth of the Roman town in AD 60 to 61. In the period prior to the revolt a few buildings developed around the central enclosure, but the extent of the settlement appears to have been very limited.[127] The town may have been no more than around ten to twelve hectares (twenty-four to twenty-eight acres) in extent at the most,[128] rather smaller in size than contemporary Londinium and the colony at Camulodunum. The streets of the town were uncambered gravelled tracks, usually without well-defined side ditches.[129] This is a situation that is broadly comparable with contemporary developments in Londinium, but the street system at Verulamium appears to be rather less regular than that at Camulodunum.

Some of the structures that have been discovered may indicate that Verulamium had a monumental centre. The known structures include one timber building, consisting of a row of at least ten rooms (figure 31), that was built early in the Roman period alongside one of the roads close to the central enclosure.[130] The individual rooms had earth floors while there was a wooden shingle or thatched roof over the whole of the structure and a colonnade forming the front of the building along the street

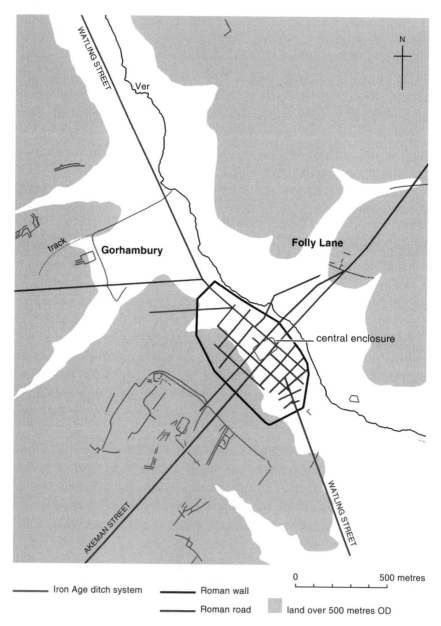

Legend:

——— Iron Age ditch system   ——— Roman wall

                        ——— Roman road   land over 500 metres OD

0   500 metres

29. Late Iron Age Verlamion and early Roman Verulamium. (*After Niblett 2001, p. 41*)

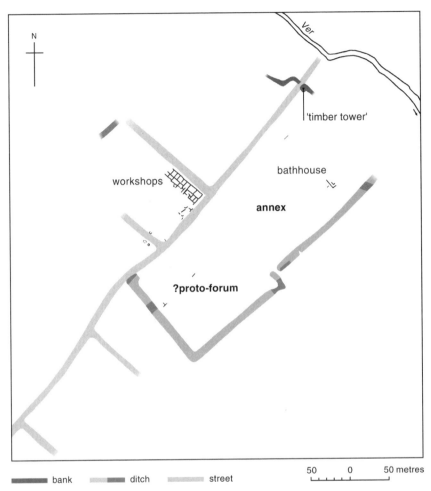

N

Ver

'timber tower'

bathhouse

workshops

annex

?proto-forum

bank   ditch   street

50   0   50 metres

30. Verulamium around AD 60 to 61. (*After James and Millett 2001, figure 18*)

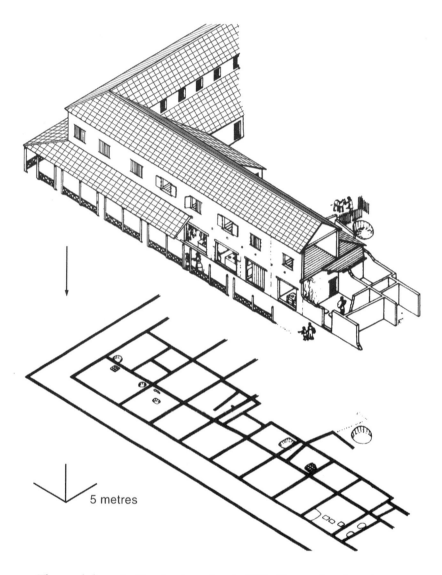

5 metres

31. The workshops in Verulamium, Insula XIV. (*Drawn by Alex Thorne, after Frere. From Niblett 2001, figure 30*)

frontage. Buildings of this type do not occur in pre-Roman contexts, indicating that this structure was a Roman innovation.[131] Several of the rooms appear to have been used to work metal and they may have been shops with connected workshops. In contrast to the colony at Camulodunum and Londinium, there may have been stone buildings at Verulamium prior to AD 60 to 61. Only a very limited area of one significant building, perhaps a bathhouse, has been excavated and this probably predated the revolt.[132] The walls of one room were decorated with plaster painted with a complex design including foliage and a lyre. In the area where the forum was built at a later date, stone walls and painted plaster have been found, possibly the remains of an earlier forum that predates the Boudican destruction of the town.[133] This was built over and replaced the central enclosure. The identification of this building is uncertain, but it may suggest that the town had two substantial public buildings prior to the revolt.

One object from the excavations may indicate the destruction of a monumental statue in the town.[134] The excavations of the shops in Insula XIV located some bronze scraps and discarded fragments in Room 1 in a context that appeared to date the finds to around AD 75–85.[135] One of the finds was particularly notable as it was derived from the drapery of a life-sized statue,[136] which, perhaps, stood in the forum. The excavator argued that the discovery of a piece of a discarded statue at such an early date strongly suggested that it was broken up at the time of Boudica's revolt, although it is possible that the destruction of the statue may relate to the damnation of the memory of Nero by the Roman Senate.[137]

The destruction of Verulamium may have been the result of native feuds and rivalries dating back to the pro- and anti-Roman stances of individual tribes at the time of the Roman invasion,[138] a form of ethnic hatred.[139] The archaeological evidence for the sacking at Verulamium appears, however, to be rather less clear-cut than that for Londinium and Camulodunum.[140] Despite some earlier claims,[141] no evidence has been found at Verulamium for extensive contemporary burning.[142] It does appear that the shops and workshops close to the central enclosure and a few other early timber buildings were destroyed by fire.[143] One of these shops had a collection of thirty-seven unused samian pots that had spilled across the veranda fronting the street. The bathhouse mentioned

above may also have been damaged, as burned timbers were found over
the top of the remains. Some other burned deposits excavated during
the 1930s have since been shown to contain pottery dating to around
AD 80;[144] they therefore do not represent destruction carried out by the
followers of Boudica.

Verulamium may well have been a town in its first stages of development at this time and perhaps there was rather less to destroy than at
the other two towns.[145] Alternatively, perhaps the destruction of Verulamium was less thorough that that of Londinium and Camulodunum.
Collections of coins and burned grain have not been found either within
or below the destruction horizon, indicating that many of the inhabitants may well have escaped with their valuables.[146] The information
from Verulamium serves as a reminder of the necessity to look carefully
at the evidence for the destruction deposits on other sites. As we have
seen, at least part of the town at Londinium appears not to have been
burned.

It has been suggested that two rural settlements close to Verulamium
(Park Street and Gorhambury) were attacked by the rebels.[147] At Park
Street, which is three miles (five kilometres) from the town, it has long
been supposed that a timber-built house was destroyed by fire, leaving
a deposit of burned daub walling material over its floor. At Gorhambury, just outside the urban area, another farm is supposed to have been
destroyed (figure 32). The excavator felt it to be inconceivable that the
rebellion had no effect on the developing settlement and suggested that
it is tempting to connect the burning of buildings on the site to the sacking of the settlement.[148] More recent assessment of these sites, however,
has concluded that it is difficult to locate destruction layers connected
with Boudica at either Park Street or at Gorhambury.[149] There is no
clear evidence that any other sites in close proximity to the three towns
were destroyed by the rebels at this time. This may suggest that Tacitus
exaggerated the extent of the destruction caused by Boudica and her followers, but future excavation in all three of the towns and on rural sites
in their vicinities will present us with a fuller and more detailed picture
of events.

Some archaeologists and specialists who study ancient coins have
argued that the tribal coinage of the Iceni can provide further evidence

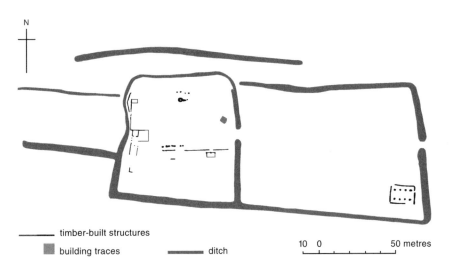

N

timber-built structures
building traces   ditch

10   0   50 metres

32. Gorhambury around AD 60 to 61. (*After Neal, Wardie and Hunn 1990, figure 45*)

for the course of the rebellion. One Iron Age coinage specialist has argued that:

> Queen Boudicca assumed leadership of the [Iceni] after Prasutagus' death, introducing an uninscribed silver unit [coin] with a Celticised head on the obverse. These were struck in great quantities to finance the revolt against Rome.[150]

This claim was made as the result of a statistical study of individual coin hoards that have long been supposed to have been deposited during the Boudican rebellion.[151] The 'Celticised' head may have referred back to the traditional Iron Age coin designs and is in stark contrast with the 'Romanised' heads that sometimes occur on the later sequences of Iron Age coins.[152] This may suggest that Boudica was drawing upon traditional Iron Age images in her fight against the Roman Empire.

Unfortunately, this attractive picture has been undermined by subsequent research that has looked at the 'Boudican hoards' in greater detail. It now appears likely that both the coins of Esuprastus and those that van Arsdell attributed to Boudica predate AD 60 to 61 by some time. Standard numismatic methods have been used to argue that it is in fact possible that all the coins produced by the Iceni date to before AD 43.[153] Perhaps the friendly kingdom of the Iceni ceased to produce coinage after the initial Roman conquest of south-east Britain. It seems that we cannot identify a coinage either for Prasutagus or for his wife, Boudica; in the past there has been too little critical assessment of this evidence.

If it is not possible to find direct indicators for the two individual leaders of the Iceni, what can the so-called 'Boudican hoards' themselves tell us about the rebellion? Eleven or more coin hoards found across the territory of the Iceni (figure 33) have been attributed to the period of the rebellion,[154] as have six metalwork hoards.[155] The coin hoards contain coins produced by the Iceni, while at least seven also contain Roman silver coins.[156] Three of the hoards that include Roman coins contain examples featuring the head of the Roman emperor Nero, who ruled at the time of the rebellion. No coins of later emperors have been found in these hoards. It has long been supposed, as a result of the coins that they contain, that these hoards were buried to keep collections of valuable metal secure at the time of the revolt.[157]

The size of the coin hoards is very variable. At Field Baulk (March,

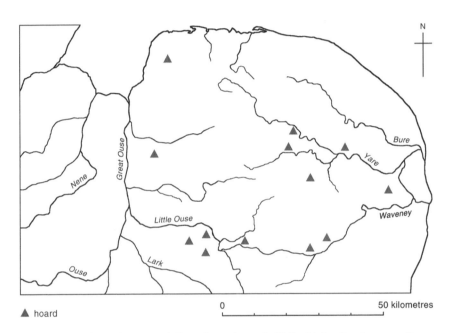

33. Iron Age hoards in Norfolk and northern Suffolk. (*After Davies 1999, figure 2.12*)

Cambridgeshire) 872 silver Icenian coins were buried in a red pot,[158] while a more typically-sized hoard at Fring (Norfolk) contained 153 Icenian coins, again contained within a pot.[159] These individual hoards contained large quantities of valuable metal. They appear to have been deposited during the first century AD, but it is likely that they were buried at various dates between the beginning of the century and AD 61, not all at one time during the rebellion.[160] This would disassociate the hoards from being deposited as a group during the Boudican rebellion, although it is possible that some of them were buried at this time.[161]

It has been argued that the six other metalwork hoards may date to AD 60 to 61.[162] Nevertheless, items of metalwork can only be dated approximately by comparing them with similar objects found elsewhere in securely dated contexts. It is possible to date certain structures in Londinium very accurately by the use of the dendrochronological analysis of wood, but none of the coin or metal hoards can be dated so accurately by any technique. It is attractive to think that some of the impressive items in the metalwork hoards, including the seven Roman silver wine cups from Hockwold-cum-Wilton in Norfolk, might have been deposited during the rebellion.[163] Perhaps they were the prized possessions of a wealthy pro-Roman native. There is, however, no conclusive evidence that the hoard dates to this time.[164] Despite the desire to find evidence that can be related to Boudica, none of these coin or metalwork hoards can be clearly associated with the rebellion. In fact the history of the study of these hoards provides a further illustration of the tendency for archaeologists to attribute objects and structures to the revolt.

Archaeologists argue about the reasons why people in Iron Age Britain hoarded their valuable items. One idea is that they hid their valuables at times of trouble and never returned to retrieve them, either because they were killed or driven off. Other archaeologists argue that the hoarding of metalwork and coinage was motivated by religious beliefs,[165] and that they were offerings to the gods and spirits. This argument is also of concern to Roman archaeologists.[166] The idea that the 'Boudican hoards' were deposited as part of people's ritual behaviour is an attractive one; they were placed in special places because they were valuable objects being offered up to the gods or spirits. This would suggest that the Icenian hoards were deposited for ritual reasons rather than to hide them.[167] They form part of a long-lived series of hoards found across these areas of Norfolk and Cambridgeshire dating from the second century BC until the first century AD,[168] part of a more widespread tradition involving the deposition of Iron Age and Roman coins and metalwork in certain locations across the whole of southern Britain.[169]

At the same time, it is not necessary to disassociate these hoards totally from the rebellion merely because they may have had a ritual association. Perhaps some of the hoards were actually offerings made to the gods to encourage their support in the uprisings against the Roman authorities that took place in AD 47 to 48 and 60 to 61. Some hoards may represent collections of valuable material sacrificed to ensure success in the conflict, much as the head of Claudius may have been a special offering made to the gods to thank them for the initial victories of the rebellion. Another object that may represent war-booty is the Roman cavalry helmet from Witcham Gravel, Ely (Cambridgeshire).[170] Archaeologists have become so critical of attempts to associate archaeological material with Boudica that many would now disagree with the idea that any of the hoards, or the possible items of war booty, are connected with the rebellion. It is unfortunate that we cannot date the individual hoards more closely, as this would give us a clearer idea of the reasons for their burial. Perhaps one day a hoard will be found closely associated with waterlogged wood and we will be able to demonstrate its association with the revolt with greater certainty.

Turning to the problem of locating Boudica's final battle, Suetonius Paulinus, the provincial governor, was campaigning in Wales when the rebellion began. He mustered an army of 10,000 men, but Tacitus tells us that he chose the site of the battle with care since he was heavily outnumbered. The Romans took up position in a narrow valley overlooking an open plain, protected to the rear by thick woodland. The Britons were massed on the plain and Dio claims that they numbered 230,000. They were so confident of victory that men brought their wives in carts to be spectators at the battle. According to Tacitus, the Britons advanced down the valley but were beaten back, where they were trapped by the carts with which they had encircled the battlefield (although we have seen that Dio gives a very different account). Large numbers of British men and women were killed. One report suggested that 80,000 people died, but that only 400 Roman soldiers lost their lives. Tacitus tells us that Boudica took poison, while Dio suggests that she fell ill and died. In any case, the revolt was over. According to Dio, Boudica was given a costly burial by her people.

During the past three hundred years various attempts have been made to locate this battle site and Boudica's burial, but there is very little historical or archaeological evidence to go on. The description of the battle given by Tacitus may be applied to hundreds of locations in southern Britain.[171] At the same time, the description itself may be accurate, as Tacitus may have had eyewitness accounts. The idea that Boudica fought her final battle in the general area of London dates back to at least 1790, but there is no evidence to indicate that this idea is accurate.

In the light of the strategic factors behind Roman military deployment at this time, it has been suggested that much of the Roman army was being moved from north Wales along Watling Street to meet the oncoming Britons.[172] Suetonius Paulinus probably campaigned with troops who had been fighting somewhere in present-day Wales.[173] Examining the line of Watling Street from the Roman settlement at Wall (Staffordshire) southwards, it has been suggested that a likely location for the battle was at Mancetter on the boundary between Warwickshire and Leicestershire. Tacitus's description suggests a place where there was a sudden change from open plain to woodland, with a sharp rise in the ground and a small valley cut into the hill side.[174] At Mancetter a ridge of old hard rock runs in a north-westerly direction, converging on Watling Street close to Atherstone.[175] The rise of the steep escarpment is the result of the presence of a fault line and there are possible locations for the valley mentioned by Tacitus. It *may* be significant that the Roman name for Mancetter was Manduessedo, a British name which appears to have been derived from the words for 'small horse' and 'war-chariot'.[176] Could it be that the name commemorates a battle in which war chariots were involved? A complex sequence of early Roman military sites existed at Mancetter and may have provided a further reason for the Roman army to have made a stand at this point.[177] It has also been suggested, improbably, that the Roman fort at the Lunt, Coventry, was adapted to provide facilities to train horses captured from the Iceni after the revolt had been put down.[178]

The idea of Mancetter as the site of Boudica's final stand is based upon little more than several layers of supposition.[179] Although the topography roughly fits the description of the battle site in Tacitus's account, and subsequent authors have accepted the site as the most likely location,[180] there is no conclusive evidence to indicate that this was the site of the battle. In fact, the suggestion for the battle site in the midlands is based on a number of assumptions. It is not clear what the Briton's intentions were at this stage. They may well have been enthusiastic to meet the Roman army, but we cannot assume this to be the case. Tacitus's account certainly suggests that the Roman army had been campaigning in Wales, but we know very little of the chronology of events. For instance, how long did it take Suetonius Paulinus to marshal his troops and to bring the enemy to battle? Dio's account suggests that this took some time, and we are also told by Tacitus that he decided not to protect Londinium. It is quite possible that Suetonius Paulinus's army was in fact in southern Britain in the vicinity of London and Verulamium when the battle took place, indicating a more southerly location for the site.

It is quite possible that the battle site will be discovered one day. Recent archaeological work in Germany has recovered a number of battle sites and the archaeological traces are very informative. One very important site near Osnabrück appears to be that of the victory of the Germanic leader Arminius who defeated the Roman general Varus in AD 9.[181] The battle was fought over several days and numerous pieces of weaponry and the remains of animals and humans have been found over an extensive area. Much of the debris of the defeat of the Roman army was left across the site by their opponents after the battle. The archaeological evidence for this battle site appears to support, at least to an extent, the account of the battle in the writings of Tacitus. It is likely that, in the case of Boudica's defeat, the Roman army would have collected the remains of the defeated Britons. The bodies of the defeated people and their animals would probably have been buried in pits, but it is unlikely that the Romans would have succeeded in collecting all the fragments of damaged weaponry and personal possessions on the site. The location of Boudica's final defeat may eventually be found by searching for relevant archaeological remains at likely sites across the south of Britain. If this site is indeed located and excavated, it will enable a more detailed assessment to be made of the accuracy of the accuracy of Tacitus's and Dio's accounts.

The historical sources also tell us about the scale of the reprisals carried out by the Romans against the Britons: that wavering tribes were ravaged with fire and sword, while a serious famine struck the province. Again it is difficult to find clear archaeological evidence for these events. New forts may have been built, or old ones reoccupied. In the midlands, forts apparently occupied at this time include Mancetter in Warwickshire and the Lunt near Coventry in the West Midlands.[182] These had been built and occupied during the original westward advance of the Roman army some time prior to the Boudican revolt,[183] although they do appear to have been reoccupied around the time of the uprising. The forts may perhaps have been bases for Roman military actions in the area during the early years of the 60s, particularly if Boudica's final battle did take place in the vicinity of Mancetter. It is also true, however, that a number of other earlier Roman forts in the West Midlands appear to be re-established around AD 60, including examples at Wall in Staffordshire and at Metchley in Birmingham.[184] These may all have been refortified as a reaction to the events of AD 60–61. Another fort has been recently discovered at Grandford in East Anglia.[185] Its location may suggest that it also dates from the period immediately following the rebellion. An important recent discovery in London indicates that a Roman fort may have been constructed just after the revolt.[186] Excavations at Plantation Place in 2000 indicate that defensive ditches and a rampart were built directly upon the ruined remains of the town, although its full extent is unclear. Further forts dating to the early 60s may well be located in future. Little other convincing evidence has, however, been found to indicate the actions of the Roman army immediately after the revolt.

It has been argued that the Roman reprisals of AD 60 to 61 set the development of the province back by a generation. Some native settlement sites in Suffolk and Norfolk may have ceased to be occupied around this time, but too few have been excavated to assess the real impact of Roman reprisals on the ground.[187] At West Stow the settlement appears to have been abandoned around this time,[188] but there is no direct

evidence that it was destroyed and it may have been abandoned peace-
fully, with the occupants moving to a new site. The major complex at
Fison Way (Thetford) appears to have been systematically demolished,
as the timbers of the structures were removed from their post-holes. It
has been suggested that a detachment of the Roman army descended
upon this site after the rebellion and demolished it.[189] There is, however,
no conclusive evidence for the destruction of this site by the Roman
army. There are a number of pieces of Roman military metalwork from
the excavation which have sometimes been associated with this idea of
demolition,[190] but we have seen above that these have been found in
native contexts at Verulamium. The Iceni were a friendly kingdom prior
to the revolt and it is quite possible that members of the tribal aristocracy were recruited into the Roman auxiliaries, as has been suggested at
Verulamium. The Roman military items from Thetford may therefore
merely represent objects deposited as offerings by local peoples at an
important tribal sanctuary. The fact that the buildings were demolished
rather than burned may suggests that the destruction was not violent
and that the sacred site was relocated. There appears to have been a late
Roman site, possible a temple, immediately to the south west of the Iron
Age site and this may illustrate continuity of use of this important
place.[191]

The archaeological evidence suggests that the towns that were sacked
recovered at different rates. At Camulodunum the colony was swiftly
re-established and, although the earlier town had been thoroughly
burned, much of the street system was reused in the planning of the
new town.[192] The occupants and government also learned from the
revolt and constructed a walled circuit, probably in the period between
AD 65 and 80.[193] At Londinium recovery was slow and many proper-
ties were left vacant for a decade or more.[194] The fort that was built
soon after the revolt may have been connected in some way with the
developing significance of London in the immediately post-Boudican
period. Gaius Julius Classicianus became the next procurator of Britain
after the rebellion and his grand stone tomb was found in London
(figure 34), which may suggest that he was based there.[195] Verulamium
may also have had a slow recovery;[196] the re-established settlement was
provided with a rampart and ditch, probably during the period between
AD 75 and 80.[197]

DIS
MANIBVS
CIVLCFFABALPINICLASSICIANI
:IIVTA:PROCPROVINC:BRIT:AISIN:
SC:XLQVIIIAINDIFILIA · ACATAI:IL:IL:IAL:
PROCPROVINCBRITANN
IVLIAINDIFILIAPACATAINDVTA
VXOR

34. A reconstruction of the tomb of Gaius Julius Classicianus, found in London. (*After Grasby and Tomlin 2002, figure 21. By permission of the Roman Society*)

All of these settlements continued to develop during the later first and second centuries and, despite the destruction carried out by Boudica and her followers, became three of the most successful towns of Roman Britain.[198] Colchester featured the rebuilt temple of Claudius,[199] London became both the largest town in the province and also the provincial capital,[200] while Verulamium came to be one of the obviously Roman towns with a highly elaborate forum complex and theatre.[201]

PART TWO

Boadicea

4

Finding Boadicea

[Voadicia/Bunduica] left such a strong mark in the memory of the people because she was commemorated ... for her marvellous virtues.

Petruccio Ubaldini (1588).[1]

Geoffrey of Monmouth, a twelfth-century writer, created a powerful myth of British origin in his *History of the Kings of Britain (Historia Regum Britanniae)*. Geoffrey's book has been described as a 'work of creative imagination',[2] but he quite evidently also drew upon some ancient sources.

Geoffrey told a number of tales that provided a direct connection with classical Mediterranean society for the population of Britain. In particular, he described the foundation of Britain by Brutus, a grandson of Aeneas who fled from Troy after the Trojan Wars.[3] We do not know very much about the sources that Geoffrey used for his *History*, but these included early medieval works. It has recently been suggested that Geoffrey's Trojan myth may have had its origin in the late Iron Age.[4] It may have represented an attempt by influential ancient Britons, perhaps a tribal chief, to draw a connection between themselves and the Trojans and, by association, with the Romans, who also claimed descent from Troy. If this suggestion is correct, the Trojan myth of origin for the population of Britain had a very early source. In addition to the myth of Brutus, Geoffrey also explored the mythical origin of Christianity in Britain (the tale of Glastonbury) and gave a detailed and fanciful account of King Arthur.

A developing knowledge of the classical sources for ancient Briton during the sixteenth century made Geoffrey's tales increasing difficult to accept. Polydore Vergil undermined the Trojan myth in a book called

Anglica Historia, written between 1512 and 1513,[5] although the first printed version was not produced until 1534.[6] He was born at Urbino in Italy around 1470 and came to Britain in the early sixteenth century in the service of the pope.[7] He used every available and appropriate classical author to write his early history of Britain.[8] Being a foreigner, his independent point of view enabled him to apply a detachment to writing English domestic history that was not possible for native writers,[9] and he dismissed the idea of Brutus as a historical character in forceful terms.[10] Vergil had a major role in the development of knowledge about the British past as he used newly-available information from the classical sources to demolish the fanciful legends of 'medieval creation'.[11] The story of Brutus retained popularity for some time during the sixteenth and seventeenth centuries[12] and even occasionally appears in modern contexts.[13] It was, however, seriously undermined by the knowledge that emerged from the rediscovery of Roman classical texts addressing the early history of Britain.[14]

The works of the Roman authors survived into the modern world because of their value to people in post-Roman times, but they had ceased to be easily available and were largely forgotten. Around 1360 Giovanni Boccaccio visited the library of the monastery of Monte Cassino in Italy. Among the manuscripts that he claimed to have 'rescued' was a work by Tacitus, although it is uncertain which.[15] After this early discovery the other remaining fragments of Tacitus's writings were collected. For instance, a substantial proportion of the *Annals* was rediscovered in 1410, while much of the *Histories* was found around 1430.[16] Printed editions of various manuscript texts began to be made in Italy during the second half of the fifteenth century and a number of editions of Tacitus's work were published between 1470 and 1533.[17] Following the recovery of his works, Tacitus came to have a profound influence on the historical and political thought of Europe from the sixteenth century onwards. His writing on the ancient Britons was now available to scholars in England. The works of various other Roman and Greek authors were also recovered and published at this time.[18]

As the myth of Brutus became increasingly untenable during the sixteenth century, questions concerning the origin of the peoples of Britain took on a particular importance with the search for new ideas of national origins and identity. By this time England had effectively annexed Wales and parts of Ireland, but Scotland remained a distinct kingdom until 1707.[19] Following the voyage of Christopher Columbus in 1492, European interests also became focused upon America.[20] The expanding knowledge of the world had a dramatic impact in Britain and Europe, particularly because of the discovery of 'savages', native peoples who were found during the exploration of the New World.[21]

Accompanying the sixteenth-century expansion of geographical knowledge were major political developments. When Henry VIII broke with the Church of Rome during the 1530s, England came under considerable international political pressure, which continued under the rule of his daughter Elizabeth.[22] Various writers and artists, including Shakespeare, responded to the new political situation by producing works that took England – its land, people, its institutions and history – as their subject.[23] The anxiety and uncertainty resulted in the creation of literature and art that served the nation,[24] raising an enquiry into the origins of the English people. What were its roots in the ancient past?[25] How did ancient peoples within Britain relate to the 'savages' of the areas of the world that were being discovered by Europeans and brought into Europe at this time?[26]

Roman civilisation provided a strong image of past greatness for many people in early modern Europe and Renaissance writers drew directly upon this inheritance of civilisation from the classical Roman world.[27] From the reign of Henry VIII onwards the image of Rome was regarded with ambivalence. Although the Roman Empire by this time had lost all political reality, its associations were still of concern to the growing number of British Protestants and to Protestant rulers. In the sixteenth century Roman imperialism was often associated with the pope, Catholicism, oppression and tyranny;[28] classical Rome being effectively tainted by the association. Some of the figures from classical literature were of potential value in this context, since the accounts made it clear that at least some ancient Britons fought against Roman rule. It would have been convenient, as a result, for the English to be able to rediscover civilised and noble ancestor figures in the ancient Britons described in the accounts of Roman authors.

The classical texts described the ancient British people encountered by Julius Caesar, Agricola and other Roman generals as savages or barbarians. The Britons appeared to be totally lacking in the type of classical civilisation that was so admired in the early modern period;[29] they seemed more akin to the native Americans encountered in colonial ventures than to the civilised and powerful people of ancient Rome.[30] A dominant view existed at this time that society had evolved from a primitive state to one of civilisation. In these terms, the appearance and actions of the contemporary native Americans were seen to provide a valid model for the ancient inhabitants of Britain, before the Romans brought civilisation. Indeed, when scholars tried to understand the ancient Britons, and to illustrate them, they often turned to contemporary images of indigenous Americans and other 'savages' for their inspiration. The accounts and drawings of contemporary explorers filled in graphic details that were not provided by the classical authors.[31] In attempting to understand the ancient Britons, the developing knowledge of people who were considered to be primitive, such as the 'Eskimos' and native Americans, became a vital source for understanding the ancient past of Britain. As a result, early modern authors and artists were compelled to build upon what has become a long-lasting idea of origins – they presented the ancient Britons as the barbarous and inferior colonised 'other'. This idea of the ancient British barbarian was itself derived from the viewpoint of the more refined and successful cultures of Greece, Rome and contemporary Europe.[32]

The investigation of the classical writings also raised the significant issue of whether the ancient Britons should be revered as virile warriors or condemned as cruel and ignorant savages.[33] Many accounts produced from the sixteenth century onwards struggled with the ideas of ancient savagery and whether the ancient Britons that were recorded in the Roman sources provided a viable, or desirable, root for the origins of the English nation. The accounts were anxious to reconcile a variety of contrasting views.[34] Many of the writers of this time show a longing to establish a respectable historical precedent and continuity for the origins of the English, looking into the past in an attempt to find the roots of their own nation. In trying to establish these ancient beginnings, English authors turned to the classical Roman accounts of Britain, including those relating to Boadicea.

The contradiction between valour and savagery lay at the heart of many accounts of the ancient past of England developed during the sixteenth and seventeenth centuries.[35] The images of Boadicea were part of this process. On the one hand, she provided an example of native savagery and resistance to Roman rule; on the other, she offered a worthy example of opposition against an oppressive imperial Rome. Along with other ancient British figures in the classical historical accounts, Boadicea presented a complicated image in early modern accounts.

All ancient people who fought against the civilising power of Rome were thought of as barbarians, but Boadicea was even more challenging than male leaders such as Caratacus. It is clear that the violence and barbarity of Boadicea and her followers were particularly embarrassing for contemporary writers. The ancient Britons in the tales of Tacitus and Dio apparently were not concerned with the masculine principles of gender hierarchy that existed for early modern writers and artists.[36] Two women – Mary and Elizabeth – came to power in England during the sixteenth century, but female leaders at this time certainly did not lead their armies into war in person, or perpetrate such acts of savagery as described by Tacitus and Dio.

Female British rulers who exercised political control in the sixteenth and seventeenth centuries were often targets for condemnation and moralising.[37] Attitudes to gender in early modern Britain, in turn, reflected those of the Roman Empire of the first to third centuries AD. Boadicea became a symbol of an early modern belief that savage excess was the inevitable consequence of female rule.[38] Following the lead of Dio, Boadicea is now often seen in these accounts as not entirely 'normal'.[39] It has been proposed that the early modern writers projected ancient British savagery onto Boadicea and other ancient queens.[40] It appears more accurate, however, to argue that these images of female barbarity in early modern Britain drew their inspiration from the classical portrayals of barbarian queens that were discussed above.[41] Early modern imagery was created in the context of the unquestioned value of the classical sources to modern people, using these sources to structure ideas of the approved role of women in society. Writers at this time were able to use the Roman literature directly to develop their arguments, since classical authors had often followed similar principles with regard to powerful women.

Male writers who wrote about women in the sixteenth and seventeenth centuries drew directly upon classical and biblical accounts, but also upon medieval thought.[42] The early modern interpretation of

Boadicea was created in the context of the unquestioned value of the
Bible and classical sources to contemporary people. At the same time, in
drawing upon classical sources, medieval accounts of powerful women
sometimes changed the point of view or even distorted the original.[43]
The classical sources were interpreted in the context of contemporary
society and used to create images of Boadicea that changed through
time. Classical accounts were reinterpreted in a contemporary context
but they also directly assisted early modern writers to develop their ideas
of gender roles within their own societies.

The first significant work to discuss Boadicea was written by Polydore
Vergil, who included an account of 'Voadicia' and 'Vodicia' in his
Anglica Historia.[44] He used the writings of Tacitus and possibly those of
Dio, and he may have drawn upon the brief reference to Boudica by
the sixth-century British monk Gildas.[45] Vergil described the rebellion
of Voadicia and identifies Mona (which he spells 'Mone') as the Isle
of Man.[46] Following Tacitus's account, he describes how Prasutagus,
king of the 'nation called the Ignei', made Nero his heir along with his
daughters.[47] He describes the rebellion and the sacking of 'Camolo-
dunum' or 'Camulodunum' and 'Verulamium' before turning to the
final battle. His attempt to identify the location of the events referred to
by the classical authors has been described as 'muddle-headed'.[48] For
instance, he locates 'Camulodunum' at either Doncaster or Pontefract,
where, he argued, there were still signs and remains of a temple dedicated to Claudius.[49] He says that the 'Igeni' were a separate people
from the Iceni and suggests that they were based in the area of present-
day Northumberland.[50] He also confused much of the evidence
provided by the classical authors; his account of Boadicea has various
errors. It must be borne in mind, however, that Vergil was writing at a
time prior to the development of any serious antiquarian interest in the
ancient monuments of Britain and his failings should be seen in this
context.

   The sixteenth-century historian of Scotland Hector Böece (died 1536)
created two distinct Boadiceas in his *The Chronicles of Scotland*[51]
Böece's account located the events of Boadicea's rebellion in Scotland.
The Roman general Suetonius is once again involved in subduing the
'Ile of Man' (the Isle of Man), which Böece takes to be the 'Mona' of

Tacitus, when the rebellion erupts. The revolt occurs as the result of the death of the king 'Aruiragus', who replaces Prasutagus in this account. Böece located 'Camulodunum' at the site of the Roman fort of Camelon, near Falkirk (Scotland). Boudica is called 'Voada' and her younger daughter 'Vodicia'. While this account shows some knowledge of the writings of Tacitus, the events are misplaced and the details of the conflict are quoted incorrectly.[52] At this time Scotland was a separate kingdom and Böece was clearly using some of the details of this rebellion in order to emphasise the ancient Scottish opposition to the Romans.[53] Before the final conflict, Voada joins the ancient British men in the fight against the Romans. She states (in Scots) that:

> Had the goddis fortunytt me to bene ane man, I mycht nocht haue sustenit sa mony importabill iniuris done be Romanis.[54]

Which has been roughly translated to mean: 'Had the gods given me the fortune to be a man I might not have sustained so many unbearable injuries done by Romans.'[55] She continues (in translation here):

> And though I may no wise devoid me of wifely image, I shall not lack men's hardiness, but armed foremost in the brunt, where most danger appears, with 5000 British ladies who were all sworn to vindicate their injuries, we shall proceed foremost in battle, not regarding fear of death, or bloody wounds or terrible slaughter of ourselves or enemies; for I can have no commiseration with those who pursued my tender friends with such cruelties, deflowering so many virgins and matrons by effeminate lust, putting so many rich cities and towns to subversion, and innocent people to murder.[56]

The Romans then defeat the Britons, Picts and Scots in a battle, and Voada kills herself rather than falling into the hands of her enemies. Her unnamed elder daughter is married off to the Roman who raped her, while the younger daughter, Vodicia, decides to take revenge for herself and her mother, and she recruits an army to continue the conflict with 'manlie courage'.[57] She is finally defeated and slain after being asked by the Roman commander how she 'does pretend such things about the spirit and courage of women'.[58]

The gender aspects of Böece's account are of interest. Both Voada and her daughter Vodicia are honourable and forceful characters who fight the Romans to avenge serious wrongs. The raping by the Romans of 'so

many virgins and matrons by effeminate lust' is a curious choice of
words. Voada is effectively manly, while the Romans are debauched but
also effeminate. In this Scottish account, Boadicea is an effective
upholder of national rights against the might of the Roman Empire, an
image that was also significant in a number of accounts written in
England during the later sixteenth century.

Elizabethan writers had an interest in worthy figures from the past,[59]
characters who had exhibited particular virtue or valour. History was
used to provide examples of ancestors to the perceived greatness of the
English, or as a form of moral instruction to the contemporary generation.[60] Boadicea appears in several texts written during the reign of
Elizabeth I (1558–1603).[61] This was a period that has been described as
'most propitious for the fame of Boudicca'.[62] Boadicea appears to have
been particularly valuable to the English during the 1570s to 1590s, at the
time of the war with Spain.[63] Although she became a popular figure at
this time, Boadicea's fame, or infamy, actually spread even more widely
after Elizabeth's death.[64] During the reign of Elizabeth, Boadicea became
a focus for attention, since she could be interpreted as a patriot who had
fought bravely against the invaders of her country. In addition, she was
derived from the same ancient British stock from which the Tudor
rulers, including Elizabeth, claimed descent.[65] Henry VII, the first Tudor
ruler, had Welsh blood in his veins and the people of Wales were
thought of as the direct descendants of the ancient Britons.

Perhaps even more significantly, owing to her gender, Boadicea could
be used to provide an interesting comparison to and contrast with Elizabeth.[66] The earlier accounts of Boadicea were sometimes used
selectively and reinterpreted to provide a commentary on contemporary
politics, but many of these effectively stress the status of Boadicea as,
first, a successful ruler and, secondly, a former queen of England.[67] Both
aspects may have been influential, but they were inaccurate.

Early modern representations of Boadicea and Elizabeth are rich in
potential comparisons.[68] Both women were seen as native rulers who led
their countries in government and war, and both vigorously opposed the
incorporation of their territories into expanding continental empires.
Both were also famous for their use of the perceived 'masculine' art of
oratory.[69] It has long been supposed that Elizabeth, as did Boadicea
before her final battle, made a speech to her assembled army by the fort

at Tilbury in 1588, just prior to the arrival of the Armada. It may even be true that the classically-educated Elizabeth drew upon the words put into the mouth of Boudica by Tacitus in making her own speech at Tilbury, although this is disputed.[70] There has often been a tendency to identify ruling women with earlier significant female figures.[71] The discovery of a powerful woman ancestor figure has sometimes been exploited, either by herself or by others, to place the new female leader within a reassuring historical tradition. The value of this historical pedigree is the result of the deep anxiety that men had about female rule at this time. Europe's intellectual elite inherited a belief in the incompetence of women in managing state affairs that was derived from the writings of Aristotle.[72] Boadicea effectively provided a historical parallel for Elizabeth. At the same time, sixteenth-century accounts were not invariably positive in their assessment of Boadicea, as indeed was also the case with Elizabeth herself.

Stephen Gosson, in *The Schoole of Abuse* (1579), presented an oration of '*Bunduica* a notable woman and queen of Englande'. He paraphrased Dio's version of Boudica's speech about the corruption of Nero's Rome in order to highlight the comparative political blessings, as well as some of the problems, of his own age under the rule of Queen Elizabeth.[73] 'God hath now blessed *England* with a Queene, in virtue excellent, in power mightie, in glorye renowned, in government politike, in possession rich …'[74] In Gosson's account, Bunduica appears to be a positive figure, even though she evidently did not possess the power or the majesty of the contemporary queen.

Raphael Holinshed's *The Chronicles of England, Scotland and Ireland* (first published in 1577), a substantial history of the British Isles, in turn served as a source for many of the plays of Shakespeare. Holinshed only dealt briefly with the ancient history of Britain in his book, but he included two long speeches by 'Voadicea', one taken directly from Dio and the other from Tacitus.[75] She appears in this account effectively as a spokeswoman of national self-consciousness and political freedom,[76] in giving a long speech on the subject of 'ancient liberty'.[77] Voadicea's first speech in Holinshed's account drew upon the words put into her mouth in Dio's version of events but was subtly updated to reflect the political concerns of late sixteenth-century England.[78]

A woodcut in the book (figure 35) shows Voadicea making her speech while standing on the tribunal in front of her troops, a hare held beneath her right arm. Holinshed describes her in the following terms:

> Her mightie tall personage, comlie shape, sever countenance, and sharp voice, with hir long and yellow tresses of heare reaching downe to hir thighes, her brave and georgeous apparell also caused the people to have her in great reverence. [79]

The image of the queen demonstrates elements of early modern queenly regalia. [80] In some ways it is comparable with the 'Ditchley Portrait' of Elizabeth I, attributed to Marcus Gheeraerts the Younger and painted around 1592. [81] In particular, the crown draws a direct comparison with that of the contemporary English queen. Voadicea in this woodcut certainly forms a direct contrast to the images of naked ancient Britons in the approximately contemporary works of Lucas de Heere and others. [82] De Heere's ancient Britons were perhaps derived from contemporary images of 'Eskimos' and native Americans, [83] but also from references to the appearance of the ancient people of Britain in the classical sources. [84] They all wear a short curved sword, of fifteenth- or sixteenth-century date, at their waists. [85] By contrast, Voadicea in Holinshed's book is well-dressed. The illustration is clearly influenced by the account of her appearance and clothing presented by Dio and her only weapon is a jousting lance, but the main inspiration both for her and the soldiers in the background is contemporary English society.

Although in some ways he presented Voadicea as a positive champion of sixteenth-century liberty, it has been argued that Holinshed also emphasised female martial activity as excessive through the involvement of Voadicea and other women in battle. [86] Holinshed used Dio's account of the barbarity of the Britons with regard to prisoners, to shock his audience, [87] recalling that: 'there was nothing with the Britains but slaughter, fire, gallows, and such like, so earnest were they set on revenge. They spared neither age not sex.' [88] He also repeats Dio's shocking story about the treatment of some Roman women. Evidently the involvement of women as military leaders and soldiers formed a major contrast between the Britain of Boudica and that of Elizabeth I, in addition to which the idea of the killing of women and children was condemned. British men in this account figure in only rather general terms, but it is stressed several times that the army of the Britons

35. A woodcut from Raphael Holinshed's *The Chronicles of England, Scotland and Ireland* of 1586, showing Voadicea making her speech to the Britons. (*Published by permission of Durham University Library*)

'consisted as well of women as men ...'[89] The Romans in Holinshed's account, on the other hand, are resolutely male. Effectively this account can be argued to represent Boadicea's rebellion in terms of gender conflict rather than of assertive native resistance to the Roman Empire.[90] Holinshed drew on the writings of Dio in particular to make these points, although he also used Tacitus's accounts.

The sharpest appreciation of the contemporary relevance of Boadicea's story during the reign of Elizabeth was shown by the Italian soldier and courtier Petruccio Ubaldini (?1524–1600).[91] Born in Florence, but with a lengthy career in England, he met Queen Elizabeth on at least one occasion when he presented her with a manuscript in 1588. This was almost certainly *The Lives of the Noble Ladies of the Kingdom of England and Scotland* (*Le vite delle donne illustre, del regno d'Inghilterra, e del regno di Scotia*), published in 1591.[92] In this work Ubaldini argued that the 'Noble Ladies' of England and Scotland provided equally positive role models as had the Greek and Roman female exemplars of virtue. He chose three women from the semi-mythical past of Britain, including 'Carthumandua' (Cartimandua) and Boadicea, the latter being represented as two women, 'Voadicia' and 'Bunduica'.[93]

Ubaldini's Voadicia is largely taken from Tacitus's *Annals*, while his Bunduica appears to be based upon Dio,[94] although it contains some other material derived from Tacitus, possibly via Böece.[95] Voadicia is of honourable and noble character. Ubaldini states that:

> Because Voadicia was provoked by a justified resentment over the treatment of her family she moved her people with her misery to such a fury and desire for revenge that they took up arms and, with her as leader and guide, they had a long and dangerous war with the Romans, with varied results ...[96]

The provocation to which Voadicia was subjected is presented in detail and there is no description of the barbarity of the actions of the Britons. Her final defeat is put down to the fact that she had an 'unlucky day'.[97] The author describes her death:

> To die free, so that she did not have to be shown in the triumph of the victors, she took poison, leaving to future generations a memory of rare strength of character and of honourable and generous prudence.[98]

By contrast, Bunduica is savage and cruel. The sacking of two Roman 'fortified places', 'Camaloduno' and 'Verulamio' and all the cruelties of the rebellion are attributed to her.[99] In particular, Ubaldini makes much of Dio's description of the cruelty of the Britons to women during the conflict. This demonstrates the dilemma of the two sides of Boadicea's character, as perceived by the writers of the period.[100] He discusses in some detail whether there was one Voadicia/Bunduica or two, concluding in a thoughtful manner that the two women were probably the same person. Ubaldini states that:

> She left such a strong mark in the memory of the people because she was commemorated amongst the great women of this kingdom for her marvellous virtues; and even the cruelty that she used against her enemies should not delete all her other praiseworthy actions, because she did these in the rage of revenge rather than because of her natural inclinations, and also because of the vices of the Roman soldiers which they learned from the evil emperor Nero ...[101]

The English poet Edmund Spenser (*c.* 1552–99) also mentioned 'Bunduca' twice in his celebration of Queen Elizabeth, *The Faerie Queene*, first published in 1590.[102] In this context she is portrayed as a native example of courage and patriotism alongside other female leaders who opposed the Romans.[103]

Antiquarian research gathered pace during the later sixteenth century as a result of the desire to uncover English historical roots,[104] and knowledge of the geography of the Boudican rebellion became rather less speculative.[105] The major figure in this growing tradition of antiquarian research was William Camden (1551–1623). He was a thirty-five-year-old school master when, in 1586, he published an historical and geographical description of Britain entitled *Britannia*.[106] This was a highly important work that was reprinted and revised on many occasions and had a huge impact upon the development of antiquarian studies in Britain. This growing tradition during the sixteenth to nineteenth centuries came to have a gradual but significant influence upon knowledge of the appearance and character of the ancient Britons in general and of Boadicea in particular.

Camden provided a generally accurate portrayal of the Roman *civitates* of Britain, and his account of Roman Britain in *Britannia* was based upon a critical use of the best information that he could obtain,

written without too much inappropriate interpretation of the information. In particular, he relied heavily upon Tacitus for the description of
the events of Boadicea's revolt.[107] He placed Camulodunum at Maldon
in Essex, arguing that the Saxon name 'Maledune' was derived from the
title of the Roman colony (which he incorrectly records as 'Camalodunum').[108] He did, however, correctly place the site of Verulamium at
St Albans.[109] Camden mentions the capture of Camalodunum and the
destruction of Verulamium by Boadicea, using several variants of her
name, 'Bunduica', 'Boadicia' and 'Booadicia'. He twice stressed the
statements of the classical authors that the ancient Britons made no dis-
tinctions with regard to gender in matters of government.[110] In a later
work, *Remains Concerning Britain* (1614), he discusses the coinage of the
Britons and mentions coins 'of the famous *Brunduica*', although he also
states that he has never seen one.[111] These coins are presumably the
same ones that were described by Speed.

In 1611 Boadicea was again used as a parallel for the now deceased
Queen Elizabeth. John Speed wrote a good deal about Boadicea in *The
History of Great Britaine*,[112] addressing her under a variety of names –
'Boudicca', 'Voadica' and 'Boduo'.[113] The last of these names is taken
from an ancient British coin series which Speed attributed to
Boadicea,[114] interpreting the legend on these coins as 'Boduo'. We now
know that the correct reading of the legend is 'Bodvoc' and that the
coins actually relate to a leader of the Dobunni tribe, which occupied an
area now centred upon the modern county of Gloucestershire.[115]

Turning to the character of Boadicea, Speed describes how:

> all indeed feared the valour of this heroick Lady: whose lawes were not mar-
> tiall to save upon ransome: whose revenge was not pacified with yeeldings or
> submission nor did she thinke there was bloud enough in the *Romans* to
> imbrue the altars of her assisting gods, or to wash off the staine of the unno-
> ble and unmanly injuries.[116]

Speed's account includes a wood-cut print of Boadicea, one of a group
of four figures, two men and two women (figure 36 and 37). The images
were inspired by the late sixteenth-century watercolours of John White
and Lucas de Heere, and by the engravings of Theodor de Bry,[117] portraying rather more realistic images of ancient Britons than Holinshed
had done.

Speed wrote at length about the first pair of figures, which are of naked ancient Britons.[118] He noted three things in particular about these people – 'their gowing *naked*', the '*staining* and *colouring* of their whole Bodies' and the '*cutting, pincking* and *pouncing* of their flesh with garnishments ... of sundry shapers and fashions'.[119] By contrast with these naked barbarians, the images of the two clothed figures that follow are discussed briefly. These latter are examples of 'the more civill Britaines'.[120] Speed tells us that the female figure is based on 'the most valiant British Lady Boudicea',[121] and this is confirmed by the fact that she carries a spear, while the hare mentioned in Dio's account is placed at her feet. The hare was to become a common association of Boadicea in later illustrations.

It is important that, in contrast to many contemporary images of naked ancient Britons, including two of the figures in Speed's account, Boadicea is represented as clothed. This may be partly because Speed and his artist wished to indicate her 'virtue' by portraying her in this way.[122] He writes that:

> The later *women* (as you see by the later portraicture) became farre more modest, that is indeed more *womenly*, hauing learned that then they openly shew most beauty: much less should they expose to the view, that which nature most endeuoured to hide, as knowing it least worth the viewing ...[123]

The 'virtue' and spirit of Boadicea are also apparent in Speed's text and it is evident that the clothing of the figure of Boadicea is also a result of Dio's description of her appearance.

Boadicea had, therefore, lost the barbaric character of an unclothed native but she does retain aspects of her barbarous background, as there are painted patterns or tattoos upon her exposed legs and arms.[124] Speed continues his account of Boadicea by drawing upon the contemporary value of her example. He wrote of the female sex as:

> naturally the weaker, yet in most *writers* there are resembrances of some, whose Actions both *politicke* and *warlike* haue beene no way inferiour to the worthiest Men, as our owne Age hath giuen testimony to the World in another *Great Lady* of British race ... whose just, wise, and resolute kind of Gouernment hath justified that Custome of our old *Britains* and *Picts* ...[125]

Speed suggested that, while ordinary women in pre-Roman Britain were not involved in martial service, some of the 'choisest' were.[126] The

36. Woodcut print of an ancient Briton from John Speed's *The History of Great Britaine* of 1611. (*Published by permission of Durham University Library*)

37. Woodcut print of Boadicea from the 1632 edition of John Speed's *The History of Great Britaine* of 1611. (*Published by permission of Durham University Library*)

Boadicea in Speed's account is really a very positive figure who is at least partly inspired by the late Queen Elizabeth.

In his detailed account of the rebellion Speed glossed over the accounts of the atrocities that Dio attributes to the Britons. His description is based mainly upon Tacitus, but with a few details added from Dio's text.[127] He described the destruction of 'Camulodunum' that, following the writings of Camden, he located in his 'table' (the index to the book) at Maldon in Essex. 'Verolanium' he correctly locates 'neere the place where *St. Alban's* standeth'. He mentions London as 'a citie even then famous for concourse of *Merchants*, and of great renowne for provisions of all *things necessary* ...',[128] but, in the company of Polydore Vergil and Ubaldini, he does not describe its destruction by Boadicea and her followers. Perhaps Speed thought that the atrocities accorded to the ancient Britons by both Tacitus and Dio, and also the destruction and burning of the now capital city of London, would have been unpalatable to his intended audience and that they might detract from the positive image that he was creating of Boadicea.

It is true that many of the accounts that we have considered here draw in detail upon the barbarity of the actions of Boadicea's followers, but a number are also positive about the relevance of Boadicea's contemporary example. She is often represented as a powerful ruling queen who waged a war against the Romans and came close to victory. In fact her eventual defeat is effectively ignored by many of the accounts. One author – Ubaldini – created a 'schizophrenic' Boadicea by splitting her into two in order to attribute the worrying aspects of her character to a less worthy companion, while Böece created two characters by the attribution of some of her actions to a daughter. Following the death of Queen Elizabeth in 1603 and the ascent to the throne of a new king, James I, assessments of the message of Boadicea's rebellion became, in general, rather more critical.

5

Subordination

Too true I find a woman curs'd with pow'r
To blast a nation's welfare ...

R. Glover *Boadicea* (1753).[1]

The broadly historical accounts of Boadicea, including those by Camden and Speed, generally appear to have used the available information to provide an accurate portrayal of the life of Boadicea. The seventeenth- and eighteenth-century stage plays about Boadicea, by contrast, manipulated the story provided by the classical sources more directly in order to make significant points about contemporary society. All plays needed to appeal to their audiences in order to have a successful run. Many people in Elizabethan and Jacobean times enjoyed stage productions and all forms of drama flourished. Some plays were aimed at a particular audience while others were intended to appeal to all social classes.[2] The plays of William Shakespeare were written for a wide audience, although he did not write about Boadicea himself.

Between 1609 and 1614 the story of 'Bonduca' was told in a play by John Fletcher.[3] This play had an enduring run, being adapted by George Powell in 1696, by George Colman in 1778 and again in 1837; it held the stage until the end of the eighteenth century and beyond.[4] Fletcher's writing shows that his knowledge was derived from Tacitus and Dio, and that he had probably read the works of Ubaldini and Holinshed. In order to fill out his story, he also followed the lead of some of the sixteenth-century stories about Boadicea in using characters that do not appear in the accounts of either Tacitus or Dio of the events of AD 60 to 61. Caratach, general of the Britons in Fletcher's play, is based upon both the historical Caratacus and the 'Caractacus, cousin of Voadicia' in the accounts of ancient Britain by Böece and Ubaldini.[5] The historical Caratacus, however, served no part in Boudica's rebellion. Indeed, he was not a member of the Iceni tribe and had been led into honourable capture in Rome ten years before the death of Prasutagus. Bonduca's younger daughter, 'Bonvica', and an imaginary nephew, Hengo, also appear in the play. Fletcher did not follow the classical accounts closely in writing his play,[6] borrowing details from other writers and inventing action to make his tale more dramatic.

Fletcher's cast list also includes 'druides'. This is the first time that druids had appeared on the English stage and this play helped to establish them in the popular imagination.[7] In Act Three they attend a sacrifice alongside Bonduca, her elder daughter, Caratach and others. The druids performed a dignified version of 'a song-and-dance act' to accompany the sacrifice.[8] Druids, as we shall see, were to become an enduring feature of the story of Boadicea from the seventeenth to the twentieth century.

In one of the early versions of the play (the second folio edition of the plays of Francis Beaumont and John Fletcher), 'Bonduca' is described as 'Queen of the Iceni, a brave Virago'.[9] In this context 'virago' means a woman with 'manly' qualities;[10] depending upon who was using the term, it could be either complimentary or unflattering. A particular irony is that the bold virago in *Bonduca* would have been played by a boy, as female actresses did not take to the stage until 1660.[11] In Bonduca's case her qualities as a virago include her courage in battle and the fortitude with which she meets death. At the same time Fletcher also portrays her as rash and headstrong – characteristics that meant she was totally inadequate to the task of dealing with the 'masculine' business of politics and warfare.[12] The women in the play generally have negative roles;[13] Bonduca's daughters entice Roman soldiers into captivity and then attempt to have them sacrificed.

The initial military victories of the ancient Britons in the play are due to the leadership of Bonduca's male cousin, Caratach, rather than directly to her own actions. In fact Bonduca is shown as boastful and incompetent in Fletcher's play.[14]

Bonduca   A woman beat 'em … a weak woman,
            A woman beat these *Romanes.*

Caratach	So it seems.
	A man would shame to talk so. [15]

Defeat eventually comes to the Britons after Bonduca has used her own initiative and condemned them to an unnecessary encounter. Caratach is heavily critical of her error in the final battle and defines it as the result of female meddling: [16]

Caratach	O ye have plaid the fool,
	The fool extremely, the mad fool.
Bonduca	Why Cosin?
Caratach	The woman fool. Why did you give the word
	Unto the carts to charge down, and our people
	In grosse before the Enemie? We pay for't ...
	Why do you offer to command? The divell,
	The divell, and his dam too, who bid you
	Meddle in mans affairs?
Bonduca	I'll help all.
Caratach	Home,
	Home and spin woman spin, go spin, ye trifle ...
	O woman, scurvie woman, beastly woman. [17]

In this way Caratach describes Bonduca as a witch (a woman commanded by the devil) and requires her disempowerment and domestication. [18] Spinning at home, a domestic activity deemed as suitable for women by James I, [19] is seen as a more appropriate occupation for Bonduca than leading warriors into battle and decision-making. [20] Caratach also shows a far more positive attitude to the Roman enemy than is demonstrated by Bonduca; for instance, on two occasions he frees Roman soldiers who have been taken captive and threatened with death by Bonduca and her daughters. [21] It has been suggested that concerns about James's lenience towards Catholics – perceived as a pro-Roman view – may have influenced Fletcher in producing, in opposition to this, the positive and valiant character of Caratach. [22]

Fletcher appears to blend the qualities of the Romans and the Britons in his account. The British become glorious when united with the admirable and efficient Romans. [23] The play was first produced just after the establishment in 1606 of two new British colonies in America.

It draws upon the relevance of the Roman conquest of Britain to contemporary foreign and domestic policy.[24]

During the reign of King James I it was politic to play down the significance of Boadicea as a military leader. This explains the use of Caratach as the general and his forthright condemnation of Bonduca's actions. A similar distrust of female military leadership is represented in Dio's account.[25] The same attitude exists in some of the Elizabethan literature that deals with Boadicea; Elizabeth's death did not alter the climate of male opinion about Boadicea very much. In general terms, women were seen as imbued with a powerful, potentially disruptive sexuality that needed to be controlled through rigid social institutions and carefully nurtured inhibitions within the women themselves.[26] In these terms, Boadicea strayed far outside the bounds of acceptable behaviour; even though her valour might be seen as admirable, it was also thought to be misguided. Fletcher's negative image of Bonduca had a major impact upon the authors of plays and books over the next one hundred and fifty years. Not all the authors who wrote about Boadicea at this time, however, were so highly critical.

We have seen that John Speed continued to draw upon the parallel between Boadicea and Queen Elizabeth to produce a positive image at the beginning of the seventeenth century. Ben Jonson's account of Boadicea in *The Masque of the Queens* (1609) is also a positive one. Jonson (1572–1637) wrote a number of court masques, short dramatic plays, for the entertainment of King James I and the nobles of his court.[27] *The Masque of the Queens* was originally planned for the royal Christmas season during 1608 but was not actually performed until 2 February 1609.[28] It was a lavish production, the sets designed by the architect Inigo Jones in the form of a 'House of Fame'. In this complex structure various seated queens and ladies revolved in front of the audience.[29] A drawing of the design survives, along with the figures of eight of the ladies who played the historical figures in the masque.

The Masque of the Queens itself featured a series of famous queens and ladies from the past, including 'Voadicea, or Boodicia; by some Bunduica, and Bunduca: Queene of the Iceni'.[30] Unfortunately, there is no surviving drawing of Boadicea herself from the 'House of Fame'.

Boadicea is described as having 'express'd all magnitude of a spirit, breathing to the liberty, and redemption of her Countrey'.[31]

Another early seventeenth-century account presents a broadly positive view of Boadicea. A pamphlet of 1617, *Esther Hath Hanged Haman*,[32] was apparently written by a woman, Esther Sowernam, although the name itself was probably a pseudonym. The so-called 'Pamphlet Wars' of the late sixteenth to early seventeenth centuries were an exchange of texts that discussed the nature of the character and role of women,[33] and works by Sowernam, Tuvil and Newstead mentioned Boadicea. Sowernam sought to demonstrate 'the estimation of the Feminine Sex in ancient and Pagan times'.[34] We do not know the identity of Esther Sowernam; it has even been suggested that the writer may well have been a man who was using Boadicea's actions ironically in order to attack women.[35] We cannot, however, be certain of this and many consider that the author of this pamphlet was in fact a woman.[36]

Sowernam had two objectives. First, she sought to 'plainly and resolutely deliver the worthiness and worth of women both in respect of their Creation as in their works of Redemption'.[37] Secondly, she demonstrates 'of what estimate women have been valued in all ancient and modern times ...'[38] She listed various admirable women from the British past and included Boadicea amongst her examples of female virtue, arguing that:

> Amongst the old Britains, our first Ancestor, the valiant Boadicea, that defended the liberty of her Country against the strength of the Romans when they were at their greatest, and made them feel that a woman could conquer them who had conquered almost all the men of the then known world.[39]

This is probably an early example of an attempt by a woman to write in her own defence against the numerous male attacks upon women that appeared around this time.[40] Later female authors were to take up Boadicea's tale in a comparable way.

Two further broadly similar accounts were produced around the same time by Daniel Tuvil in 1616 and Christopher Newstead in 1620. Tuvil, in his study *Asylum Veneris: or A Sanctuary for Ladies Justly Protecting Them from the Foule Aspersions and Forged Imputations of Traducing Spirits*, drew upon a variety of women from ancient and medieval history to support his 'account of vertue in women'.[41] He illustrated this by considering the ideal characteristics of women, including beauty, chastity, modesty, humility, etc. At the end of a long list of female virtues he includes a chapter headed 'Of their Valour and Courage', and in this part of the work he considered 'Voadicia':

> Have wee not in our owne Confines, that princely Voadicia ... who with her warlike Amazonians maintained the reputation of her State, and kept it long on foot against the fierce invasion of the Romanes?[42]

Newstead's account of 'Voadicia', in his *An Apology for Women: or Women's Defence* (1620), is broadly comparable. It was dedicated to 'The thrice excellently vertuous Lady, Mary, Countess of Buckingham' and intended to act as a way of 'repulsing your sexes wrongs' in terms of a number of other authors who seek to 'disgrace women'.[43] The women from the ancient and medieval world who are quoted by Newstead as examples fall into many of the same categories that had already been used by Tuvil. In the section on 'fortitude and magnanimity' we are told that: 'The ancient inhabitants of this Ile, the Brittaines, Voadicia being the General, shaked off the Roman yoke, and most of their prosperous battels were when women did leade them.'[44]

Thomas Heywood produced a similarly positive view of Boadicea in his *The Exemplary Lives and Memorable Acts of Nine the Most Worthy Women of the World*, published in 1640. Heywood examined nine women in rather greater detail than the previous authors, choosing three Jews, three Gentiles and three Christians to elucidate his points. His book was dedicated to two prominent women and also 'To all noble and brave spirited gentlemen, with the excellent and vertuously disposed gentlewomen in general'.[45] One of the women chosen by Heywood is 'This Bunduca (cald also by severall Authours, Boodicia, Boudicea, Voadica and Bownduica)'.[46] An illustration of Bunduca (plate 1) shows her wearing the court dress of the period, with a plumed hat and a pearl necklace.[47] On the opposite page is the verse:

> How much O Brittaine, are we bound to thee
> Mother, and Nurse of magnanimitye:
> Of which thou from antiquity haft lent
> Unto all ages famous president,
> Witnes this British Queen, whose masculine spirit
> Shall to all future, glorious fame inherit,[48]

He suggested that Bunduca:

> was not as some have described her a martiall Bosse, or Amazonain Giantesse, but tall of stature, and moderately fat and corpulent, her face excellently comely, yet with all incomparably terrible, her complexion very faire and beautifull, which who will wonder at in a lady born in Brittaine.[49]

Heywood presents Bunduca effectively as a liberated warrior.[50]

The petition made by the Levellers in 1649 and 1653 also made reference to Boadicea.[51] These mid seventeenth-century radicals sought the abolition of the monarchy and the House of Lords and also equality before the law, while female Levellers also opposed the oppression of women.[52] Although the four accounts of Tuvil, Sowernam, Newstead and Heywood, together with the Levellers' reference, used Boadicea and other women to present a positive view of womankind, the majority of pamphlets on the subject were more critical.[53]

Antiquarians also began to debate about the site of Boadicea's grave at this time, following up Dio's reference to her costly burial. In 1624 the antiquarian Edmund Bolton proposed that she had been buried at Stonehenge.[54] In 1640 Thomas Heywood repeated the idea but did not come to a clear conclusion.[55] The idea that Stonehenge was built for Boadicea was swiftly rebutted,[56] but it re-emerged in Edward Barnard's account of 1790. He was unable to choose between the idea that 'Stonehenge was erected as a monument to commemorate the heroism of Boadicea' and the alternative suggestion that she was buried close to London.[57]

Although many early seventeenth-century accounts of Boadicea did not follow the highly critical approach adopted by Fletcher, John Milton used an equally negative image. In his *History of Britain* (1670) he provided a rather confused version of the story of Boadicea taken from Tacitus and particularly from Dio. He describes Boadicea's lack of modesty and shame, her 'loose bodied gown' and the 'hare at her bosom' and suggests that she was a 'distracted Woeman, with as mad a Crew at her heeles'.[58] Tacitus's and Dio's accounts of the rebellion are criticised by Milton. In particular he attacks their accounts of Boadicea's speech which, he suggests, were their inventions. He argues that: 'this they do

out of a vanity, hoping to embellish and set out their Historie with the
strangeness of our manners, not careing in the mean while to brand us
with the rankest note of Barbarism, as if in *Britain* Women were Men,
and Men Woemen'.[59]

Milton casts doubt upon the description of Boadicea and her actions
presented by the classical authors. In its place, he presents a tempered
version of Dio's description that plays down Boadicea's warlike attributes.[60] At the end of his account of the rebellion, however, the disorderly
acts of Boadicea and the Britons 'manifested themselves to be right *Barbarians* ...',[61] and this is taken as the reason for their downfall.

It has been suggested that the image of Boadicea underwent a general transformation during the Restoration in England, with the
re-establishment of the Stuart monarchy in 1660. Her savagery was
reduced as she was brought into line with late seventeenth-century
ideals of subordinate womanhood.[62] Heywood's image in 1640 of a
'comely ... beautifull ... lady' is perhaps also to be seen in the light of
changing views of womanhood. Aylett Sammes, amongst a series of
more peculiar speculations,[63] created a comparable portrayal of 'Boadicia' in his *Britannia Antiqua Illustrata* (1676).[64] Sammes used the
accounts both of Tacitus and Dio directly in his writings. He gave Boadicia a reduced role in the rebellion and the tribesmen of the Iceni are
attributed with a collective desire to avenge her and her daughters.[65]
This is actually largely a result of Sammes's preference for Tacitus's text
over Dio's. He mentions that Tacitus, in contrast to Dio, 'wrote next
to these times, and ... may be supposed to have truer intelligence ...'[66]
The attitude of Sammes to the accounts of the two classical writers mir-
rors the comments of some modern analysts. Included in Sammes's
account is a picture, a 'Sculpture of Boadicia' (plate 2), drawn by
William Fairthorne and based upon Dio's description of Boudica,[67] but
also applying ideas of dress and appearance derived from seventeenth-
century society. It was not until the mid eighteenth century that a more
antiquarian depiction of Boadicea began to emerge.[68] In Sammes's book
the verse below the illustration reads:

> To war, this QUEEN doth with her Daughters move,
> She for her Wisdom, followed, They for Love;
> What Roman force, Such joined powers could quell;
> Before so murdering Charmes whole Legions fell.

> Thrice happy Princess, had she rescued so,
> Her Daughters honour, and her Countrys too;
> But they being ravish't, made her understand
> 'Tis harder, Beauty to secure, than Land.
> Yet her Example teaching them to dye,
> Virtue, the roome of Honour did Supply.[69]

This verse emphasises Boadicia's wisdom, love, charms and honour rather than the violence and lack of control stressed by some of the earlier accounts. Sammes evidently, however, had some concerns with Boadicea's image, as his translation of Dio's description of her shows: 'Of stature bigg and tall, of a Grim and Stern visage, but withal modest and chearful, a rough and hoarse voice ...'[70]

Fletcher's play *Bonduca* inspired later playwrights. In 1696 it was updated and given the title *Bonduca: or The British Heroine*[71] and was performed at the Theatre Royal. The actor George Powell (1658–?1714) wrote the dedication to this work in which he noted of the play: 'tis a Fabrick of Antiquity; a Foundation of that Celebrated Poetical Architect, the Famous *Fletcher*. But with several Alterations ...'[72] He suggested:

> where can our Noblest English Memoirs be more gracefully or more suitable lodged, than in the Hands of the Noblest English Honour? And it has this further Advantage, as being an English story; That the Glory of Worthies and Heroes sounds Sweetest, where the Musick is tuned at Home.[73]

Powell also wrote a note 'to the reader' in which he recalled that the adaptation was undertaken by a friend of his, and that the whole play had been revised in a fortnight.[74]

Henry Purcell (1659–95) composed music for this adaptation of the play, completing it a month before his death;[75] it is one of Purcell's most celebrated productions.[76] Much of the music was instrumental and incidental to the action, but it also included a number of songs, including two patriotic ones, 'Britons, Strike Home' and 'To Arms, to Arms'.[77]

'To Arms, to Arms' appears in Act III, where it is sung by druids during a sacrifice to ensure victory. The words are:

> To Arms, To Arms! Your Ensign straight display,
> Now, now, now, set the Battle in Array,

> The Oracle of War Declares,
> Success Depends upon our Hearts and Spears.[78]

'Britons, Strike Home' was sung just after 'To Arms, to Arms'. The words are:

> Britons, Strike Home: Revenge your Country's Wrongs,
> Fight and Record your selves in Druids' Songs.[79]

These songs and their tunes remained a popular part of the patriotic repertoire for a long time.[80]

While much of Fletcher's original text remained, *Bonduca: or The British Heroine* shifts some attention away from Bonduca to her daughters and to the general Caratach.[81] The three women still have a role in the violence of war, but their behaviour is rather less extreme than in the original play. For example, following on from the altercation between Caratach and Bonduca in which the general suggests that his queen should go home to spin, Bonduca now asks for Caratach's forgiveness.[82] Caratach, played by George Powell, replaces Bonduca in making the penultimate speech of the play, prior to his suicide. At this stage, the gender roles in the conflict are neatly reversed in a conversation between Suetonius, the Roman general, and Caratach. Suetonius offers his friendship to Caratach and the British general proclaims:

Caratach	No *Roman*! No! I wear a *British* Soul:
	A Soul too great for slav'ry ...'
Suetonius	Was *Rome*, too poor a Mistress,
	To wed thee to her Arms? ...
Caratach	*Rome*, Sir, ah no! She bids a Price too small,
	To bribe me into Life. My bleeding Country
	Calls me to Nobler Wreaths ...
	And when her Caratach dies in such a Cause
	A *British* Tomb, outshines a *Roman* Triumph.[83]

Britain, as represented by Caratach, is resolutely male, while Rome is now seen in female guise.

Despite the downplaying of the role of Bonduca in particular and of women in general, the play provided an opportunity for a woman to play the role of Boadicea. The first professional actresses appeared on the British stage in 1660,[84] and plays about Boadicea created some of their first roles. In this particular production Mrs Frances Mary Knight was cast as Bonduca and Jane Rogers as her daughter Claudia,[85] while her other daughter was played by Miss Cross.[86]

A new play, *Boadicea, Queen of Britain,* was written by Charles Hopkins in 1697 and acted by His Majesty's Servants at the theatre in Lincoln's Inn Fields. This play was influenced both by Fletcher's *Bonduca* and by Powell's reworking of the play. Hopkins's play shows no additional knowledge derived from the Roman account of events.[87] As in the case of Fletcher's work, Hopkins does not follow the classical sources closely but develops an inherited tale for dramatic effect. For instance, Boadicea has a general named Cassibelan (after the historical Cassivellanus) and her daughters are named Camilla and Venutia. The role of the druids is developed, and they sing at a sacrifice of some oxen:

> Throw now the strugling Victim on,
> Press, press him hard, and keep him down:
> Pierce his Sides deep, and let them pour
> Into your Golden Bowls their Gore,
> 'Till they can shed, can bleed no more.[88]

The druids increasingly became a major element of the story of Boadicea. Their inclusion in Hopkins's play is to be seen as part of the process by which they became a source of popular fascination in the seventeenth century and in particular during the eighteenth and early nineteenth.[89] It is not surprising that they were introduced into the story of Boadicea or that the classical references to their practice of human sacrifice[90] were developed.[91] Despite this, the only classical reference that describes druids in the context of the events of AD 60 to 61 relates to their suppression by Suetonius Paulinus on Anglesey before the start of the rebellion. Webster and others used this to suggest that the rebellion had a partly religious motive,[92] although there is no direct evidence to indicate this. This is one of the enduring myths that has developed around the story of Boudica. We have seen that Fletcher first included the druids in the tale of Boadicea and others, including Hopkins, have continued this tradition.

John Dryden, writing to a female friend in the 1699, remarked that Hopkins's play was one 'which you fair ladyes lik'd'.[93] This liking may have resulted from the fact that Boadicea was portrayed in what the author saw as a rather more flattering light than in some earlier seventeenth-century renditions. Hopkins's Boadicea is represented as a far more positive and maternal figure than Fletcher's Bonduca. The part of Boadicea in Hopkins's play was created for the talented actress Elizabeth Barry (1658–1713). Barry was one of the most popular of the first group of English actresses and is known to have performed 142 named parts between 1673 and 1709. She was also famed for her toughness of character and assumed a public 'masculine' role in theatrical affairs.[94] This may well have given her the appropriate public image to play Boadicea. The heroine displays military efficiency and handles diplomatic negotiations with shrewdness and courtesy.[95] Nevertheless she leaves many of the significant decisions and actions in the play to men.[96] In effect, in his rendition of both Boadicea and the ancient Britons, Hopkins sanitised the accounts in the classical texts by omitting both the violence and the lack of control that are evident in Tacitus's and Dio's accounts. For example, Decius (a Roman general) threatens Boadicea that unless she allows Rome to take over her kingdom war will be inevitable. He also mentions that:

> Those Souldiers are incens'd, whole desperate Bands
> Dare act whatever Rage, and Lust commands.
> They'l set your temples and their Gods in Fire,
> While Heav'n in vain sees the bold Flames aspire.
> Chaste matrons, shall like common Strumpets burn,
> And Infants from the Breasts they suck, be torn.[97]

In fact, some of the violence in the play is the result of Roman action, while some of the atrocities that were attributed to the Britons by Dio are transformed into threats from the Roman commanders.[98]

In 1753 a further play entitled *Boadicea* was produced by Richard Glover in Dublin.[99] Glover's Boadicea was depicted in an almost totally hostile manner and her failings are repeatedly associated with her gender.[100] She is effectively an exaggerated version of Fletcher's Bonduca.[101] An illustration of Boadicea reproduced with a late eighteenth-century edition of Richard Glover's play shows the actress, Mrs Powell, in the title role (plate 3).[102] It shows a determined woman standing on the edge of the raised tribunal platform with a spear in her hand; she wears a crown and breastplate that are totally out of context in first century Britain.

The hero of this play is her brother-in-law, Dumnorix, leader of the 'Trinobantians' (Trinovantes), who was played by the great actor-manager David Garrick (1717–1779).[103] The action of the play takes place after the killing of 70,000 Romans by the Britons.[104] Boadicea's character is exemplified by her speech at the start of the play, which draws upon Dio's account of her actions. In this speech she replies to a Roman ambassador, who is suggesting peace between the two sides, by saying:

> May stern Andate, war's victorious goddess,
> Again resign me to your impious rage,
> If e'er I blot my suff'rings from remembrance;
> If e'er relenting mercy cool my vengeance,
> Till I have driv'n you to out utmost shores,
> And cast your legions on the crimson'd beach.
> Your costly dwellings shall be sunk in ashes,
> Your fields be ravag'd, your aspiring bulwarks
> O'erturn'd and levell'd to the meanest shrub;
> Your gasping matrons, and your children's blood,
> With mingled streams, shall dye the British sword;
> Your captive warriors, victims to our altars,
> Shall croud each temple's spacious round with death:
> Else may each pow'r, to whom the Druids bend,
> Annul my hopes of conquest and revenge![105]

Boadicea is responsible for serious military errors in Glover's play. She argues with her sister Venusia and brother-in-law Dumnorix about the fate of Roman prisoners of war. Boadicea wants to have them sacrificed, despite the fact that they were caught trying to save her own daughter from the advances of another Roman soldier. Dumnorix does not permit their deaths and, as a result of this, Boadicea refuses to support Dumnorix in a military action against the Romans, as the result of which he is defeated. Boadicea later attacks the Roman camp herself at night in an ill-advised manner, is defeated and poisons herself. By the end of the play all the leading Britons are dead and Britain falls to the Romans, although Dumnorix rather than Boadicea has the final action.

In this play we are left in no doubt of the potentially devastating consequences of female rule.[106] Dumnorix says of Boadicea:

> Too true I find a woman curs'd with pow'r
> To blast a nation's welfare ...[107]

> Frantic woman!
> Who hopes with fury and despair to match
> The vigilance and conduct of Suetonius.[108]

By contrast, the character of Boadicea's non-combatant sister, the fictitious Venusia, wife of her general Dumnorix, is presented in a positive light.[109] She commits suicide with her husband, but just before she does this she states:

> Though my weak sex by nature is not arm'd
> With fortitude like thine, of this be sure,
> That dear subjection to thy honour'd will,
> Which hath my life directed, ev'n in death
> Shall not forsake me ...[110]

In the context of the third quarter of the eighteenth century, as the contribution of women to the economy of the household diminished, a fashion arose for admiring what has been termed 'palpitating sensibility and languishing grace, rather than robust health and rational judgement'.[111] The character of Venusia may be seen in this context. To stress a comparable point, far from indicating a greater tolerance for female rule, images like that produced by Glover for the characters of Boadicea and Venusia mark the 'eclipse' of female rebelliousness as a source of national concern as women became generally less involved in public activities.[112]

Glover's play created an impassioned response from an anonymous pamphlet writer, *Female Revenge: or The British Amazon Exemplified in the Life of Boadicia* (1753).[113] This pamphlet, which sold for six pence, argued that Glover had abused the evidence of the classical historians in his portrait of Boadicea. *Female Revenge* is an early example of a work in which someone, who clearly had a good knowledge of the classical accounts, objected to a popular portrayal of Boadicea to the extent that he or she felt driven to publish his or her views. We will come across similar examples of attacks upon popular images later. The author

1. Bunduca, from Heywood's *Exemplary Lives* of 1640. (*By permission of the British Library, shelfmark 276.e.1 Bunduca*)

2. Boadicia, by William Fairthorne, from Aylett Sammes's *Britannia Antiqua Illustrata* of 1676. (*Published by permission of Durham University Library*)

3. 'Mrs Powell as Boadicea' in Richard Glover's play of 1753, from *Boadicea, British Theatre Volume II* by R. Glover, 1797. (*Published by permission of Durham University Library*)

4. 'Boadicea in her Chariot'. The frontispiece to volume 1 of Tobias Smollett's
A Complete History of England of 1758, by Charles Grignon, after Francis
Hayman. (*By permission of the British Library, shelfmark Chariot E. 2050*)

5. 'Will you follow me, men?' Illustration of Boadicea by A. S. Frost. From *Our Island Story* by H. E. Marshall (1905), opposite p. 20.

6. Miss Elizabeth Kirby as Boadicea in a 1909 production of Cicely Hamilton's *A Pageant of Great Women.*

7. An image of Boadicea in stained glass, from a window in Colchester Town Hall, dating to around 1901–2. (*Copyright Colchester Museums*)

8. Thomas Thornycroft's statue *Boadicea and her Daughters*, erected in 1902. (*Photograph Richard Hingley*)

stated that the pamphlet was 'Calculated to instruct the Reader of this celebrated Tragedy, in the true History of one of the most memorable Transactions recorded in the British Annals; and to shew wherein Poetical Fiction has deviated from Real Facts'.[114] The writer used the accounts of Tacitus and Dio to produce a positive image of Boadicea that contrasted directly with Glover's rendition. Tacitus is used to show that Boadicea and her daughters were used 'in the most barbarous Manner' by the Romans.[115] It was noted that the Roman historians themselves acknowledged the violence and injustices of the Roman actions. The 'most horrible cruelties' were committed by the Britons, but these acts were deemed to be due to provocation.[116] The author felt that Glover's play was inaccurate in historical terms and also 'too full of Horror to work upon the tender Passions of a polite Audience',[117] and that Boadicea herself was portrayed as fit for the madhouse rather than as one who could preside over a nation or lead an army.[118]

Another scholarly eighteenth-century account of Boadicea is contained within John Horsley's important work, *Britannia Romana* (1733). This book, which has been said to mark 'the beginning of the study of Roman Britain as we know it',[119] provided a sound account of the rebellion based upon the writings of Tacitus with few flights of fancy.[120] Horsley may have been more responsible than anyone else for popularising the spelling 'Boadicea',[121] as he discussed the form of her name in some detail before indicating this as his own preference. Again, Horsley locates Camulodunum at Maldon in Essex,[122] while Verulamium is sited correctly.[123]

The theme of 'Boadicea in her Chariot' was illustrated on the frontispiece to Tobias Smollett's *Complete History of England*, first published in 1757 (plate 4). The illustration was produced by Charles Grignon, based upon the work of Francis Hayman.[124] This depiction of Boadicea, compared to many of the earlier images, demonstrates the influence of growing antiquarian knowledge. The work of the English antiquaries during the second half of the seventeenth and the eighteenth centuries had revolutionised the understanding of archaeological monuments and of the possessions of the prehistoric inhabitants of Britain.[125] Boadicea is shown seated, bare-breasted, wearing a chain necklace and carrying a wicker shield, a spear and a hare. Some of the details are, perhaps, rather more appropriate to the ancient British context than the earlier images that we have discussed. Unlike many contemporary images, there is no crown on Boadicea's head; the artist has been able to use archaeological knowledge to inform his illustration rather than being entirely inspired by contemporary society. In the illustration Boadicea has a male attendant, who is also carrying a spear. Her chariot has four wheels, two smaller ones at the front and two larger at the back, all fitted with spikes, or scythes, a feature that later was to become a tradition in portrayals of Boadicea.

A group of druids behind Boadicea are evidently blessing her undertaking against the Romans. These figures are influenced by the developing tradition of depictions of druids, following on from the research of William Stukeley in the early to mid eighteenth century.[126] Smollett himself provides two and a half pages of description of the rebellion of AD 60 to 61, mostly taken from Tacitus's account. Boadicea is described as 'a woman of a masculine spirit and irresistable eloquence'.[127] Inflamed by the druids who survived the slaughter on Anglesey, the Britons rose against the Romans. The destruction of Camulodunum and Verulamium, together with the final battle, are described but the sacking of Londinium is not mentioned. Dio's description of the warrior queen is given in full in a footnote.[128] Around the same time Boadicea was included as one of the six subjects for paintings suggested by the committee that was set up by the Society for the Encouragement of Arts in 1758–59.[129]

Neither of the plays of Glover or Hopkins had the success of Fletcher's production. Perhaps the portrayal of her assertive deeds and speeches made Boadicea's transgressions and failures too obvious.[130] Fletcher's play had the longest run and held the stage until the end of the eighteenth century and beyond.[131] In the various plays about Boadicea produced during the seventeenth and eighteenth centuries, the ancient British leader and her daughters were often progressively removed from major roles in decision-making and savage warfare. They were relegated to a less public position in the story of the rebellion.[132] In the accounts in which she does have some part in initiating military strategy, Boadicea's role is invariably disastrous. In the context of these plays, she was effectively 'disarmed' as an effective female warrior.[133] In some other accounts, Boadicea commonly becomes the upholder of characteristics that were seen as quintessentially feminine by the male authors who wrote about her. For instance, in Sammes's poem she is portrayed as an upholder of honourable female virtues (love, charm, chastity and honour). As time went on Boadicea was transformed from a very public character to a rather more private figure, a process that mirrored the declining power of women in the political sphere and their increasingly domesticated role during this time.[134]

The early modern period in England saw a change in Boadicea's image that was not simply a transition from a worrying martial figure to a comforting maternal one, but to one that involved conflicting ideas. Perhaps the most significant of these is the positive version of Boadicea that was produced in the account of Esther Sowernam. This pamphlet effectively stresses Boadicea as a symbol of women's strengths and illustrated Sowernam's determination to fight for the interests of women in the face of male criticism.[135] Speed also drew upon recent history to create a more positive image for her. Of the more extreme versions, Glover's monstrous Boadicea was not acceptable to at least one of his contemporaries.

One vital element in these early modern accounts of Boadicea was a developing idea of British nationhood. During the sixteenth century, the English were seeking to develop a strong concept of their identity as a people in the context of a difficult international situation. In accounts of the sixteenth to eighteenth centuries there was a struggle to reconcile at least two contrasting positions. On the one hand, there is a longing to establish a respectable historical precedent and continuity for English identity, while on the other there was a desire to exorcise primitive female savagery from national history.[136] A new element in these early modern accounts related to developing British nationalism. In their struggle to write a history of Roman Britain sixteenth- and seventeenth-century writers were influenced by the idea of the legitimacy of British nationalism and the concept of Boadicea as a patriotic defender of British rights was developed. This is why many accounts of this date talk of nations and country in their accounts of Boadicea.

Writings about Boadicea at this time represent attempts to tell stories about the prehistory and early history of Roman Britain. Sixteenth- and seventeenth-century authors were, however, influenced by the idea of the legitimacy of the English nation and its roots in the ancient past. As a result the idea of Boadicea as a patriotic defender of English rights was developed. This connecting of Boadicea to the image of English (or British) nationalism is partly derived from the classical sources. As we have seen, Tacitus in *Agricola* and Dio describe Boadica as effectively a native British leader who rose with her people to drive the Romans out of Britain. Tacitus's account in the *Annals*, however, tells a rather different story. In this work we are told that she was the leader of one British tribe, the Iceni, supported by others; she did not rule throughout Britain.[137]

At a deeper level, the new ideas of nationalism that were developed in the early modern world had no link with the Roman Empire. In the Roman Empire of the first century AD the types of ideas about nationhood that were being developed in the sixteenth- and seventeenth-century did not exist. The evolving image of Boadicea as a patriot, however, had increasingly important repercussions from the late eighteenth century onwards. She was transformed at this time from a quieter domesticated figure into a strong and independent character in many works of literature and art. This use of Boadicea to develop ideas of English nationhood and imperial ambition drew upon the classical sources, while at the same time exploiting the seventeenth- and eighteenth-century developments of her image.

6

Imperial Icon

In the past, I beheld Buddig – Victoria – intently listening to the Arch-druid's wonderful Prediction. In the present, I behold our great and good Queen Victoria realising the marvellous fulfilment of the Prophecy . . .

M. Trevelyan (1900, xii).

During the late eighteenth and nineteenth centuries Britain's empire expanded across much of the world (figure 38). Many commentators at this time drew direct comparisons and contrasts between the empires of Britain and Rome.[1] The Roman parallel appeared to be particularly important for the ruling classes of Britain who were educated in classical languages and texts. This was considered to be a vital part of their learning and experience in a tradition that ultimately derived from the Renaissance.[2] The language, writings and art of Greece were an important part of cultural experience,[3] but classical Rome was also thought to be an important source of identity.[4] Rome was of particular significance due to the fact that the invasion of Britain in AD 43, and the subsequent domination of Britain by Rome, was seen to have been the process by which Graeco-Roman civilisation was imported to the British Isles.[5]

Nevertheless, for much of the eighteenth and nineteenth centuries association with imperial Rome was a difficult one. In 1776–88 Edward Gibbon published his account of classical Rome – *The History of the Decline and Fall of the Roman Empire*, a historical masterwork that has had a deep influence for centuries since.[6] This work focused on the image of imperial decline and fall, but also emphasised that the collapse of the Roman Empire was the result of its moral corruption and degradation. Gibbon disliked the idea of 'imperialism' and he did not consider that the Roman Empire provided a direct parallel for the British.[7] This awkwardness of comparison with the Roman Empire

remained until the 1870s, both due to critical views about the degener-
ate character of classical Rome and also because the French had
developed the concept of imperialism in direct association with their
own ambitions.[8] The imperial character of the rule of the emperor
remained a challenge to many critics writing during the early and middle nineteenth-century. They felt that the idea of Roman despotism did
not associate well with England's inherent 'freedom', which was often
thought to have derived from the supposed Anglo-Saxon origins of the
English race.[9]

A generally progressive view of cultural evolution developed during
this period, associated with the concept that society progresses through
time. Greece and Rome were effective cultural icons for the educated
classes because education and culture stressed the vital contribution of
these classical societies to contemporary European nations. British
writers and critics increasingly felt, however, that the British had managed to improve upon the examples that classical civilisation had
provided. For example, in discussing the Roman Empire in his book,
The Roman Wall, first published in 1851, John Collingwood Bruce wrote
that:

> Another empire has sprung into being of which Rome dreamt not ... In this
> island, where, in Roman days, the painted savage shared the forest with the
> beast of prey – a lady sits upon the throne of state, wielding a sceptre more
> potent than Julius or Hadrian ever grasped! Her empire is threefold that of
> Rome in the hour of its prime, but power is not her brightest diadem. The
> holiness of the domestic circle irradiated her. Literature, and all the arts of
> peace, flourish under her sway. Her people bless her.[10]

As confidence increased with the successful expansion of the British
Empire, many felt that the British were surpassing the successes of the
Romans, at least in geographical sway and governmental terms.[11]

During the late nineteenth and early twentieth centuries the image of
Rome was associated with the disturbing facts that the pride of native
Britain had once been humbled by a Roman army, and that most of the
island had been effectively converted into a colony.[12] This idea about
the Roman invasion is evident from the sixteenth century onwards, but
it was developed more fully at this time. Children's novels and history
books, which became common during this period, occasionally
addressed the difficult idea of previous phases of 'foreign' (Roman and

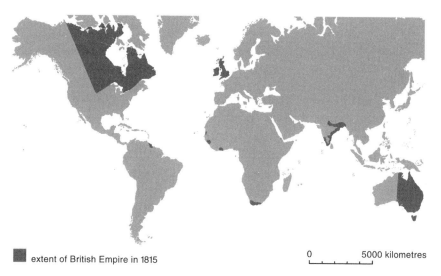

extent of British Empire in 1815

0   5000 kilometres

38. The British Empire in 1815.

Norman) domination. Many authors focused on medieval and modern England, when the country had remained free from conquest,[13] and often struggled with the idea of a native British defeat. For instance, in his *Stories of the Land We Live in: or England's History in Easy Language*, published in 1878, William Locke suggested that:

> I dare say every one of our forefathers, when they saw the Romans come first, were discouraged, and thought all was over with them; they should never be happy any more, their towns and castles taken, many of them killed and their enemies very proud and haughty. But those very things were meant for their good. Their savage customs and barbarous manner of life were thus changed. There we find the first steps on the ladder that has conducted Englishmen to such power and greatness ... Let us heartily thank God for it ...[14]

While showing evident embarrassment with a period of former foreign domination, these comments relate Britain's late Victorian greatness to its earlier history. A number of writers, including children's authors, discussed the Roman impact on Britain for a variety of reasons. In the context of these works national pride could be reasserted in a number of ways; for instance, by exploring the active opposition of the ancient Britons to Rome.[15]

This tendency had an origin in the late eighteenth century when Boadicea was increasingly drawn upon as a figure of patriotic heroism and as an inspiration for national and imperial literature and art. From this time poets, playwrights and artists championed the resistance of the British to Rome, and Boadicea and Caratacus – the other British war-leader who opposed Rome – were often drawn upon.[16] The most significant work in this context was William Cowper's poem of 1782, *Boadicea: An Ode.* Cowper (1731–1800), was one of the most succeful poets of this age.[17] It has been argued that his *Boadicea* fostered an asexual image of British triumph and heroism.[18] The poem was published at a time of British territorial expansion and political ambition following a period of lengthy conflict, including the American War of Independence,[19] and Boadicea was adapted to fit this context. The poem helped to project Boadicea into the context of the British Empire by suggesting that her actions had assisted with the development of British imperialism,[20] effectively creating her as an imperial icon.

Drawing upon a tradition that arose from earlier plays, a druid speaks to Boadicea after she has been flogged by the Romans and before the start of the uprising. The druid states:

> Rome shall perish – write that word
> In the blood that she has spilt;
> Perish hopeless and abhorr'd
> Deep in ruin as in guilt.
>
> Rome for empire far renown'd,
> Tramples on a thousand states,
> Soon her pride shall kiss the ground –
> Hark! The Gaul is at her gates.
>
> Other Romans shall arise.
> Heedless of a soldier's name,
> Sounds, not arms, shall win the prize,
> Harmony the path to fame.
>
> Then the progeny that springs
> From the forests of our land,
> Arm'd with thunder, clad with wings
> Shall a wider world command.
>
> Regions Caesar never knew
> Thy posterity shall sway:
> Where his eagle never flew,
> None invincible as they.[21]

Boadicea then rushes into battle and the poem ends with the statement:

> Ruffians, pitiless as proud,
> Heav'n awards the vengeance due,
> Empire is on us bestow'd
> Shame and ruin wait for you.[22]

The clear reference in the druid's prophetic words and also in the final statement is to the decline and fall of the Roman Empire and to the rise of its British successor.[23] By this device the poem finally provided an acceptable image of Boadicea;[24] it removed those aspects of her actions regarded as unfeminine by ascribing her ambitions and aggression to the male druid.[25] She seeks his council but the only words that are actually spoken are those of the druid. Boadicea is transformed into an exceptional figure from British history whose gender contributes to her symbolic sacrifice. The offering that Boadicea makes then becomes firmly linked with the forthcoming imperial development of Britain itself.

The cruelty of the ancient Britons in victory and Boadicea's ultimate defeat are pushed aside by the substitution of British for Roman imperial ambitions.[26] The poem reflects British self-confidence, which had been fostered by an unprecedented series of military successes. Once an empire had been established that is more extensive than that of the Romans, the importance of their previous domination appeared to be of less concern.[27] At the same time, the poem raises significant issues.[28] In order to justify the claims of the poem it was necessary to argue that Britain owes its greatness to a more humane treatment of its subjects as well as to its superior technology; Cowper never articulates this idea, perhaps because he felt unable to substantiate it.[29] Elsewhere in his writing, Cowper raised concerns about the contemporary state of Britain and its empire, and with slavery in particular. He considered that the energy of imperialism did not generate any export of freedom or virtue from Britain to the empire.[30] It is possible that Cowper was attempting to resolve his anxieties about the British Empire by transferring them into the context of the story of Boadicea.[31] His concerns about the savage elements of British imperialism are not clearly stated in *Boadicea*, but these may indeed have been behind his thoughts.[32] Once more, Boadicea provides a valuable source because of the ambiguity of her example.

Whatever motivation drove Cowper to write his poem, it had a profound impact that effectively led to the reinvention of Boadicea as a champion of British imperialism.[33] The poem linked her to the expansion of the British Empire and, during the nineteenth and early twentieth centuries, she was recruited as a British imperial folk heroine. These accounts developed Boadicea as a figure of patriotic purpose, although the earlier associations that drew upon the classical accounts persisted. Fletcher's play *Bonduca*, adapted for performance both in 1778 and 1837, included the two songs written by Henry Purcell that helped to cement an association between Boadicea and British imperialism. One of these songs, 'Britons Strike Home', was particularly popular and was often performed separately from the play at times of national crisis.[34] It is likely, however, that Boadicea's growing popularity as a figure of imperial inspiration finally led to the end of her stage presence,

as the re-enactment of her assertive speeches and deeds made her transgressions and failures too obvious for contemporary taste.[35] It has been
suggested that only by quitting the stage during the early nineteenth
century could she be transformed into an imperial icon.[36]

Perhaps partly owing to the influence of Cowper's writing, representations of Boadicea around this time have less to do with the barbarian
world and refer more directly to the society in which they were created.
These new images placed her in a less specific historical context.[37] An
illustration by Francis Robert West in Edward Barnard's *History of England* (1790) shows Boadicea wearing a full-length robe, draped with a
shawl trimmed with fur or wool, referring to her perceived barbarian
status (figure 39).[38] Thomas Stothard and William Sharp portray her
more in the guise of a classicised heroine, while the later image produced by Robert Havell for Meyrick and Smith's *The Costumes of the
Original Inhabitants of the British Isles* (1815) is based more soundly upon
antiquarian research.[39] This attempt at historical accuracy did not, however, distract other illustrators from producing more fanciful versions of
Boadicea,[40] an activity that would continue into the twentieth century
and beyond.

Boadicea was clearly an increasingly popular figure among illustrators at this time, but her image was not an entirely positive one in
all cases. Alfred Tennyson wrote an influential and critical poem
about her actions.[41] In his 'experimental' poem *Boädicéa*, written in
February 1859 and published in 1864,[42] the ancient British queen is a
violent and uncontrolled figure who shows a particularly savage taste
for battle.[43]

> While about the shores of Mona those Neronian legionaries
> Burnt and broke the grove and altar of the Druid and Druidess,
> Far in the East Boädicéa, standing loftily charioted,
> Mad and maddening all that heard her in her fierce volubility,
> Girt by half the tribes of Britain, near the colony Cámulodúne,
> Yell'd and shriek'd between her daughters o'er a wild confederacy.[44]

Boädicéa produces a bloodcurdling speech that is partly based on
Tacitus and Dio. She commands her forces to:

> 'Burst the gates, and burn the palaces, break the works of statuary,
> Take the hoary Roman head and shatter it, hold it abominable,

Cut the Roman boy to pieces in his lust and voluptuousness,
Lash the maiden into swooning, me they lash'd and humiliated,
Chop the breasts from off the mother, dash the brains of the little one out,
Up my Britons, on my chariot, on my chargers, trample them under us.'[45]

The barbaric actions which Dio attributes to the ancient Britons are here put directly into the mouth of Boädicéa as a command to her followers. There is a direct sexual and anti-maternal element to Boädicéa's immorality in this context, part of a device for distinguishing ('decent', moral) war from savagery.[46]

   Boädicéa also draws upon Cowper's earlier poem in her speech as a device to allow the prediction of the rise of the British Empire, following the decline and fall of its Roman predecessor.

'Fear not, isle of blowing woodlands, isle of silvery parapets!
Though the Roman eagle shadow thee, though the gathering enemy
     narrow thee,
Thou shalt wax and he shall dwindle, thou shall be the mighty one yet!
Thine the liberty, thine the glory, thine the deeds to be celebrated,
Thine the myriad-rolling ocean, light and shadow illimitable,
Thine the lands of lasting summer, many blossomed Paradises,
Thine the North and thine the South and thine the battle-thunder of
     God ...'[47]

Despite Tennyson's far more critical rendition of the character of Boädicéa, the imperial inspiration of her actions during the mid nineteenth century was too strong for him to ignore. The poem concludes:

So the silent colony hearing her tumultuous adversaries
Clash the darts and on the buckler beat with rapid unanimous hand,
Though on all her evil tyrannies, all her pitiless avarice,
Till she felt the heart within her fall and flutter tremulously,
Then her pulse at the clamouring of her enemy fainted away.
Out of evil evil flourishes, out of tyranny tyranny buds.
Ran the land with Roman slaughter, multitudinous agonies.
Perish'd many a maid and matron, many a vainglorious legionary,
Fell the colony, city and citadel, London, Verulam, Cámulodúne.[48]

Tennyson's image of Boadicea was inspired by Thomas Stothard's engraving of 1812. This shows Boadicea haranguing the Britons. A copy of the engraving had been sent to Tennyson in February 1859.[49] The

39. 'An Antient Briton' and 'Queen Boadicea'. From *Portraits and Dresses of the most Remarkable Personages and Sovereigns in England Prior to the Norman Conquest*, plate I. From Edward Barnard's *New Complete and Authentic History of England* of 1790. (*Authors' copyright*)

poem also shows some influence from Tacitus but, following the lead of Cowper, Boädicéa's speech is moved to the start of the rising. His critical view of Boadicea's barbaric character and actions may be seen in the context of the 'reflected barbarism' that Tennyson saw around him in contemporary Europe.[50]

   Boädicéa must also be considered in the context of the events of the 'Indian Mutiny' of 1857.[51] Indian rebels laid siege to British communities and slaughtered many of the inhabitants.[52] The reference to the destruction of the colony of 'Cámulodúne' and of Roman civilisation in general by Boädicéa and her followers was surely written with knowledge of these events. Tennyson's poem *The Defence of Lucknow* (written and published in 1879) described a siege during the Indian Mutiny.[53] In this case the British garrison and community resisted their attackers successfully and the poem is a glorification of their efforts. It is apparent that Tennyson had been encouraged to write a poem about the Indian Mutiny during 1858,[54] but it took him twenty years to complete the piece. The tone of the poem *Boädicéa* suggests that Tennyson had the events of the Mutiny in mind early in 1859, possibly encouraged by Stothard's engraving.

   It is unlikely, however, that Tennyson was directly comparing the reasons behind the Mutiny with the causes of Boadicea's rebellion. There is no easy way to make a comparison between the empires of Rome and Britain in Tennyson's work.[55] Another of his compositions, *The Idylls of the King* (completed in 1888), was a fable of benevolent colonial government based on the fictitious court of the semi-mythical King Arthur – a model for the British Empire.[56] By contrast, the Roman Empire in *Boädicéa* and *Idylls* is barbaric.[57] Tennyson effectively rediscovered the furious Boadicea of Dio, Fletcher and others and reinterpreted her for a new imperial context. In his work she is patently a barbaric and negative figure, a contrast to the 'venerated moral serenity and middle-class propriety' of the contemporary queen, Victoria.[58] At the same time it is important to recall that other aspects of the British Empire at the time may have been seen as more ambivalent by Tennyson.[59] In any case, within Tennyson's poems the positive imperial associations of Cowper's Boadicea are entirely lost to view.

   Although *Boädicéa* was one of Tennyson's favourite poems, it was never one of his most popular, perhaps partly due to its difficult metre,[60] possibly also because it was not in keeping with the late nineteenth-century attitude to Boadicea and the British past. Other authors, however, found Boadicea hard to praise. In 1903 the historian B. W. Henderson directly compared the sacking of Camulodunum during 'The Great Rebellion of Boudica' with the Indian Mutiny in his *The Life and Principate of the Emperor Nero*:

> We English, too, have had to face the doom in India, which fell out of a sunny heaven upon amazed Camulodunum, and we too may know how the Romans died. They waited the oncoming tide of fury with the courage not only of despair, but of grim Roman tenacity and discipline.[61]

Apparently:

> Iceni, Trinobantes, Brigantes, the tribes to the number of a hundred and twenty thousand men, swept down upon the defenceless Roman settlers as Indians upon New England homesteads, as cruel and as relentless ... The men died fighting, the women, tortured by the malice of fiends, mutilated, impaled, perished in a lingering agony of suffering, amidst the mad revelry and wild orgies of the savages.[62]

He suggested that:

> Neither, for all the glamour of patriotic art, may we justly lament for the conquered cause ... It were not withstanding but maudlin sentiment to deplore the Roman victory. The revenge was one of greater races than the Britons, of time rather than of the avenging sword ... But the Roman conquest was Britain's first step along the path to her wider Empire.[63]

Although it is unclear, Henderson appears to have argued that, as a result of both the Roman victory over Boadicea and the Anglo-Saxon victory over the Romans, the seal was set on the future greatness of the English.[64]

Cowper's poem *Boadicea* had a particularly important role in the development of the late Victorian and twentieth-century image of Boadicea. It was learned by thousands of Victorian and early twentieth-century schoolchildren and quoted widely in later times.[65] The image also helped to foster a strong perception of Boadicea as a national heroine in England. 'Boudica' in Celtic meant 'Victoria', and so on occasions during the reign of Queen Victoria it was natural that she was compared with the ancient British ruler;[66] although, as seen in the writings of Tennyson and Henderson, Boadicea was not considered to be an unconditionally positive figurehead. Her image as a national heroine was reused and redefined in the late nineteenth and early twentieth centuries in a range of works and it can be argued that it was elevated into a coherent representation – an image that has been regularly invoked, redefined and contradicted ever since.

Francis Barker produced the lengthy poem (210 pages) *Boadicea* in the same year (1859) that Tennyson's poem was written. Barker's work had a clearer patriotic purpose. The preface states:

TO THE BRITISH PEOPLE

Pardon my presumption, my countrymen; but to whom can I so appropriately dedicate a poem, whose subject is Boadicea, as to you, in whose veins still runs, however, mixed and mingled, the blood of the ancient inhabitants of Britain.[67]

This work is deeply caught up with ideas of British freedom and the Christian Church. According to the author, the past peoples of Britain struggled so that we can enjoy the fruits of their labours.[68] Some of the significant characters of the tale are Christian and a whole series of details is invented, including information about Boadicea's two daughters, who are named Kerma and Brenda. The ancient Britons are severely provoked into their actions. Brondo, king of the Brigantes, describes Boadicea as:

> She who loved peace and lived
> In peace, so long as it could be preserved
> With honour; but now justly incensed,
> Stands forth undaunted, in her country's cause.[69]

Boadicea herself makes an impassioned speech to the assembled Britons:

> Men! Britons! Fathers!
> I appeal to you: for yourselves, your wives,
> Your children; and for the honour, of our
> Common country. I call upon you all,
> To arouse yourself, and struggle for freedom,
> To the death. Soon, soon, then, will you enjoy
> The palm of victory; and your children,

> And your children's children, will bless you; as
> They boast themselves, the offspring of the free.[70]

Barker's poem is an example of a growing body of work in the later nineteenth century that represented Boadicea in a patriotic manner. In effect, an 'imperial cult of Boadicea' developed in late nineteenth- and early twentieth-century Britain that drew upon Cowper's poem for its inspiration.[71]

One particularly important source of inspiration for late Victorian and Edwardian children was the historical novel.[72] During this period the British redefined their celebrations of national heroes, including Boadicea, Caratacus, various medieval kings, knights, modern soldiers and imperial explorers.[73] A range of children's history books and works of fiction mention Caratacus and Boadicea and their, ultimately unsuccessful, struggles against the Roman invaders. These include C. Merivale's *School History of Rome* (1877), A. J. Church's *Stories from English History: From Julius Caesar to the Black Prince* (1895), G. A. Henty's *Beric the Briton* (1893), H. E. Marshall's *Our Island Story*, (1905), C. M. Doughty's monumental and mythic poem *The Dawn in Britain* (1906), and E. O'Neil's *A Nursery History of England* (1912). Boadicea and Caratacus joined Arthur and Alfred not as native chieftains but as patriotic heroes, staunch defenders of Britain against the evils that might beset her from outside.[74] Although Caratacus was a significant figure at this time,[75] in the late Victorian context he came to be overshadowed by Boadicea.

G. A. Henty, the leading author of adventure stories for boys, wrote over 140 books and many articles. In 1893 he published a novel about ancient Britain and the Roman Empire entitled *Beric the Briton: A Story of the Roman Invasion*. The novel is about the life of its fictitious hero, Beric,[76] who in the early part of the story has a major role in Boadicea's rebellion. After his mother has described the Roman seizure of the property of the dead British king Prasutagus, Beric declares that: 'The gods have clearly willed ... that we should rise against the Romans.'[77] Boadicea herself is described as 'of different stuff to her husband', who had 'curried favour with the Romans'.[78] It is clear that she will seek to right the wrongs that have been committed against her and that 'there shall be such a rising as the Romans have never yet seen'.[79] The Britons are fully united in their hostility towards the Romans. Beric suggests that the Roman desecration of the shrines of the Britons will cause them to 'lay aside their jealousies and act as one people'.[80] Later, after the Romans have 'grossly insulted' Boadicea's daughters, and, following a meeting involving various groups of ancient Britons, druids and Boadicea, the rebellion begins.[81] Boadicea is described as 'tall and stately, large in her proportions',[82] while the drawing of her in the novel (by William Parkinson) shows a young woman, unaccompanied by her daughters, displaying the marks of the Roman rods on her upper body (figure 40). Speeches are made by both the chief Druid and Boadicea before battle commences. Boadicea is a stately and gracious figure in the novel but has no active role in the atrocities that are committed against the Romans by the Britons during the course of the story.[83]

Although *Beric the Briton* is a work of fiction, its author had a good knowledge of the accounts of Tacitus and Dio, although much of the action in the novel is clearly influenced by the Victorian context in which it is set. The stress on national unity in the novel is evident. At the end, when Beric returns to his tribe, we hear that many flocked to greet him:

> They were proud of him as a national hero; he alone of their chiefs had maintained resistance against the Romans, and his successes had obliterated the humiliation of their great defeat.[84]

Throughout the book the Britons are at their best when they act in unison.

Boadicea and Caratacus were partly utilised by late Victorian and Edwardian writers to obliterate the memory of a period of foreign rule over the country whose inhabitants 'never shall be slaves'. The ancient British population who were the followers of Caratacus and Boadicea in fighting against the Romans were also useful in this regard. Authors often felt that these ancient Britons had bravely defended their liberty. Fletcher and Kipling suggest that Caesar's account of his invasion of Britain 'leaves us with the impression that the spirit of the dear motherland had breathed valour and cunning into the whole British people'.[85] These comments reflect the emphasis in Henty's book and in other works on the unified character of the British resistance against Rome.[86] In fact, as the ancient Britons lived in many distinct tribes who

40. 'Boadicea shows the marks of the Roman rods.' Illustration by William Parkinson, from *Beric the Briton* by G. A. Henty (1893), p. 72.

united only finally when faced with the powerful Roman army of conquest, any worship of 'motherland' was a modern attribution rather
than an ancient British attitude. It is clear from these observations that
the invocation of ancient British national folk heroes was felt to counter,
or at least to moderate, the impact of the idea of the Roman domination of Britain and to project a British national spirit into the modern
context of the literature of imperialism.[87] As such, the image of the
ancient British hero fulfilled an important role in the creation of empire
in the modern period.[88]

A. J. Church's children's novel *The Count of the Saxon Shore* (1887)
also features Boadicea, although the story takes place in the late Roman
period, just before the Romans abandon the province of Britain. We
learn that in the early fifth century AD, as the Romans were preparing
to leave,

> Caradoc [Caratacus] and Boadicea, and other heroes and heroines of British
> independence, were household words in many families which were yet thor-
> oughly Roman in spirit and manners ... these loyal subjects of the Empire,
> as all the world believed them, cherished in their hearts the memory of the
> free Britain of the past and the hope of a free Britain in the future.[89]

In reality, as we have seen, knowledge of Boudica was probably lost by
this time, although she is mentioned by Gildas. Church's comments
reflect British concerns over Celtic nationalism in the late nineteenth
century and the political situation in Ireland in particular.

Perhaps the most striking late Victorian or Edwardian image is the
statue of *Boadicea and her Daughters* by Thomas Thornycroft, situated
near the western end of Westminster Bridge,[90] a rendition that has
been called 'the apotheosis of Boadicea'.[91] Thornycroft (1816–1885)
was a successful Victorian sculptor and *Boadicea and her Daughters* is
his most ambitious work;[92] this massive statue of Boadicea and two
daughters in a war chariot was in production from 1856 until 1871.[93]
Thornycroft also designed other statues of figures from British history,
including Alfred the Great and Charles I.[94] He discussed the relative
merits of realism and inspiration with Albert the Prince Consort. The
Prince took a direct interest in the project, lending horses from his own
stable for models, and often visiting the studio to see how the group
was progressing.[95] Albert's comments appear to have had a direct

impact upon the modelling of the statue, for Thornycroft wrote to a friend that:

> The comparative advantages of realistic treatment were contrasted against the artistic and poetic views: and his decision was decidedly to the latter. He would make the chariot regal: 'You must make', said the Prince, 'the throne upon wheels.'[96]

Thornycroft recalled of Boadicea's daughters:

> I make one eager gaze forward, the other shrinks back appalled at the battle cry. The Queen with outstretched hands and swelling chest, urges her scythe-armed chariot upon her foes. The vehemence of her movement would be impotent did it not excite a similar disturbance in the figures clinging to her garment.[97]

He explained his conception of the daughters of the queen as 'young barbarians who would regard their violation simply as an insult to be avenged'.[98] These comments suggest that Thornycroft had a attitude to Boadicea that was comparable to the 'reflected barbarism' expressed by Tennyson in 1859.

In the 1870s it appeared that Thornycroft might receive a much-needed commission from the state to complete the Boadicea group. His proposed statue was praised in the *Times* newspaper in July 1871 as 'the most successful attempt in historical sculpture of this barren time …', but the government did nothing to assist its completion at this stage.[99] In 1883 Thornycroft continued work on the statue, but died in August 1885. It was not cast in bronze until after it was presented to the nation by Thornycroft's son, John, in 1896.[100] London County Council raised the money for the casting by direct public subscription. The committee which was set up to help with the process consisted of well-known Members of Parliament, leading painters, councillors, journalists and, significantly, Welshmen.[101]

One proposed location for the statue was a tumulus, or barrow, on Parliament Hill Fields, traditionally known as 'Boadicea's Grave'.[102] This earthwork is on the northern slope of Parliament Hill between a shallow valley on the west and Parliament Hill on the east.[103] The excavator, Charles H. Read, explained that the origin of the attribution of the tumulus to Boadicea is unclear and that he had discovered only modern references to the idea.[104] Edward Barnard, however, had described the earthwork in 1790 in his book *The New Comprehensive, Impartial and Complete History of England*. He discussed two possible locations for the final battle between Boadicea and the Romans and for the subsequent burial of Boadicea – Stonehenge and Parliament Hill. He argued that some

> think that the important contest was decided in a large open space which are now fields between Hampstead, Highgate and London, near the centre of which, about a mile and a half north of Clerkenwell, is a small projecting bank, which some persons yet call Boadicea's camp.[105]

This would appear to be the tumulus referred to by Read as 'Boadicea's Grave'.

Read, who was a prominent member of the Society of Antiquaries of London, began the excavation of this tumulus on Monday 29 October 1894 at the instigation of London County Council. He excavated a trench through the body of the barrow but found no trace of an original burial, although he did find evidence for a burned layer, probably on top of the old ground surface. The excavation revealed a complex structure with several phases of construction. Read concluded:

1. That it was without question an artificial mound, raised at a spot where there was originally a slight rise in the ground.

2. That a great quantity of additional material was added to it, chiefly on the northern and eastern sides, and probably within the last two centuries.

3. That the tumulus had not been opened before.

4. That it is very probably an ancient British burial mound, of the early-bronze period, and therefore centuries before the Christian era. The burial was probably by inhumation, and the bones have entirely disappeared.[106]

As a result of these excavations, the Society of Antiquaries rejected the identification of the mound as the burial place of Boadicea. Her association with this general region of London has, however, continued. More recent folk stories nominate King's Cross Station as her burial place, a site located in the south-eastern zone of the 'large open space' discussed by Barnard in 1790.

Following the rejection of the site on Parliament Hill Fields, alternative sites for the statue were discussed before Westminster Bridge was finally chosen.[107] Thornycroft's statue was placed on the Embankment in front of the House of Commons in 1902 by London County Council (plate 5). The statue was erected shortly after Britain's military victory over the Boers and one year after the death of Queen Victoria. It shows a 'full-bodied and amply draped queen' standing in a chariot with scythe blades projecting from the wheel hubs.[108] We have seen that there was already a tradition of representing the scythes on the wheels of the chariot in earlier images of Boadicea, although it is unclear from where the idea originated. The chariot itself is based upon a Roman model and is very unlike the native versions that are known from later archaeological excavation. Thornycroft deliberately made no real effort to incorporate the growing archaeological knowledge of ancient Britain into his group. Boadicea is portrayed as a wild warrior who wields a spear in her right hand while raising her left skywards. Her two half-naked and unarmed daughters crouch sheltering behind her. The statue represents a poetic rather than a realistic image of regality and once again shows the inspiration of earlier sculptures in that Boadicea is wearing a crown.[109]

Despite the presence of her children, this image of Boadicea does not really stress her maternal role; rather, she is represented as a powerful warrior.[110] The two horses drawing the chariot rear up and have wild eyes but, despite this, Boadicea has such control that she can stand upright without holding the reins. It has been suggested that the statue created an emotive patriotic stir at the thought of the 'virago of a queen' defying a great but alien power.[111] Her perceived attraction is that she is a patriot, woman and mother, seeking to avenge political, sexual and familial wrongs.[112] It has been also suggested that this statue was deliberately placed to provide a symbolic defence for the House of Commons in the face of an attack from over the Thames to the south,[113] although this perhaps overstresses British paranoia at this time. It does stand adjacent to Westminster Bridge, watching over all those who cross it into London and was apparently particularly popular with children.[114] It remains a source of fascination for Britons and foreign visitors alike.

On the front (south side) is an inscription in gold letters which reads:

> Boadicea
> Boudicca
> Queen of the Iceni
> Who died AD 61

> After leading her people
> against the Roman invader

While on the east side of the pediment is an inscription that quotes Cowper's poem:

> Regions Caesar never knew
> thy posterity shall sway.

In this context Cowper's poem was used by the London County Council effectively to recruit Boadicea for the establishment. [115]

A further image involving the glorification of Boadicea as a national heroine is provided by Marie Trevelyan in her extraordinary book *Britain's Greatness Foretold: The Story of Boadicea, the British Warrior-Queen*. 'Marie Trevelyan' was the pen name of Emma Mary Thomas. Born in 1853, she was the daughter of a stonemason from South Glamorgan. She created a massive collection of Welsh folklore during her lifetime and produced several books on this subject; three of her works are available from a website. [116] Her book *Britain's Greatness Foretold* was published in 1900 and, although there is little indication that it had very much success, it is a useful indication of the way that Boadicea was perceived by some at this time. The front cover of the book featured a Union Jack, above the words:

> Britain's Greatness Foretold
> Regions Caesar never knew
> Thy posterity shall sway
> The Prediction Fulfilled.

The two middle lines are taken from Cowper's poem, while the final line refers, as we shall see, to a major theme of the book.

Trevelyan became deeply interested in the queen of the Iceni and at the age of eighteen wrote a poem about her that was later developed into a novel. [117] She wrote:

> My desire to follow the career of Boadicea grew intense. I felt that there must be a peculiar interest in going to the sources whence sprang the patriotic spirit of a race who, eighteen centuries ago, fought boldly against the Romans – who saw empires and monarchs vanish – who bravely held their own against all the warlike nations of Europe – whose soil is the dust of patriots – whose exhaustless vitality through all ages supplies renowned

commanders on land and sea, and whose logs and roll-calls record the names of those who have distinguished themselves at the head of our gallant sailors and soldiers in maintaining the honour of Britain.[118]

She recalled the history of the design of Thornycroft's statue and looked forward to it being displayed. This occurred two years after the publication of *Britain's Greatness Foretold*; a photograph of the sculpture forms the frontispiece to the book. Trevelyan also suggests: 'In those struggles for national liberty and justice we trace the foundations of our present freedoms. In elements of their unanswering devotion we behold the origins of the great and unparalleled patriotic revival of 1899–1900 ...'[119] Presumably the 'revival' that she is referring to was represented by British victories at this time over the Boers in South Africa. In reality, this 'revival' did not appear to have become as dramatic and glorious as its supporters had hoped it would be.[120] Despite Trevelyan's optimism, the Boer War continued until 1902 and was associated with a major crisis of British self-confidence. The events of 1899–1900 are directly reflected in the content of her book. Trevelyan suggested that, as a result of the Boer War: 'the ancient fires of British valour and patriotism were replenished, and blazed forth with the strong, unwavering light that in the past bewildered the Romans, and in the present astonishes Europe'.[121]

Trevelyan used the preface of her book to stress the patriotism of the Welsh people, and their dedication to the British cause, and to argue that the war effort had been the result of British, rather than solely English, work. The events of 1899–1900 are said to have 'in a measure effaced the names of England and the English, and restored to us – ours by birth-right – the broader names of Britain and the British'.[122] Indeed, she places much emphasis on the Welsh as the upholders of ancient British racial claims. She had heard the story of the rebellion of Boadicea during her childhood in Wales and knew the Welsh language from an early age – in her own words, the language in which Boadicea thought and spoke.[123] It is often supposed that the present-day Welsh population is derived from the original Iron Age peoples of Britain, while the Anglo-Saxon English have replaced the former British population throughout England.[124] Trevelyan claimed Boadicea as an ancestor figure for the Welsh rather than for the British as a whole.

Perhaps the most remarkable element of her book, until we remember that Trevelyan was a collector of folklore, is the prophecy which is spoken by the fictitious 'Arch-druid of London', Arianrod. This is 'The Prediction Fulfilled' of the title of the novel. In this context, Trevelyan is evidently drawing upon some of the earlier images of Boadicea's rebellion in the early plays or in Cowper's poem. She recalls that the Arch-druid's predictions of the future greatness of Britain has been 'immortalised' by historians and poets. [125] In Trevelyan's novel Arianrod makes this prediction after several British military victories over the Romans and the burning of London:

> 'Slumber now!' said the Arch-druid, looking sadly towards the smouldering city of Caerlud [London],'slumber and take rest, while warring hosts struggle and perish. But the time shall come when Britain shall be avenged! The Romans shall vanish, other invaders shall be laid low, and thou, O city, rising from the dust and ashes of purifying fire, shall ascend and become the fairest queen and mother of cities in a vast empire on which the sun shall never set!'
>
> As Arianrod uttered the prediction which, in ages to come, was brilliantly fulfilled, the rising sun, like an emblem of eternity, bore witness to the prophesy. [126]

Arianrod and a druid chorus then predict the future in greater detail:

> Never for us comes a twilight of ages,
> Never a shadow to mar the grand triumph
> Of glory that comes, and shall never see sunset. [127]

Arianrod's words drew upon that of the druid in Cowper's poem, which is reprinted in full at the start of Trevelyan's book. Trevelyan wrote that the evidence for the early struggles of British valour is to be found in this Arch-druid's prediction, immortalised by historians and poets 'and rendered familiar to later generations by Cowper's celebrated and deathless ode ...' [128]

The prediction, which is repeated at several different stages in the book, has no basis in the classical sources but is treated throughout as a historical fact. The writer Edwin Collins provided an introductory piece for Trevelyan's novel, entitled 'The Prediction Fulfilled', in which he appeared to be unaware that there was no reliable historic basis for Arianrod's prophecy. He wrote that since the prophecy was made in the first century: 'through all that lapse of time the characteristics of

the British race have been tending towards bringing about its fulfilment.'[129] After considering the progress of the Boer War, and other
imperial topics, he concluded his piece by arguing:

> Surely it is not inappropriate to preface an imaginative work which portrays
> an heroic period in Britain's past by the foregoing sketch of some recent his-
> torical events, which seem, by their realisation, in solid facts, of a prediction
> uttered over eighteen centuries ago, to show how close is the relation
> between the imagination and history.[130]

In the case of Arianrod's prophecy both Trevelyan and Collins appear
to have projected a work of mythical history as fact.[131]

Trevelyan's Boadicea is not the barbarian of some earlier works.
Trevelyan countered the view of critics who wished to see Boadicea as a
'barbaric queen, surrounded by fierce warriors and *masculine* women'.[132]
She recalled how the Iceni had come to terms with the Romans and
at the time of the invasion 'had almost entirely forfeited the name
of Britons' and afterwards had 'remained unfaithful to the National
cause'.[133] She argued that it is likely that the 'refining influences' of
Roman civilisation formed an important element in Boadicea's early
training and subsequent position as wife of King Prasutagus.[134] The
Boadicea of Trevelyan's novel is stately, civilised and kind. The atrocities
mentioned in the classical sources are not discussed in any detail.
Boadicea even shows clemency in treating some captured Roman soldiers as 'state-protected prisoners of war'.[135] Trevelyan draws directly
upon Tacitus in this regard and Dio's account is less in evidence.

After the defeat of Boadicea and her followers, Trevelyan recalls how:

> In their cherished dreams they had beheld an empire of shadowy vastness, a
> monarch of monarchs, a victory unparalleled, a triumph incomparable, and
> freedom – unlimited freedom for Britain.[136]

This, however, does not happen for some time after the final action in
the novel. Although Boadicea is defeated and dies by her own hand at
the end of the novel, the action finishes in a positive fashion as the
granddaughter of Caratacus, Princess 'Golden Beauty', marries a Roman
and becomes a 'Nazarene'.[137]

Thornycroft, Trevelyan and Collins's portrayals of Boadicea drew
directly upon Cowper's poem in projecting a nationalistic motivation
through the glorification of the ancient British queen as an upholder of

British nationality at a time of foreign oppression. They also drew upon the association that Cowper created between Boadicea and the expansion of the British Empire. In effect, Boadicea was reinvented as an upholder of Britain's imperial might. Works of literature and art helped to familiarise children and adults with an imperial image that was reproduced in various ways during the twentieth and twenty-first centuries.

Other images of Boadicea at this time draw upon her attributed maternal nature and determination. Henrietta Elizabeth Marshall, writing under the name 'H. E. Marshall', wrote *Our Island Story: A History of Britain for Boys and Girls*, a highly influential book of 1905, which provided inspiration for at least one later writer. Marshall tells the 'story of a warrior queen' in a manner which she considers to be suitable for young minds; she says that the work represents 'not a history lesson, but a story-book'.[138] Some of these stories, the author admits, are fairy tales and not history, but these too are considered to be part of 'Our Island Story'.[139] It is no surprise, therefore, that in addition to the mythical tale of Albion and Brutus, the account of Boadicea contains some fairy-tale elements. Marshall draws upon Tacitus, although some of the detail is modified, as in the incident when the Romans 'beat her with rods and were rude to her daughters'.[140]

We are told that, after her speech to the Britons, Queen Boadicea looked so beautiful and fierce, with her golden hair blowing in the wind, 'that the hearts of her people were filled with love for her, and anger against the Romans'.[141]

> her proud head was thrown back and the sun shone upon her lovely hair and upon the golden band which bound her forehead. Her dark cloak, slipping from her shoulders, showed the splendid robe that she wore beneath, and the thick and heavy chain of gold round her neck. At her feet knelt her daughters, sobbing with hope and fear.[142]

Boadicea is illustrated in Marshall's book (plate 6) as a maternal figure with her daughters behind her. She addresses her soldiers with her children sheltering behind her and a protective male ancient Briton guards all three. She is unarmed apart from a dagger in her right hand. She has a gold band on her head which is really a crown, presumably to remind young readers of her royal status.

After her speech, the Britons 'marched forward to battle, forgetful of everything but revenge ...'[143] Led by Boadicea, they were determined 'to

avenge their Queen, to fight and die for her and for their country'.[144]
As a result, Marshall tells us that the Britons utterly destroyed the towns
of London and St Albans. Strangely, there is no mention of Camulodunum. Finally, the Roman leader is so downcast that he travels to the
British camp, bearing in his hand a green branch as a sign of peace. The
tradition of the Roman commander sending a representative to talk to
Boadicea prior to the final conflict dates back to Glover's play of 1753
but has no source in the ancient literature. In reply to his request for
peace, Boadicea states: 'You shall have peace, peace, but no submis-
sion. A British heart will choose death rather than lose liberty. There
can be peace only if you promise to leave this country.'[145] Eventually,
the Britons are defeated and Marshall has Boadicea and her daughters
commit suicide.

7

In the Modern World

Boadicea, as national legend has it, was a great British queen who led
her people to battle against the Roman invaders. Her scythed chariot
and rearing stallions, together with a sense of victory and patriotism,
are embedded in our national memory.

S. Macdonald (1987).

Prior to the late nineteenth century Boadicea was drawn upon from time
to time for particular reasons and to make significant points, but she was
not a popular figure for much of the period. During the late nineteenth
and early twentieth centuries she was transformed in the popular imagination to create a historical ancestry for British national pedigree and
imperial greatness; from this time forward her popularity was assured.
During the twentieth century accounts of Boadicea proliferated, portraying her in contrasting ways. They include scholarly books, plays,
poems, drawings, museum exhibitions and other representations.

The image of Boadicea during the twentieth century is not coherent
and well defined. During the early to mid twentieth century, as the
British Empire gradually went into terminal decline,[1] it might be supposed that the uncomplicated image of Boadicea as a British imperial
icon and upholder of national identity would have ceased to be popular. From the early twentieth century it was increasing common for
women to write accounts of Boadicea that sometimes challenged the
assumptions made by previous generations of male authors. At the same
time the role of Boadicea as a national icon survived well into the twentieth century and still continues to provide a context for both popular
and academic images of the early British leader.

This was a period in which the serious archaeological investigation of
the events began. Growing antiquarian knowledge contributed to the
informative aspects of some of the drawings and engravings that were

produced from the seventeenth century onwards. This also gradually provided a more realistic understanding of the society within which Boadicea, or Boudica, lived. A greater degree of professionalism was applied to the archaeological study of the British past from the late nineteenth and early twentieth centuries,[2] and from the 1920s onwards evidence associated with Boudica was studied seriously. This was a result of discoveries of associated objects and the important archaeological excavations that were carried out in the former Roman towns of Verulamium, Camulodunum and Londinium.

Archaeologists interpreted Boudica in different ways throughout the twentieth century. In some accounts she has been seen as a problematic figure.[3] More recent assessments are sometimes less morally judgmental in their opinion of her actions. Scholars of the Roman world have become interested in the idea of active and passive resistance to Roman rule within the empire.[4] Some academics now stress that rebellion and revolt may have been quite common occurrences within the Western Roman Empire, especially during the later first century BC and first century AD. It is likely that, in the past, rebellion and resistance have been played down within an academic tradition of study keen to emphasise the progress of society under Roman rule.[5] Boudica's image has therefore been reinvented by new generations of archaeological scholars.

The Boudica of contemporary popular culture is generally a positive figure. Searching the internet suggests that her popularity is increasing; we shall examine some of these websites below. Many of these images appear to have been created, in effect, as ironic reflections on the outmoded Victorian official image. Boadicea has, once again, become something of an anti-establishment figure in the modern world, but one with a positive image.

Prior to the early twentieth century it was very rare for women to write accounts of Boadicea. Ester Sowernam, as we have seen, had presented Boadicea as a positive figure who made the Romans feel that she could conquer them. During the early years of the twentieth century the Suffragists effectively used the same approach, highlighting the achievements of powerful women, to support their claim for the right to vote;[6] the valour and bravery of Boadicea was a source of strength to their movement. The Artists' Suffrage League designed banners to 'celebrate the memory of great women of all ages',[7] including one that represented Boadicea by a scythed wheel and the points of spears embroidered in gold silk.[8]

Dora Montefiore, a leading Suffragist,[9] made a number of speeches between her release from Holloway Prison and going abroad in January 1907. Writing about meetings of the Women's Social and Political Union in 1906, she recalled that:

> One of my best meetings was close to the statue of Boadicea in a prohibited part of London, as no meetings were allowed to be held so close to the Houses of Parliament. It had long been my wish to hold a meeting there, as Boadicea in her chariot always appeared to me to be advancing threateningly on the Houses of Parliament, and she was therefore a symbol of the attitude towards Parliament of us militant women. Toward the end of 1906 tramlines were being laid at that part of the embankment, and the traffic was obstructed by piles of wood blocks, and these I saw would make a most capital rostrum from which to speak ...[10]

On this occasion Montefiore spoke for an hour and a half,[11] but she did not leave a detailed account of what she had to say. The fact that she gave this speech from a wooden platform, or tribunal, may suggest that she drew directly upon Dio's account of Boudica.

At a dinner given by the National Union of Women's Suffrage Societies to welcome released prisoners of the militant Women's Social and Political Union, each guest was presented with a drawing showing an altered version of Thornycroft's statue. In the borders are two inset cameos, one of a madonna-like mother and baby, the other of a mother and child reading a book together.[12] The central female figures in the chariot are not as wild as Thornycroft's originals and Boadicea's spear is transformed into a banner that reads 'Votes for Women'. In her other hand Boadicea carries the scales of justice, while an angel presents her with a laurel crown, a symbol of victory.[13]

Boadicea was also one of the warriors in Cicely Hamilton's *A Pageant of Great Women* (1910). First staged at the Scala Theatre in London on 10 November 1909,[14] the play went on to tour the country.[15] It featured a number of Great Women from the past, including Joan of Arc, Black Agnes (Countess of Dunbar), Elizabeth I, Catherine the Great, Victoria, Florence Nightingale and thirty-eight other famous women. These characters were grouped into categories – learned, artists, saintly, heroic, rulers and warriors, very much following the example of some of the seventeenth-century pamphlets. Actresses who were to play the heroines in *A Pageant of Great Women* were provided by Suffragist societies. Miss Elizabeth Kirby played the part of Boadicea (plate 7). She presented a robust figure with a long flowing cloak of many colours, with a garland in her hair and a spear in her right hand to emphasise her military role – an image that draws upon Dio's description but one that has been given a clear Edwardian spirit.

The text to accompany Boadicea's contribution to *A Pageant* includes:

> Oh, look on her who stood, a Briton in arms,
> And spat defiance at the hosts of Rome.[16]

The moment when Boadicea appears is particularly significant.[17] The character of Prejudice was played by a man. He acknowledges that women are able to rule but claims that force is a male prerogative:

> Force is the last and ultimate judge: 'tis man
> Who laps his body in mail, who takes the sword –
> The sword that must decide! Woman shrink from it,
> Fears the white flint of it and cowers away.'[18]

At this point, the Warrior Women, led by Joan of Arc and followed by Boadicea and a number of other women, are paraded in rebuttal of Prejudice's case. Struck dumb by the force of their argument, he 'slinks away' humiliated, in defeat.[19]

Next to Boadicea in the act of the disempowerment of Prejudice was the 'Ranee of Jhansi', played by Munci Capel. The Ranee was 'Killed fighting against the British during the Indian Mutiny'.[20] Hamilton's positive and forceful comparison of the actions of Boadicea and the Ranee draws a striking contrast to Henderson's earlier critical comparison of the rebellion of AD 60 to 61 to the Indian Mutiny. In Hamilton's *A Pageant* both Boadicea and the Ranee are presented as powerful female figures of inspiration for modern women. For those who were courageously fighting for their rights during the early twentieth century, Boadicea had a very different significance from the violent and uncontrollable savage of Tennyson's and Henderson's accounts.

The rise of Boadicea as an imperial icon in Victorian and Edwardian times may be the reason for her adoption by the Suffragists.[21] As a powerful and attractive figure from national history she could serve the Suffragists' purpose more effectively. Her physical embodiment in the form of Thornycroft's statue on Westminster Bridge was of particular significance in that it enabled these women to strike right at the symbolic heart of Briton's male-dominated political structure.

The significance of Boadicea as a Welsh patriot had been raised by Marie Trevelyan in 1900; the same association was exploited by a sculpture that was produced during 1910–16 and placed in Cardiff City Hall.[22] Boadicea forms the dominant central figure and is dressed in a flowing Grecian-style gown. She has her arms around her daughters, who stand one to either side. The statue, by James Harvard Thomas, was one of a number of figures from Welsh history provided for the new Marble Hall at Cardiff City Hall.[23] Her rendition in this context evidently draws upon the idea of the Welsh as the inheritors of ancient British valour. Elsewhere Boadicea appealed to people because of her regional significance; for example, in Colchester Town Hall she is commemorated by a colourful stained-glass window that was installed during the construction of the building in 1901–2 (plate 8).[24]

Since the late 1920s archaeological research into Boudica or Boadicea's rebellion has advanced. This archaeological focus is the result of the discovery of objects that may have been derived from the revolt, the excavation of archaeological sites that may have an association with her, and the publication of scholarly books. An interest in locating events connected to her is evident from attempts during the nineteenth century to locate Boadicea's burial place, but it is only after 1900 that serious research was carried out on the archaeological traces related to the events.

Interest in this physical evidence developed with the discovery of significant objects connected with the sacking of the Roman towns of Londinium, Verulamium and Camulodunum. In the first few decades of the twentieth century occasional discoveries were attributed to the revolt. In 1909, writing about the early Roman phases at London, it was observed that:

Some have professed to see, in the wood-ashes excavated from a low level at

various point of the city, tangible evidence of a conflagration following on
from the revolting cruelties perpetrated on the inhabitants.[25]

This is an early recording of the destruction layer which was later to be
located in all three of the towns reportedly burned in AD 60 to 61. In
1907 the head of a statue was found lying in the muddy bed of the River
Alde at Rendham in Suffolk. After an interval of about eighteen months,
on 3 December 1908, the famous artist Sir Lawrence Alma-Tadema presented the object to a meeting of the Society of Antiquaries in London.[26]
It was suggested at this time that the head might have been Viking
plunder that had been lost upstream and carried to its findspot by the
flow of the river.[27] Francis Haverfield, the foremost Roman archaeologist of his time, made a far more likely proposal when he argued that
the head might be from a statue of Claudius that had been 'torn from
the temple of Claudius in the *colonia* by British pillagers and thrown
away later on'.[28]

During the late 1920s interest in the rebellion became more focused
as a result of several new discoveries and the interpretations of old
finds. In 1926 George Macdonald published an influential article in the
Journal of Roman Studies in which he supported Haverfield's suggestion that the head of Claudius was war-booty from the revolt of AD 60
to 61. He suggested that the statue might have been broken up by the
rebels and the head preserved to be carried on a pike in triumph before
being deposited in the River Alde at a later time.[29] The idea that the
head was removed from a statue of Claudius standing in Camulodunum
is still accepted by many archaeologists. Macdonald's account of the
statue may have led to an increasing interest in the rebellion, as 1927–29
were important years in the development of archaeological research,
particularly in Colchester, where M. R. Hull undertook significant work
over a number of years. During August 1927 workmen constructing a
new café in Colchester brought a large collection of pottery into Colchester Museum from a site that came to be known as the 'First Pottery
Shop', located in the part of the Roman town that has been termed
'Insula XIX'.[30] Further excavation of 'two pits' in 1929 revealed that
the shop and its contents had been burned down during the middle of
the first century AD,[31] an event that was thought at the time to be
associated with the rebellion.[32] Although more accurate dating of the
samian pottery now suggests that the stock of pottery was about

five years old in AD 60, it remains likely that the shop was indeed destroyed at this time.

During 1927 another significant site was located in Colchester when a large deposit of pottery, including four hundred fragments of samian, was found during building work.[33] It was thought that this probably represented the stock of a further pottery shop, the 'Second Pottery Shop', located in Insula XXVIII. During 1928 the tombstone of a soldier, called Longinus Sdapeze, was discovered by workmen in Colchester, but no additional archaeological work was undertaken on the findspot at this time.[34] In archaeological accounts, the damage to Longinus's tombstone became associated with the rebels, although this is no longer felt to be necessarily the case.

Lewis Spence's book of 1937, *Boadicea: Warrior Queen of the Britons*, was an attempt to create a scholarly account of the evidence.[35] He presented the first study on a 'major scale of what can be gleaned of her life and times',[36] but also mythologised Boadicea.[37] His account was both inaccurate and fanciful. He explored the idea that Boadicea's last battle took place in the vicinity of what is today King's Cross Station,[38] and also suggested that the 'Caledonians' had chariots with scythed wheels.[39] Nevertheless, this book continues to inspire the content of some websites.

Spence's work did, however, draw attention to some archaeological evidence from Colchester and London to support the idea of the burning of towns. He mentioned in the foreword of the book that in recent years 'much fresh material has been forthcoming ...'[40] Archaeological knowledge for Boudica's revolt grew further around this time, as excavation became a more professional undertaking. Perhaps the most influential archaeologist during the 1930s was Mortimer Wheeler. In 1930 Wheeler had written about the Boudican destruction layers in London. He recalled that:

> Here and there about the City, between the line of the Walbrook and London Bridge, excavators cutting new foundations from 10 to 20 ft below the street-level sometimes come across a thick layer of ashes, the remains of houses built of timber and clay, with fragments of roofing, of gaily painted wall-plaster and with early coins and pottery that must have been made before the day of Boudicca's vengeance.[41]

During the 1930s archaeological work on early Roman sites became more focused and, as a result, knowledge of Boudica developed. Wheeler and his wife Tessa worked at Verulamium in the early 1930s and in 1936 they published *Verulamium: A Belgic and Two Roman Cities.*[42] This was a milestone in Roman studies since it used state of the art archaeological methodology.[43] The Wheelers found little evidence for the early Roman phases of the town during their extensive excavations and argued that 'little can be known without further excavation'.[44] On the basis of the limited evidence for 'huts with clay floors' and the character of the early pottery assemblages from the town, they concluded that 'Verulamium was slow to forget its pre-Roman origins'.[45] The fact that they found no direct evidence for the destruction of the town in AD 60 or 61 appears to have been due to their main excavation being located outside the focus of the pre-Boudican occupation. The Wheelers concluded that Verulamium was destroyed at this time,[46] but without the writing of Tacitus it is highly unlikely that they would have claimed any evidence for the event.[47] Hawkes and Hull also argued for Boudican destruction as a result of the excavations at Sheepen (Colchester) during the 1930s. By 1958 Hull was able to point to five clear examples of burned layers that indicated destruction at this time within the colony of Colchester itself.[48]

More convincing evidence for the Boudican destruction in Verulamium was located by Professor S. S. Frere during his excavations in the town between 1957 and 1961. In Insula XIV, a block of shops was located that had been built alongside the Roman road called Watling Street, possibly during the late 40s AD.[49] Frere's excavations also located a destruction deposit indicating that these shops had been destroyed by fire, apparently dating to the rebellion of AD 60 to 61. As a result of the burning some of the timber and daub structure of the shops survived in very good condition,[50] enabling the buildings to be interpreted in detail. Little convincing evidence for a Boudican burning of the town has been found since this time,[51] and the extent of the destruction is unclear. Frere also found extensive evidence for a further fire that dated to around AD 155–60,[52] indicating that fires in Roman towns were not always the result of enemy action.

In 1962 Donald Dudley and Graham Webster produced a scholarly account of the evidence in *The Rebellion of Boudicca* that included a full discussion of her role in history and tradition. This book helped to refocus archaeological attention on Boudica during the 1960s and 1970s. The discovery of apparent evidence for the sacking of Verulamium in

AD 60 to 61 led archaeologists to search for similar information in the other two towns that Tacitus tells us were destroyed. During the 1970s the destruction layer was located in Camulodunum during the development of new buildings. Since this time a number of excavations have examined this deposit.[53] Extensive evidence for a similar deposit has been located in Londinium during excavations over the past thirty years. As a result of this work, an understanding of the early phases of the three towns burned by Boudica has gradually emerged.

In 1978 Graham Webster produced a further book, *Boudica: The British Revolt against Rome AD 60*, a rather less challenging account than the work he had written with Donald Dudley. It concentrates on the archaeological evidence and far less on the development of the image of Boadicea since the Renaissance; it has, however, been republished several times, most recently in 2000. Between 1980 and 1982 an excavation at Fison Way, Thetford in Norfolk, was conducted by Tony Gregory. This site may well have had Boudican associations and have represented a tribal centre of the Iceni. A concise and useful popular account of the of the archaeological and historical evidence was produced by Paul Sealey in 1997, *The Boudican Revolt against Rome*.

The books by Dudley and Webster, Webster and by Sealey have helped to spread the knowledge of twentieth-century archaeological discoveries to the public sphere and have had some impact upon popular images. In particular, Webster promoted the spelling of 'Boudica' for the name of the ancient British ruler and argued for the replacement of the inaccurate version 'Boadicea'.[54] It is, however, some indication of the small degree to which academic writing influences popular images that there are far more references to 'Boadicea' on the internet than there are to 'Boudica' or 'Boudicca'. References to Spence's book of 1937 also remain common, although this work was unreliable when published and is now entirely out of date. Other more recent accounts provide far more up to date and accurately researched images.

Despite the contributions of archaeological works carried out since 1920, the nationalistic use of Boadicea's image continued well into the twentieth century. Cowper's poem had a particularly important role in reinforcing twentieth-century images of the warrior queen. Learned by thousands of Victorian and early twentieth-century schoolchildren, and

quoted widely in later times, the poem was 'known to every schoolboy'
as late as 1962.[55] Other images, such as that created by H. E. Marshall,
also continued to be influential.[56] In this context the image of Boadicea
as a British patriot continued to be significant at least until the late 1980s.

In Lewis Spence's book of 1937 the author addressed the contemporary meaning of her example. Spence describes the rebellion as having
'attained almost the proportions of a national uprising'.[57] He followed
a long-established tradition in comparing the rebellion of Boadicea to
the Indian Mutiny:

> In both cases a number of contemporary small garrisons, separated by great
> distances, were threatened by a merciless and infuriated native population
> and faced with problem of making contact with one another or being cut off
> in detail.[58]

Spence's conclusions were, however, rather different from those of the
earlier authors who had compared the two rebellions. In drawing morals
from the tale, Spence was continuing the tradition set by Cowper. He
argued that:

> In Boadicea's noble and patriotic effort I think we behold the first example
> of that love of liberty which has ever distinguished this island of ours and
> which has developed in the course of centuries the most enlightened, the
> most just and the most humane system of government and administration
> known to mankind.[59]

He was thoroughly inspired by Boadicea's actions, feeling that she
'revealed in her spoken sentiments those self-same qualities which the
great majority of British wives and mothers, even in these latter days,
are known to possess ...'[60] He continued:

> Even at the present the lessons of that effort are self-evident. Let us cherish
> with no common pride the memory of a woman and queen in whom the
> native virtues of courage and love of country shone with a fervour well-nigh
> unexampled in our annals. Let us honour her name and deeds along with
> those of our greatest, let us see to it that her heroic saga receives a more
> fitting and honourable place in our national records.

> > Regions Caesar never knew
> > Thy posterity shall sway;
> > Where his eagles never flew,
> > None invincible as they![61]

In Spence's account Boadicea is a patriot and example of moral decency to contemporary Britons. He constantly reminds us of her 'Celtic' identity and links her with other figures from Celtic mythology and history, but he states that the value of her example is in the present. In drawing on the poetry of Cowper at the end of the book, Spence reinvents Boadicea as an imperial figurehead for the whole of the British people. He acknowledges the cruelty of some actions by the ancient Britons but reminds the reader that they were driven to them by Roman provocation.[62]

In 1949 C. H. Abrahall published a novel entitled *Boadicea, Queen of the Iceni*. At the end of the novel a group of ancient Britons gather around Boadicea's grave and vow that they will never forget the cause of freedom for which she has striven and died. The author concludes that:

> It was many years before their words came true, but Boadicea had not died in vain, for the seed that she had sown grew and grew, and, coming to flower, spread all over the land.
>
> And men remembered Boadicea, first Queen of Britain, as the one who struck the blow for the freedom which later became theirs.[63]

Spence and Abrahall's writings are excellent examples of the way in which some authors read contemporary relevance into historical events. Boadicea's objectives were in fact far removed from any modern ideas of nationhood or imperialism.[64]

With the decline of Britain's empire Boadicea's image in the published accounts often changed from this type of nationalistic and imperialistic image, although it was still used to provide moral lessons in troubled times. In 1956 Winston Churchill wrote about Boadicea in his *A History of the English-Speaking Peoples*. He stated that: 'Her monument on the Thames Embankment ... reminds us of the harsh cry of "Liberty or death" which has echoed down the ages.'[65] He suggested that Boadicea's revolt is perhaps the 'most horrible episode' which our island has known. He continued by remarking: 'We see the crude and corrupt beginnings of a higher civilisation blotted out by the ferocious uprising of the native tribes. Still it is the primary right of men to die and kill for the land they live in ...'[66]

James Scott's popular account of Boadicea, published in 1975, follows a similar logic but develops the arguments in greater detail. Scott assessed both the positive and negative ideas of Boadicea and argued that:

> Boadicea rose against oppression, against an omnipotent conqueror. That has very strong appeal, bolstering national pride. Such defiance has inspired our finest emotions, our best prose.[67]

For Scott, however, Boadicea still remained a character full of contradictions. He suggested that one element had been 'snatched out of the fire she lit', that of resistance against oppression and wrong-doing.[68] In fact, her voice was the last cry of 'something old and savage rather than the first expression of noble feelings'.

Scott viewed Boadicea as representing a negative force in British national history. He remarked that:

> What she [Rome] had to offer in culture, administration, standard of living ... would have been missed or at least postponed ... Put another way, Rome was a civilisation, Britain a collection of barbaric tribes. The influence of Rome must have been progressive ... Boadicea was ... a retrogressive influence in slowing down Romanisation.[69]

Scott adapted Churchill's concept of a 'higher civilisation' and, as a result, Boadicea was considered a 'retrogressive influence', slowing down the process of 'Romanisation'.[70] Despite Boadicea's heroic example, she is ultimately seen as 'a bad thing' because her actions delayed the 'civilisation' of Britain – if her efforts to drive out the Romans had been successful, she would have removed the civilising power of Rome from the shores of Britain. Here we have repeated the contradiction of Boadicea as, on the one hand, a figure of native valour and, on the other, a troublesome barbarian who would hold back the progress of Britain. These comparable ideas of progress continued to haunt images of Boadicea produced later in the twentieth century.

The archaeologist and Roman scholar Graham Webster used Boudica's example to inform contemporary politics and drew directly on a close association between contemporary Britain and classical Rome. In the book he wrote with Donald Dudley in 1962, the authors compared Boudica's rebellion with the Mau Mau tribal insurrections of the 1950s (during the final stages of British rule in Kenya).[71] In the epilogue to his later book Webster considered the relevance in greater detail.[72] He wrote that the 'tragic events' of AD 60 to 61 can 'teach us something about our present difficulties'.[73] Indeed, Webster felt that 'If we could understand more fully the factors behind the Revolt, and especially the attitude of the Roman government, we would be in a much better position to evaluate present politics'.[74] Besides the 'Mau-Mau atrocities' in Kenya and the perceived Communist threat, he also refers to Ireland. Antonia Fraser developed Graham Webster's argument about the value of historical comparison when she stated that the association between the events of AD 60 to 61 and the Mau Mau rising was 'certainly a valid one'.[75] The writings of Webster and Fraser indicate that by the 1960s to 1980s the Mau Mau rising in Kenya had taken on a greater contemporary relevance than the 'Indian Mutiny' as a major source of contemporary comparison. Webster and Fraser are arguing that the tale of Boudica can be used to aid the understanding of political and religious hotspots and to inform contemporary actions. Although Webster relegated such discussion to the end of the book, from the way that he writes it was evidently a highly relevant consideration for him. As in many more popular accounts, the past is seen to be of use to the ways that we can understand the present.

This process of historical association can sometimes draw the past into an inappropriate context. Garrick Fincham's recent attempt to 'deconstruct Boudica' shows how far interpretations have changed since the end of the British Empire in the 1960s and 1970s.[76] He argues that Webster's account of the revolt functions as a colonial document that draws upon parallels between the attitudes of the colonial English and those of the imperial Romans, traditions that this English elite actually derived from Roman sources through education in the classics.[77] Tacitus's account of the burning of Colchester by the followers of Boudica, and the version of events drawn by Webster from Tacitus's writings, reveal all the characteristics of western portrayals of colonial conflict within recent empires.[78] Boudica, the Mau-Mau and the terrorists in Ireland are all defined as the 'other', barbarians in Roman and British terms. Fincham suggests that the colonial context both of the Romans in Britain and of the British in their colonial possessions (particularly India) created comparable responses to common problems. This led both classical Romans and colonial Britons to seek similar solutions and to draw similar comparisons. The ancient British rebels were people

who needed to be effectively managed and controlled through the use
not only of political might, but also of historical knowledge.

Webster suggests that, in reading Dio's account of the ways in which
the Britons treated their captives, 'one still cannot read his words without revulsion'.[79] Fincham remarks that this revulsion results from the
fact that we naturally draw upon our own experiences in interpreting
the past and are aware of modern colonial contexts in which comparable events have occurred.[80] But why did Webster feel such a close
connection with the Roman victims of the revolt? This is because a parallel is being drawn in his mind between the modern world and the
ancient, between Romans in Britain and Britons under attack in India,
Kenya or Ireland. Webster was aligning himself in support of the Roman
conquerors – unlike earlier authors such as Trevelyan and Spence who
sympathised with Boadicea. Nevertheless, for Webster the story of
Boudica still had a moral lesson. Webster was an authoritative academic
representative of a major western power who had a clear historical
concern and a particular story to tell.

It is of interest that all of these authors have taken sides in the debate.
Webster was fascinated with the lessons that this rebellion against Rome
had for contemporary Britain. The relevance of Boudica's example has
been transformed from being a message of glorious opposition against
wrongful imperialism into a mechanism by which a modern imperial
power may avoid costly, dangerous and unpleasant revolts.[81]

It may be inevitable that we draw morals from the past and, in addition, it is natural to be disturbed by Dio's account of barbarity, although
we may well not fully believe all the details. Webster creates a clear identification with the Romans ('we are Romans'). This is partly inevitable
as the classical sources are all derived from a Roman context and no
native account of the rebellion exists. It is also, however, a result of
Webster's use of Rome as an origin myth for contemporary Britain.
Rome is perceived to have brought us to where we are now. Webster is
taking sides in the debate – Boudica was an example of a destructive
force that needs to be comprehended and understood in the present if
we are to remain safe.

Webster's account of Boudica becomes a colonial document because
of his use of the past to help with understanding modern colonial contexts. This drives the interpretation of events in one judgmental

direction, while it is now fashionable to study the conflict in terms of its complexity. It is not appropriate to draw such simple messages from history if it is our aim to understand the subtlety of past events. 'Scholars' write accounts that have a realistic context with regard for evidence from the past, an objective achieved by Webster's account. At the same time, however, the idea that scholars can distance themselves from the attitudes of society in general is not realistic, as a further example will help to demonstrate.

The perceived patriotism of Boadicea's actions remained influential until the 1980s. In her book *Boadicea's Chariot: The Warrior Queen*, published in 1988, and recently republished, Antonia Fraser explains her early interest in Boadicea, which eventually culminated in the writing of her book. She recalls that she was inspired by reading H. E. Marshall's rendition of the story of the warrior queen in *Our Island Story* during the 1930s.[82] For Fraser, any comparison of Boadicea's revolt with the Mau Mau rising did not detract from the patriotic value of her actions and its potential to provide lessons for contemporary Britons. Fraser wrote:

> It was Boadicea the patriotic heroine whose story first thrilled me; I wept for her treatment – and that of her daughters – and wept again, but this time in admiration for her death.[83]

In this context Fraser felt that both Boadicea's gender and 'patriotism' were relevant factors that encouraged her popularity.

We have seen that from the 1980s a strong interest has developed in the ways that Boadicea's image evolved after the rediscovery of the Roman sources during the Renaissance. Scholars who have studied this topic are mainly English literature specialists and historians, and we have used some of their arguments. Seminal writings during the period that Margaret Thatcher was Prime Minister included a chapter in Simon Shepherd's *Amazons and Warrior Women*,[84] a section in Marina Warner's book *Monuments and Maidens*,[85] and an article by Sharon Macdonald.[86] Accounts by these authors and Antonia Fraser all drew a parallel between Thatcher and Boadicea.[87] All four of these works emerged during the period of office of the first female Prime Minister in British history. Fraser praises Thatcher's example, while Warner and Macdonald are more circumspect about her contribution to British

society. By taking Britain to war against Argentina in a dispute over the
Falkland Islands in 1982, Thatcher was seen as effectively taking on the
mantle of past female warrior leaders and queens.[88] Parallels between
Thatcher and Boadicea (figure 41) in turn drew upon the earlier image
of Boadicea as a figure of national and imperial inspiration.[89]

Following the example of these four authors, articles on the reception
of Boadicea from the sixteenth to the eighteenth century have proliferated since 1990. In fact, it would appear that there is far more written
today about the historical reception of the image of Boadicea than
about the ancient historical and archaeological evidence. In particular,
Fletcher's misogynistic play *Bonduca* has become a significant focus for
scholarly attention. Jodi Mikalachki's book *The Legacy of Boadicea*,
for example, published in 1998, deals with how Boadicea was used in
early modern England. This refocus of interest on historical representations of Boadicea is also reflected in the information accessible on the
internet.

Most of the archaeological and ancient historical work regarding
Boudica has been produced by men,[90] while works concerned with her
historical representations since the Renaissance are primarily produced
by women. Apparently, the gender of writers continues to be a significant factor in how they approach Boudica or Boadicea. Popular
accounts during the twentieth century were produced by both men and
women, as is evident from a review of historical novels and the internet.
Popular publications on Boudica or Boadicea, both of the scholarly and
more popular type, have been prolific since 1980. In particular, historical novels became very common in the late twentieth century, while
playwrights have drawn on a long tradition in choosing her as a lead
character.

A database of historical novels about Rome, *The Fictional Rome Website*,[91] is maintained on the internet by the Richard Stockton College of
New Jersey. In July 2002 this listed works by twenty authors who have
been published since 1900 on the subject of Boudica or Boadicea. A
search on the computer index of the National Library of Scotland in
2003 indicated some additional examples. If we combine these lists,
although not all the novels that have been published about Boudica or
Boadicea during the twentieth century will have been included, we can
see that the interest of historical novelists appears to have peaked

41. George Gale's cartoon of Margaret Thatcher as Boadicea, from *The Daily Telegraph* of 11 June, 1987. (*By permission of the Telegraph Group Ltd*)

between 1960 and 1979. From four novels in the first twenty years of the
century, and one between 1920 and 1939, there were five published
between 1940 and 1959 and no less than fourteen between 1960 and 1979.
Only two more appeared between 1980 and 2000. Since 1980 some other
forms of publication have become more common and the warrior
queen has remained highly popular.

Of these historical novels, those of Rosemary Sutcliff and Henry
Treece are probably the most widely read.[92] Although many authors
stress that their novels are not works of history,[93] readers' ideas of the
past are often deeply influenced by popular images. Sutcliff's Boudicca
is a complex character, headstrong and valiant, but also in many ways
barbaric. The author was forced to invent information to supplement
the historical evidence and, in particular, appears to draw upon the
image of native American Indians when describing her ancient British
warriors as painted 'braves'.

In Sutcliff's novel, as in earlier accounts, Boudicca goes too far. Her
anger and revenge are provoked by unforgivable Roman cruelty, but the
heroine promises that she will sacrifice men, women and children to the
'Great Mother' following her victories, and her savagery effectively leads
to her defeat. Here the author is evidently drawing upon Dio's account
of the atrocities committed by the Britons. After the sack of Camulodunum, the narrator, 'Cadwan of the Harp', remarks with concern:

> I will not tell, I will not remember, how they died, those women. But after it
> was all over, I saw their bodies hanging there, like dreadful white fruit hang-
> ing from the branches of the dark and ancient trees, and I knew what
> Boudicca had promised to the Great Mother when I saw her dancing there
> two nights ago. And I knew why the woods had grown full of fear.[94]

Boudicca's barbarity in victory is of concern to some of her followers,
including her loyal harper. When she is defeated the reader feels sympathy for her but also that in a significant way she deserves her tragic
end, which the author makes clear is the ending of the ancient British
way of life. The commentary on her defeat is provided by Cadwan,
but also by the Roman Agricola; while Cadwan's way of life will evidently now come to an end, Agricola (who became governor of Britain
twenty years later) points the way forward for the British. Sutcliff's
novel is intended to be exciting for the reader, but is ultimately rather

depressing. It was unlikely to provoke the kind of patriotic feelings that were encouraged by the writings of Cowper and Marshall, and by Thornycroft's statue. Instead, it provides a more realistic image, supported – where possible – by the available historical and archaeological evidence.

Terry Deary provides other, more believable, images in the 'Horrible Histories' volume *The Rotten Romans*.[95] The front cover shows a tall and ferocious-looking Boadicea brandishing a sword and confronting two Roman legionary soldiers; 'You first Brutus', says one to the other. Inside, we learn that: 'Boudicca always looked pretty fearsome with her huge mass of bright red hair, her rough voice and her king-sized body'.[96] Deary presents a balanced picture of the rebellion – its causes are given from both the British and the Roman point of view – and argues that we need not be swayed by Roman writings about Boudica.

> If the Brits had been able to write then, they would have given a very different account of the battle. The Romans were very good at blaming other people for things. The truth is usually that there are good arguments on both sides …[97]

Deary presents both sides of the argument in cartoon form (figure 42). Unlike many previous authors and current museum displays, he does not take a side in the debate.

Twentieth-century plays include *Boadicea* by Monica Lissak, first performed at the King's Head Theatre in Islington, London, on 27 April 1996. At the beginning of the play the author addresses the question of 'What changes Boadicea from a fun-loving wife and mother into the killing machine of history?' The reasons for Boadicea's revolt are given in detail. Unlike Tacitus, Lissak shows the Celts as musical, artistic and spiritual. Boadicea has a good and happy life; she is not in the mood for war, but a druid priestess, determined to overthrow the Romans and regain her own power over the British, insists that war is in Boadicea's stars. When this fails, the priestess undermines Boadicea's confidence by lying to her about the behaviour of her Roman lover. Boadicea then embarks on her role as a 'killing-machine'. Evidently, this play, in the company of earlier dramatisations, does not adhere closely to the historical information. *Boudicca's Babes*, written by Greg Lyons and directed by Ivan Cutting, was performed by a touring theatre company

42. A balanced view of Boudicca. Drawn by Martin Brown. From *Horrible Histories: The Rotten Romans* by Terry Deary, pp. 46–47. (*By kind permission of Terry Deary, Martin Brown and Scholastic Ltd*)

in East Anglia during 2002. The play portrays Boudica as Madonna – 'all pointy bras and chariot, a first-century material girl!'[98]

Television programmes about Boadicea have occasionally been produced since the 1980s. In 1986 *Imaginary Women*, produced by Marina Warner, was screened on Channel Four.[99] The rock-singer Toyah Willcox appeared driving a chariot, her hair coloured a violent punk red. Wilcox had accepted the role of Boadicea in a play the previous year and described the ancient war leader as a 'free and liberated sexual woman'.[100] This image strongly contradicts the mythological development of Boadicea associated with the time during which Margaret Thatcher was Prime Minister.

Boudica's popularity is once again on the increase. In 2002 two further television documentaries about her were produced. The *Guardian* newspaper of Saturday 27 April 2002 ran a feature on *Boudicca, the Warrior Queen*, a film for television that was subsequently shown on ITV1 in September 2003. It was written by the award-winning dramatist Andrew Davies and the title role was given to the high-profile actress Alex Kingston. During a television interview at the Montreux Film Festival in Switzerland in April 2002, Davies suggested that the film would emphasise some of the parallels between the problems of the Roman Empire and the present situation in world politics. Davies described how Boudicca's battle against the Romans resulted in the defeat of the British, but that 'she gave the Roman Empire a tremendous fight'. He suggests that there 'are piquant parallels between the Druids', who were involved in the tale of Boudica, 'and the Taliban'. The *Guardian* concluded that Davies's record in his career (from *Moll Flanders* to *The Way We Live Now*) suggests that film on Boudica would comprise more action than accuracy; indeed, Davies stated in his interview that the film is 'not going to be old-fashioned history'. The Boudica of Davies's film was therefore developed as a figure that was intended to resonate with people in Britain today.

Boudica is also the subject of a number of current exhibitions in museums, including those at Norwich, Colchester, London and Verulamium. The displays at Norwich and Colchester each develop entirely different aspects of the events of AD 60 to 61, while those at London and Verulamium adopt other approaches.

At the museum in Colchester Castle, an exhibition created in 1992–93 deals with the development of late Iron Age and Roman Colchester from the origins of the settlement. Information is provided on the Iron Age *oppidum*, the Roman conquest, the fortress and the colony.[101] The negative treatment of the native Britons by the Roman soldiers and colonists is described, with a display of human skulls bearing weapon marks from the ditch of the legionary fortress.[102] The exhibition then moves on to a significant display about the events of AD 60 to 61, entitled 'Revolt'. A dramatic and colourful audio-visual display focuses the visitor's attention on the destruction of the town, the killing of 30,000 people and, in particular, the sacking of the temple of Claudius by the rebellious Britons. It features a conversation between two Roman soldiers trapped within the besieged temple. One, who is injured, criticises the Roman government's mistreatment of the Iceni that has led to their rebellion. The other, who feels aggressive towards the Britons, finally rushes out to battle, while his wounded companion is burned alive as the temple collapses in flames. The substance of this audio-visual is derived from Tacitus's account in the *Annals*.

Moving further into the gallery, a panel describes 'The Myth of Boadicea'. This explains that 'After her death the story of Boadicea became the stuff of legends ... Every age invented their own version. Sometimes villain but more often heroine.' Some of the old accounts of Boadicea are mentioned, including those of Milton, Cowper and the Suffragists, together with a variety of modern advertisements and posters that utilise Boudica or Boadicea. A promotion for the Mitsubishi Colt 1800 GTI suggests that Boadicea had a reputation as a leader of men, a 'go-getter who inspired confidence', and that the Colt is the type of car that such present-day 'Boadiceas' should drive.

In the same part of the exhibition is a display case full of artefacts associated with the destruction of Camulodunum. This is the fullest collection of destroyed possessions from the sacking of the three Roman towns in any display. The items include burned samian pottery, material from important buildings (including Purbeck marble and imported marble from the Mediterranean), daub building material, glass and coins. The background to this display features a colourful reconstruction of the burning of the temple of Claudius that recalls the violent scenes shown in the audio-visual display. The accompanying text emphasises the idea that the town was taken by surprise and that 30,000 Roman men, women and children perished in the onslaught. The sacking of Londinium and Verulamium is also mentioned before attention turns to the defeat of the rebels. We are told that the Britons also demonstrated their hatred of their conquerors by desecrating memorials to the Roman dead, exemplified here by the tombstones of Longinus and Facilis. The exhibition then turns to the discussion of 'a fresh start' as the colony is re-established on the original site.

The Colchester exhibition focuses the visitor's attention on the horror of the rebellion and the consequent loss of human life.[103] It does draw attention to the provocation to which the native Britons were subjected in an attempt to present a balanced account, but the main emphasis is placed on the destruction of a developing Roman town that later had to be refounded in order to recover.

Norwich Museum and Art Galley, within Norwich Castle, includes an exhibition opened in 2001 entitled *Boudica and the Revolt against Rome*. This presents a very different, indeed entirely positive, view of Boudica as 'a Norfolk heroine'. It also lays a very direct territorial claim to Boudica and her actions. In Colchester she is an outsider who wreaks havoc on the developing Roman town, while in Norfolk she is considered a local heroine.

The Norwich exhibition is an imaginative and thoughtful interpretation of the events of the rebellion, gradually unfolding the story of Boudica in an interactive way that evidently provides an exciting account for both adults and children. A notice at the entrance informs visitors that they are entering the land of the Iceni. Adjacent to it is a video screen displaying a sequence of images of Boudica or Boadicea from the past 400 years, each gradually morphing into the next. The visitor then enters the exhibition through a timber doorway representing the entrance to an Iron Age roundhouse with shields hung on its interior wall. Passing through another doorway to exit the roundhouse, the visitor then enters an area displaying ideas about the 'Celtic' people. *Life on the Land* argues that the Iceni lived in harmony with the landscape prior to the Roman invasion of Britain. A three-dimensional reconstruction features a life-sized model of a kneeling man in the act of offering a sword to the gods by placing it in a sacred pool. The interpretation then moves on to the first contacts with Romans, when the

Iceni became a friendly kingdom of Rome. Highly impressive ceremonial gold neck-rings from Snettisham, on long-term loan from the
British Museum, and others from Bawsey and Sedgeford, are on display.
These are linked to Boudica by Dio's reference to her wearing a gold
necklace.

Close by is a full-scale reconstruction of the type of chariot that
Boudica might have used. Visitors are invited to stand on the chariot's
platform to watch a video film of the approach to a battle, viewed from
behind the chariot horses' heads. Various artefacts from East Anglia
associated with Iron Age horseriding and chariots are displayed nearby.
The objects in these parts of the exhibition are mainly native and
Iron Age in origin, in direct contrast to the artefacts in the Boudica
exhibition at Colchester Castle.

The gallery in Norwich then deals with the gradually deteriorating
relationship between the tribe and the Romans, and a growing discon-
tentment that led to the rebellions of AD 47 to 48 and 60 to 61. In 47 to
48 the Iceni, a 'proud and independent people', were forced to give up
their arms. The most dramatic aspect of the gallery is an audio-visual
display in which an older woman with red hair (perhaps intended to
suggest that she is one of Boudica's daughters) relates the story of the
rebellion of AD 60 to 61 to a group of boys and girls, one of whom is
her grandchild. This is the place in the gallery in which the native story
of the revolt is developed most fully, but the substance of the folk-tale
of events long ago is actually derived almost entirely from the writings
of Tacitus in the *Annals*. It is not truly a native account of the revolt.
Displayed close by is the fragment of a horse's leg derived from a bronze
statue and found at Ashill (Norfolk). Finally the gallery deals with how
people in Norfolk slowly adopted Roman culture after the rebellion had
been put down. In fact, one of the boys in the video says to the older
woman: 'But now we live at peace with the Romans, we nearly *are*
Roman'. Roman artefacts and information upon the *civitas* capital at
Caistor-by-Norwich (Caistor St Edmund) and some of the villas of
Norfolk are presented to reinforce the ways in which the people of East
Anglia gradually took up Roman ways after the revolt.

The Norwich exhibition displays the evidence in an accessible and
entertaining way. A website launched before the gallery was opened
makes some claims that are worth exploring. It suggests that the

exhibition tells Boudica's tale through 'the eyes of the Iceni' while, correctly, making it clear that the story has at other times and places been told through the eyes of her enemies. It is suggested that Norfolk is where Boudica lived and ruled after the death of her husband and that in Norfolk 'the Iceni version [of the story] has survived but [has] never been told in full to the wider public ... until now'.[104] This is problematic because, as we have seen, the main elements of the native account of the rebellion at Norwich Museum are actually derived from the Roman author Tacitus; there is no known evidence that a native version of the story survived during post-Roman times in Norfolk.

Dr John Davies, the Chief Curator and Keeper of Archaeology at the Museum, argues that:

> Her story is told in Colchester and London but she was only there because she sacked them. There is nothing wrong with them telling the story there but it is our story, this is where she lived. We are reclaiming Boudica as a local heroine and trying to tell the story in the place it should be told in.[105]

He also suggests that 'The story of Boudica is coming home, reclaimed from cities where her story is told through the eyes of an invader to a place where her deeds are recalled by her own people'.[106] The city of Norwich, however, originated in the medieval period, and the county of Norfolk did not exist in the first century AD; in fact the territory of the Iceni covered a rather larger area. Although there is no convincing evidence to link her with the Iron Age settlements at Thetford, Caistor-by-Norwich (Caistor St Edmund) or the many other places in which she might have been based, Boudica presumably would have visited and been familiar with at least some of them. In addition, when people think of Boudica they often remember the sacking of Colchester and London, or Thornycroft's statue by Westminster Bridge. The Norwich Gallery was intended to remind people of Boudica's origins.[107] In defence of this claim for her as a Norfolk heroine, there have been far more outlandish claims from other parts of Great Britain.

Boudica is given only a passing treatment in the exhibition at the Museum of London that was installed in 1996. Near the beginning of the gallery dealing with the history of London there is a single small case entitled 'Chariots of Fire', presenting a brief account of the events of

AD 60 to 61. We learn that the first London was 'destroyed by fire' and that the archaeological evidence lies in a burned clay layer derived from the remains of the houses that made up the settlement. It is stated that London was burned, along with two other towns, by the Iceni and the Trinovantes when they rebelled against Roman cruelty. The Roman governor Suetonius Paulinus came 'to the rescue', when he raced to London with his cavalry, but was only able to evacuate the inhabitants who were able to leave. Those left behind were massacred. So far the description has, yet again, followed Tacitus's account in the *Annals*. The display then uses the same source to describe the murdering, hanging, burning and crucifying of up to 70,000 citizens and 'loyal Romanised Britons' in the three towns. It is noted that Tacitus may have exaggerated for political reasons, but at the same time the display encourages visitors to have a negative view about the actions of Boudica. A colour picture of Boudica's attack on London is accompanied by a caption that states 'Boudica led the Iceni and Trinovantes in an attack which totally destroyed the first settlement in London'.

To understand the reason for this negative view of the actions of Boudica we need to look at the general nature of the galleries at the Museum of London.[108] Laid out chronologically, they deal with the story of the development of the city of London through time. The Roman exhibition is placed towards the beginning of the sequence and in a very prominent position. It contains writing, furniture and pictures of historical figures from the period – things that we can relate to directly.[109] The impression is given that the history of London is a straightforward sequence, from its foundation by the Romans through its early medieval, medieval and post-medieval form to the modern city. This concept emphasises the fact that London became the capital city of the Roman province of Britannia, probably after the time of Boudica. This idea of the linear history of London ignores the fact that there was a major desertion of the city in the post-Roman period and that seventh- and eighth-century London lay principally outside the Roman walls of the town, to the west.[110] This picture of the gradual evolution of London through time is likely to lead any visitor without preconceptions to a negative view of Boudica.

The London display, together with that at Colchester, is effectively pro-Roman – the rebellion destroyed a developing city with a great future. The reference to the possibility that Roman provocation lay behind the events does not fully enable the visitor to make a reasoned assessment of what happened. Indeed, the fact that in the Museum of London the rebellion is only given a single small display implies that it is not important to understand the events of AD 60 to 61 in order to appreciate the early history of London. The failed rebellion is deemed to be, virtually, a historical aside.

The Museum of London also displays artefacts that are intended to present a more direct image of the destruction of London. The caption referring to one of the human skulls from the Walbrook Stream states that 'perhaps it belonged to one of the victims decapitated in the massacre of AD 60'. Now, however, it appears unlikely that these skulls are connected directly with Boudica's rebellion. Also on display are various other objects connected with the burning of London: seventeen coins struck during the reign of the Emperor Claudius and the samian dish in which they were found during an excavation in King William Street; additional fragments of burned samian pottery, blackened grain and baked clay; and a clay pot which contained four rings with intaglios from a jeweller's shop in Eastcheap that was caught up in the conflagration. The bronze arm from the excavation carried out at Gresham Street in 2001 is also on display.

The museum in Verulamium provides scant coverage of the revolt of AD 60 to 61. The audio-visual at the start describes Verulamium, while a single information panel deals with the impact of the rebellion upon the developing Roman town. This is accompanied by a dramatic colour reconstruction of the attack by the Britons that shows, in the foreground, a woman with black hair holding a sword. Throughout the gallery attention is drawn to the cooperative attitude of the local population to the Roman government and to the idea that Boudica and her followers were outsiders who brought destruction to the pro-Roman population of the area.

The museum displays at Norwich and Colchester present directly contrasting pictures of Boudica and the rebellion. They are influenced by many earlier images that have been examined in this book. They also communicate these images to new audiences who visit the museums to be presented with ideas about the past. The displays at London and Verulamium tell us more regarding what archaeologists think about the development and history of these towns than about the rebellion itself, effectively lessening the significance of the events of AD 60 to 61.

Museums and books are not the only ways that people learn about Boudica and Boadicea. Some accounts on the internet follow an earlier tradition in creating imaginative and speculative ideas about both the past and the present. The image of Boudica or Boadicea in the early twenty-first century is largely a positive one, as a search for both versions of her name on the internet indicates, with several thousand websites available on a wide variety of topics. A quick search in June 2004 produced 59,700 sites referring to 'Boadicea' and another 29,700 to 'Boudica'. These include serious accounts of her life and actions, attempts to develop discussions about the site of her final battle (often at Welsh sites), speculations concerning her Welsh identity, a robot called 'Boadicea', a play, a travel company, a fashion label, information about the television series *Star Trek*, a web designer called Viviane 'Boadicea' Reber, and merchandising (including books and CDs).

Several websites discuss the location of Boudica's final battle. One supports Webster's suggestion that the battle took place in the vicinity of Mancetter in Warwickshire.[111] Bob Trubshore's webpage argues that Webster's idea is based on 'several layers of supposition' and that 'Until some suitably high-powered academic chooses to challenge Webster, then most "respectable" writers seem happy to take his speculation as more-or-less proven theory'.[112] Other writers are more fanciful: Broc Beag considers a romantic account from the nineteenth century that Boudica died at Gop Hill, to the north west of Trelawnyd in Flintshire (Wales).[113] Evidence supporting Gop Hill as Boudica's burial place apparently includes the local tale that the ghosts of the adversaries Suetonius Paulinus and Boudica still walk the lanes of Flintshire, while an elderly man witnessed Boudica in her chariot, presumably a ghostly apparition, racing down the hill at night.[114] Another website describes some of the historical and archaeological evidence while suggesting that Boadicea 'remains to this day, the greatest of the heroines of Britain'.[115] Others support the opinion that she was buried on the site of what is today King's Cross Station, London; some are even more specific in proposing that her remains lie beneath Platform 8.[116]

We also find that Boadicea is a 'Beowulf-like, parallel computer cluster' at the Fluid Mechanics Group at the University of Zaragoza in Spain;[117] a small, six-legged pneumatic walking robot, designed by Mike Binnard, with mechanics that are modelled on a cockroach;[118] a newsletter for disabled women in London;[119] and a music publisher appealing to 'nationalists'.[120] The television fantasy *Xena: Warrior Princess* features a character called Boadicea.[121] The Iceni Brewery, based in Ickburgh in Norfolk, produces a 'Boadicea Chariot Ale', which has a strength of 3.8 per cent and is a 'well-balanced session bitter with hop and fruit flavour and a dry aftertaste' (figure 43).[122] Dr Gillian Carcas, an English composer, has recently produced a chamber opera on the subject of Boudica.[123] 'Boadicea of Marshwood' is the name of a Shetland pony,[124] while *Little Bo* is a children's story, written by the actress Julie Andrews, about a kitten whose father gives her the 'big name' of 'Boadicea' that he shortens to 'Bo'.[125] One website compiler believes that the historical Boadicea might have been her forty-seventh-great grandmother.[126]

Boadicea has also been recruited for the promotion of tourism in Essex.[127]

Two thousand years after terrorising the Romans in Essex, Queen Boadicea has ridden once again in support of the county. Accompanied by her Celtic warriors, Boadicea has taken Essex County Council's fight back against the effects of Foot and Mouth right to the door of Number 10 Downing Street!

From the County Hall in Chelmsford, Boadicea made a dramatic dash up to London to Downing Street and then on to the House of Commons where she and a delegation from Essex County Council delivered a personal invitation to discover Essex to the Prime Minister and his tourism minister, Janet Anderson.

Boadicea in a chariot drawn by two horses and surrounded by a tribe of warriorlike Celts from the Essex-based Britannia Society made an impressive sight as she crossed Westminster Bridge before drawing up at Downing Street where she handed over the invitation together with a dozen oysters from West Mersea and wine from Carter's Vinyard near Colchester.[128]

Ed Gregory, from Essex County Council's Tourism Department, who organised the event, stated that:

It was just an amazing day and we really think we have gone a long way towards raising the profile of Essex as a tourist destination at what is quite a

43. The label design for 'Boadicea Chariot Ale'. (*By permission of Iceni Brewery*)

difficult time for our local tourism industry. It was fantastic to see the first
lady of history in Essex riding once again in support of our country.[129]

Why Boudica, who probably lived somewhere in present-day Norfolk,
should be an appropriate ambassador from the county of Essex is not
explored by this website. Presumably, the Westminster Bridge route was
partly chosen because of the presence of Thornycroft's statue. The pres-
entation of oysters to the Prime Minister is an obvious association, as
the Romans exploited British oysters on a large scale, but wine was
unknown in Britain prior to contacts with the Mediterranean during
the later first millennium BC. It is also ironic that the wine in question
was produced near to the former location of the Roman colony of
Camulodunum, one of the towns burned down during the revolt.

Fascination with Boudica and Boadicea appears to be growing. The
novelist Fay Weldon has written a monologue, *I Boadicea,* that was read
by Vanessa Redgrave and broadcast in October 2002 on BBC Radio 4.[130]
In an interview about this piece, Weldon mentioned that she loves 'that
statue down on the Embankment of Boadicea and the chariot ... I like
to think that she's advancing on Parliament ... But I fear she's stuck
where she is'.[131] This last remark is an ironic twist on the Suffragists'
image of Boadicea of the early twentieth century.

Weldon muses that the Romans must have been 'very impressive'
when they came to Britain:

> They had these baths, and white robes and clothes and togas and decoration.
> And we were living in mud huts!' she shudders. 'Food was hard to come by.
> You were cold. You were dirty. You had furs. You didn't have any of this
> wonderful stuff.'[132]

She suggests that, as a result of the Roman atrocities in AD 60 to 61, it
stands to reason that 'You'd want to murder them in their baths, change
the water and have a bath yourself ... then you could have the pleasure
of it without being indebted to them. After that you could work out how
to make the bath'.[133] At the end of the interview Weldon mentions that
she has always wanted red hair 'but it must always have been so dirty
and uncomfortable and covered with lice and completely revolting and
disgusting'. The interviewer agreed with Weldon that it is lucky indeed
that the Romans have left us baths.

Fay Weldon's comments are evidently tongue-in-cheek, but they refer to a common attitude towards English national history that will be discussed in the final chapter. Weldon conveys a highly simplistic view of Iron Age life, while such fiction is sometimes promoted as history by radio and television programmes and on media websites. The tourism-motivated invasion of London in 2001 and Fay Weldon's interview both raise a number of issues that we shall examine again in the final chapter.

Popular accounts, including those on the internet, have some similarities. In the contemporary world Boudica or Boadicea is drawn upon by both men and women, but there often appears to be a difference in the ways that she is used. The robot 'Boadicea' has been designed by a man, and attempts to locate Boadicea's final battle appear to be made mostly by men. At the same time, there is evidently a greater interest in Boadicea among women, as most plays, novels, operas, dramas and websites about Boadicea are produced by women. In many of these productions Boadicea is a character of international significance, a noble and upright person, who strives against the imperial might of Rome and in the face of savage mistreatment. This image has historical roots that we have explored. Some of the internet images draw upon the idea of Boadicea as a marginal and mystical figure, in addition to her established role as a powerful female warrior.

Boadicea's positive and negative associations both resonate in many of these accounts. Some of the popular imagery about Boadicea shows a lack of concern with any detailed knowledge of both the ancient history and the archaeological evidence. Does it matter that popular images are often created without much appreciation of the actual evidence? Alternatively, should we just accept that much of the recent popular outpouring of imagery associated with Boadicea is harmless in addition to being highly entertaining? The answers to these questions are not simple and concern the nature of myths of origin and our attitudes to the nature of history.

8

A Woman of Many Faces

It is in our schooldays that almost all of us learn our ancient history. This is uninspiring to the schoolboy. Then he comes upon a person – a woman! – who rose against the Romans and dashed about in a chariot with scythes on the axles cutting the legs off the people whose dead language he has to endure in another uninspiring lesson.

J. M. Scott, *Boadicea* (1975).

Throughout time, as we have seen, one aspect of Boadicea that has remained constant is that she is a woman who led her people into battle.[1] This association of a particular woman with war has often appeared problematic for the mainly male authors and artists who have represented Boadicea. Gender, as a variety of writers have stressed, forms a major element in all representations of Boudica and Boadicea from the Roman period onwards.

We shall now explore three themes that draw some of the above accounts together, helping us to see how the image of Boudica and Boadicea has been both adopted and adapted in the past. They are not discrete, but overlap, support and contradict each other in a variety of complex ways[2] and are all associated by subtle means with her gender, which is fundamental to all; Boudica or Boadicea as barbarian, national heroine and freedom fighter.

She has been created as a barbaric figure. Tacitus and Dio, writing from a male-dominated classical Mediterranean perspective, tell us that it was not unusual for women to be war leaders in ancient Britain. It is not certain that this was the case – both authors may have used this argument to stress their attitudes to the barbarity, and otherness, of ancient Britons. Female leadership was an anathema to Roman authors. Whatever the truth of the situation with regard to war leaders in pre-Roman

Britain, early modern and modern society has followed the example of the Roman authors in viewing Boadicea as different. She is an anomaly because she crossed what were seen as the acceptable boundaries of the female role.

From the early modern period she was regarded as a retrogressive influence on the progressive development of society in Britain. This view of Boadicea effectively takes the Roman perspective and is in agreement with the Roman authors who condemned her barbarity and savagery. This point of view originates in the Roman accounts, particularly in Dio's writings and Tacitus's description in the *Agricola*. During the immediately post-Roman period such ideas were used by the writer Gildas in his condemnation of the efforts of the 'treacherous lioness' to hinder Roman domination of Britain. In early modern times, concern about Boadicea's barbarity is evident in a number of accounts, particularly in the writing of Ubaldini about Bunduica (1591) and also in the plays of Fletcher (1609) and Glover (1753), which show an increasingly strong anxiety about her actions. In all these works she is represented as a negative influence on the development of Britain and perhaps intended as a warning for the contemporary population. Her barbarity is deeply bound up with her gender, projecting paranoia about the idea of female rule – concerns that directly paralleled the attitudes evident in the Roman sources.

Such reservations concerning women and power have been continued through to the modern world. In Tennyson's poem *Boädicéa* of 1859 his heroine shouts and screams before her attack on Colchester and encourages universal slaughter, while in 1903 Henderson related her actions in a very one-sided manner to the fate of British victims of the 'Indian Mutiny'. Scott in 1975 thought her actions admirable but that she was a negative force in hindering the progress set in motion by the Romans. In all of these nineteenth- and twentieth-century accounts the authors take the perspective of the conquering Romans. As we have seen, Webster did the same in 1978 when he asked what Boudica's example could tell us about modern 'religiously-inspired' conflicts. Sutcliff's Boudicca goes too far by slaughtering Roman and pro-Roman women during the revolt; in this story the Roman, Agricola, is left to point the way into the future. Fay Weldon admired Boadicea's bravery but disliked the idea that her actions might have left the ancient (and modern)

Britons without the benefits of baths, running water and an adequate supply of food.

These accounts of Boadicea do not all argue precisely the same point. During the seventeenth and eighteenth centuries there was an expressed concern about female control of public life that is rather less apparent in recent accounts. Several of the authors admired Boadicea's bravery and spirit while having reservations about her barbarity. What all these accounts have in common is that they connect with the powerful and problematic idea that the Romans' mission in Britain was to bring civilisation to the ancient Britons. This image, which can be summed up by the expression *What the Romans Did for Us*, suggests that the Roman Empire was a 'Good Thing' (Sellar and Yeatman 1930, 10–11) that disseminated a culture and a civilisation that we have directly inherited. Owing to her initial victories over the Romans and her attempts to drive them out of Britain, Boadicea has been placed in the position of threatening the benefits that the Romans had brought to us – things that are seen as being vital today.

Two recent works of popular culture portray this schoolbook image of the value of Roman rule to the Britons and set Boadicea's example in context. In a cinema production that shocked some – Monty Python's *The Life of Brian* – the contribution of the Roman Empire to European society (and by association to Britain) is recalled.[3] The People's Front of Judaea is debating the demands to be made to Pontius Pilot when Reg, their leader, sums up their feelings about the Romans: 'They've bled us white. They've taken everything we had. And what have they ever given us in return?'[4] Someone in the group mentions the aqueduct, another sanitation. A dozen interventions later, Reg is forced to admit, grudgingly, the better sanitation, medicine, education, irrigation, public health, roads, fresh water, baths and public order, but he still demands to know 'What have the Romans ever done for us?' The inference in the Pythons' account is that the Roman Empire was a vital element in the development of society within the Mediterranean lands, Europe and Britain, representing the positive value of the example set by the Romans. In these terms, the claims that Reg makes are made to appear to be unbalanced.

Howard Brenton was the author of the play *The Romans in Britain* that so badly shocked Mary Whitehouse in the early 1980s. Brenton develops his own critical account of the initial actions of the Romans in Britain. He writes that they are often considered to have been a positive force because they built straight roads and 'brought law',[5] so the Roman invasion is represented as a *good thing*. Brenton's own views of the motivation and actions of the Romans was in fact far more critical and this is why the action of his play was felt by many to be shocking: it drew upon the author's concern about the character of British rule in Ireland. Brenton uses Rome in a critical fashion and the supposedly positive aspects of Roman rule are viewed in an ironic manner.

Even though both Brenton and the Pythons were placing a critical or an ironic twist on their versions of this popular primary school image, recent television programmes and popular books such as *What The Roman Did for Us* serve to perform a similar, less ironic, purpose today.[6] The concept of 'what the Romans did for us' stresses the positive innovations that Rome is supposed to have brought to Britain and also the apparent similarity and continuity between the Roman past and modern times. Rome is therefore felt to have been central to the development of the character of our own society. In these terms, the idea that the Roman conquest was a 'good thing' provides a popular myth of origin of huge power and significance.[7]

Many of those with an archaeological understanding of the past are highly critical of this type of idea. A century and a half of archaeological research into the society of the pre-Roman peoples of Britain has demonstrated that they did not live in the primitive, unclean state that has been assumed by many. Iron Age peoples evolved their own culture, including their own methods of hygiene and food supply. Negative representations of Boadicea connect with images of the barbarity of the ancient Britons in general, ideas that still sometimes influence popular representations now. Partly derived from the Roman sources, these images give a Roman perspective, one that stresses the civilising influence of Rome rather than its barbarity and cruelty.

The barbaric image of Boudica may be moderated through a consideration of the context of her actions and character. Tacitus's account in the *Annals* gives the most positive version of the story by explaining the serious provocation to which Boudica and the Britons were subjected. This has often been the favoured account of the rebellion, allowing critics to derive a more balanced perspective. In many accounts from the Renaissance to the present day the fact that Boadicea was provoked into action has been used to moderate both the barbarity of her character and the violence described in the Roman accounts of her actions. In his account of 1591, Ubaldini stressed the serious provocation to which the noble Voadicia was subjected and many later authors followed the same tradition.

We have also seen that Dio's account describes her as well clothed, a factor that had a role in her early domestication. Julius Caesar described the ancient Britons as being dressed in skins and adorning their bodies with blue dye from the plant woad, while other classical authors comment on their nakedness. Barbarity and nakedness became associated with the idea of the primitive through sixteenth-century contacts between Europeans and the various peoples of the New World who dressed themselves according to their own traditions and environments. We have seen that, in the early seventeenth century, Speed used Dio's description of Boadicea's clothes to develop the idea that both she and her female contemporaries were rather more civilised – more modest, and therefore more 'womanly' – than their forebears. They were seen as people who had progressed, perhaps partly under the influence of Rome. Clothing therefore becomes a signifier of an increased level of civilisation.[8]

This more positive image, derived from a clothed Boadicea, chimes with her social status in Speed's account. As an ancient British queen, she provided a counterpart to Queen Elizabeth I. Boadicea's status as a member of the native aristocracy, stressed by Tacitus in the *Annals*, may have led to the development of the idea that her actions could not have been as uncivilised as they had been portrayed by Tacitus and Dio. At the very least Tacitus's writings could be used to suggest that the ancient Britons had an excuse for their barbarity. In many accounts of the sixteenth century, and in some of those of the seventeenth, the barbarity that was mentioned in the classical texts was dismissed, played down or ignored entirely. How could this early British queen be so barbaric? Perhaps the Roman authors had overemphasised her behaviour for their own reasons, as Milton suggested in 1670.

Associated with this view of Boadicea was the idea that she provided a strong and positive example for contemporary English people. This image as a national heroine had a long duration, developing from the sixteenth century onwards. During the second half of that century, and in the turbulent sphere of international politics, Boadicea and Caratacus served as figures of inspiration for the English. Boadicea's valiant efforts to free Britain from the Roman invaders communicated a strong image of native independence that was paralleled with Elizabeth I's fiercely-proclaimed devotion to her people and her native land.

This image can be described as 'nativist', as opposed to the pro-Roman ideas studied above. It views Roman influence in a far less positive light and supports the ancient Britons in their struggles against the invading Romans. As such it contrasts directly with the image of Boadicea as a barbaric woman. It is perhaps significant that such images of Boadicea's role in the development of national greatness came to a head at two particular times – during the reigns of two highly influential and powerful British queens, Elizabeth I (1558–1603) and Victoria (1837–1901). In both periods, Boadicea was used to set these monarchs in historical context by providing both parallels and contrasts. Artists, writers and historians from these times have used the available information about Boadicea in an attempt to present an authentic account of the virtues and strengths of their respective monarch in a comparative perspective. They drew upon the past to bolster the image of a contemporary powerful woman. Perhaps the evidence from classical accounts for the ancestry of female rule in Britain was used to assist Elizabeth and Victoria to develop their own authority.

At the same time, the parallel was unconvincing. These later leaders did not personally lead troops into battle, nor, in the views of their contemporary societies at least, did they directly countenance savage acts of barbarity against women and children. Boadicea was, therefore, never an entirely positive parallel. Many accounts, however, do play down the barbarity of Boadicea's actions, which are often outweighed by the role that is developed for her as a national heroine. Images of Boadicea that were influenced by ideas about Elizabeth I include those produced by Gosson, Holinshed, Spenser, Speed and Jonson. Versions created by Henty, Thornycroft and Trevelyan came from the reign of Victoria. Such a use of Boadicea's image was not, however, restricted to the reign of these two female monarchs, as the positive images in Cowper's poem of 1782, in Spence's book of 1937 and references to Boadicea during Margaret Thatcher's period of office indicate.

The image of Boadicea as a national icon was associated with the idea of her as an honourable mother.[9] Evidently, this is also derived from the Roman sources, from Tacitus's description of the treatment of Boudica and her daughters. From the late seventeenth century onwards a number of authors began to develop the idea of Boadicea as an honourable British lady whose actions had been greatly provoked by Roman outrages to her motherly sense of propriety.[10] Other later accounts blamed the barbarity on factions among the ancient Britons such as the druids, rather than attributing it directly to Boadicea herself – effectively 'emasculating' Boadicea in political and military terms. By using such associations, writers were able to create a maternal figure with a concern for the independence and freedom of Britain. An early example is Hopkins's play of 1697, but this image becomes fully exploited during the late Victorian period. In Henty's *Beric the Briton* of 1893 Boadicea is a forceful, stately and gracious figure who has no part in the atrocities carried out against the Romans. Marie Trevelyan's Boadicea has been affected by the 'refining influence' of Roman culture and is seriously goaded into action; she even affords captured Roman soldiers the rights of prisoners of war.[11] In H. E. Marshall's *Our Island Story* she is shown as a proud maternal figure, carefully sheltering her young daughters behind her while calling on the Britons to revenge themselves on the Romans. Harvard Thomas's statue in Cardiff also shows her protectively embracing her daughters. In some later works Boadicea continues to be portrayed as a concerned mother. In Lissak's play of 1996 she is a 'fun-loving wife and mother' who has to be pushed particularly hard into seeking revenge for the wrongs that have been done to her. Many images on the internet stress the way that she was sorely provoked into her actions against the Romans.

This image of Boadicea as a national icon is unsupportable from a critical modern perspective. It is just as flawed as the idea of Boadicea as a primitive barbarian who delayed the progress of Roman civilisation. As we have seen, Boudica became the ruler of a single ancient British tribe and she appears to have rebelled against the Romans due to serious provocation. The concept of England or Britain as a unified entity did not exist in the first century AD. Any cohesion that the ancient

Britons achieved in their resistance to Rome during the invasion of AD
43 and the rebellion of AD 60 to 61 resulted from a wish to avoid being
controlled by the Romans in their daily lives rather than from any spirit
of national unity or purpose. It is unrealistic to assume a nationalistic
motivation for these actions. Indeed, as we have seen, Boudica was not
necessarily a 'queen' at all and, furthermore, concepts of Iron Age rule
cannot be equated with the Elizabethan or the modern institution of
queenship. It was, perhaps, inevitable that Boadicea would be drawn
upon during the reigns of Elizabeth and Victoria, but the association is
not convincing.

The two general and contradictory ideas of Boadicea as presenting
either a negative or a positive image force the authors of many
accounts to take sides. The Roman sources include descriptions and
opinions that were used to reinforce both perspectives; many authors
use elements of both. At the same time, they are not entirely exclusive
of one another and this is one of the reasons for the popularity of
Boadicea – she provided a complex and partly contradictory image.
Even for those who used the image of Boadicea in a positive fashion,
the negative connotations could not be entirely ignored. The Boadicea
of the Elizabethan age is a reflection of the contemporary queen but one
that also emphasises Elizabeth's virtues more fully through comment
on what were perceived as the limitations of the ancient British female
ruler. In a contrary fashion, the late eighteenth-century poet Cowper
used Boadicea to ask critical questions about the imperial situation of
his own time.

In fact, during the sixteenth century, two writers found the contrasting views of the Roman authors to be so problematical that they created
the imaginative solution of two Boadiceas – one with mainly positive
attributes and one with negative. Böece duplicated her by writing about
a mother, Voada, and her daughter Voadicia, while in 1591 Ubaldini created a virtuous Vodicea and a negative Bunduica. In this way,
sixteenth-century authors were able to avoid the contradictory elements
of the positive and negative versions of the story presented by Tacitus
and Dio. The idea of twin Boadiceas declined with the development of
a fuller understanding of the ancient written sources. In this context,
however, other later authors also used contrasting positive characters to
exemplify Boadicea's barbarity; for example, in his play of 1753, Glover

made use of Venusia to emphasise the serious moral shortcomings of Boadicea.

Perhaps the maternal representations of Boadicea have helped to develop a third image – that of a freedom fighter. With the passing of the British Empire it has become less common in popular culture for Boadicea to be portrayed either as a barbaric figure or as a national icon. Instead, for many, she has become effectively a figurehead of opposition to dominant forces, including powerful regimes and centralising national identities. Behind the ways that Boadicea was used to cement national unity was ultimately the objective of strengthening the bonds that tied the nation together. By creating an ancestry for national feeling, writers and artists from the sixteenth century to the twentieth have sought ways to promote national unity. In contrast, the idea of the freedom fighter casts Boadicea as a figurehead for those who want to challenge what they regard as oppressive. In this way Boadicea is often used to champion the rights of groups within society rather than the interests of the independent nation. In this guise she has become a forceful icon of female independence and also of regional identity. The idea of Boadicea as a freedom fighter is not a single image but a series of ideas that are united by the role that they define for her as a symbol of opposition against some wider power.

These newly-defined roles are not very evident in accounts before the twentieth century. They do find an echo in Ester Sowernam's writings of 1627 and the Levellers' use of Boadicea in the seventeenth century when campaigning for the equality of all people before the law. The Suffragists were instrumental in turning the late Victorian and early Edwardian use of Boadicea as a figure for imperial inspiration back against the men who had developed it. During the twentieth century, enfranchisement and an increasing role in the workplace have given women more of a voice in society and Boadicea has remained popular, as searching the World Wide Web indicates.

In the age of the internet, Boadicea has come to represent, in most cases, a challenge to any sense of national identity. She has become a girl from Essex in an attempt by Essex County Council to invigorate the county's tourism after the effects of the Foot and Mouth crisis of 2000 to 2001, riding to London to make a local claim on a national institution.

In a similar manner she is also a local heroine for people in Norfolk who are encouraged to celebrated her cult in Norwich Castle. In the words of one archaeologist from the museum, this is the right place to celebrate her life as she was a local girl. As an ancient Briton she is also claimed by some Welsh interests as an ancestor of the current 'Celtic' population of Britain. The site of her last battle is unknown, yet several accounts suggest, improbably, that it occurred at a location in present-day Wales. Some Londoners also make an equally improbable claim on her through the commonly-held myth of her burial on the site of what is today King's Cross Station, a favourite story of London taxi-drivers.

She has been used directly in popular culture, having been reinterpreted as a punk in Toyah Willcox's representation and more recently on the stage as an early version of Madonna. Her name has been taken by a newsletter for women wheelchair users, presumably due to the fact that she represents an empowered woman and that wheelchairs are sometimes known as 'chariots'. Her name has also been given to a powerful computer in Spain and to a dextrous robot. Her Norfolk connection has been used to name a beer, while her valour has inspired the naming of a courageous kitten in a novel for children. In all these guises she has broken away from her former roles as either a barbarian or a national figurehead in order to establish a variety of more local and fragmented identities. She has been reclaimed from her dominant late Victorian and Edwardian image in ways that involve a reversal of and opposition to her earlier images.

The role of Boadicea as a freedom fighter may, however, prove to be increasingly ambiguous. The people in her story rebelled against a foreign power that was dominating Britain. In the early twenty-first century we have our own conflicts, involving warlike action in Afghanistan, Iraq and the Near East. These contemporary situations involve western powers, including Britain, in dominant military roles. The ambiguity of Boudica's example again comes to the fore. She has been used to examine aspects of rebellion that relate directly to our own national experience. She may become problematic in this context because of growing concerns about national security and world peace.

Boudica's story also allows us to consider how academic works relate to popular ones. Simplistically, scholars sometimes suggest that there are two types of accounts – on the one hand, serious, detailed scholarly writings and images that try to adhere to the evidence and, on the other, popular stories and images about the past that have very little connection with the available evidence. The former are felt to be the work of 'experts' or 'scholars', while the latter are usually considered inaccurate and speculative, at least to some degree. 'Specialists' feel that many popular accounts are actively imaginative, as their authors do not appear to have made much effort to use the sources. Accounts that do use relevant evidence have not always tried to obtain accurate information from the earliest surviving written texts, or from archaeological writings, but have depended on the distorted later versions of a myth passed on by others.

In fact, scholarly criticism of the overliberal use of information about Boadicea began as early as 1753 with an anonymous attack on the historical accuracy of Glover's play. In this critique it is claimed that Glover abused the evidence of the Roman texts by making Boadicea unrealistically barbaric. In 1849 John Akerman undermined the idea that Iron Age coins marked with the name BODVOC referred to Boadicea; he argued this on the grounds of their distribution. Other more recent accounts have derided various popular images for paying scant attention to the evidence.[12] For example, the 'Boudica Celebrations' were a series of summer events that took place in St Albans in Hertfordshire during 1989, based around the burning to the ground of the neighbouring Roman town of Verulamium in AD 60 or 61.[13] We learn that:

> The theme was therefore 'Fire'. The central feature ... was the staged production of a play, *Boudica*. The festival opened with a fireworks display, the theme of which was Star Wars. Other attractions included a torchlight procession, a display of vintage fire engines, folk dancing, a Bavarian evening, and a Wild West shoot-out. The most bizarre event of the programme was the PC (personal computer) users' race ... The logo for this season of bricolage-leisure was a very benign-looking dragon, whose talents included driving a Roman chariot.[14]

Portrayals of this type set out to be amusing, but they evidently concern some critics. Kevin Walsh argues that there is a serious problem with this type of approach to history in which, effectively, all accounts of the past become equally valid and a loose theme can unite disparate events. This is because it is very difficult for someone without a prior knowledge of a historical theme to understand the information that historians and archaeologists attempt to collect and analyse.[15] The type of approach represented by the 'Boudica Celebrations' conveys no valuable information about the past. It may be entertaining, but it represents an entirely uncritical perspective with no information value.

Academics and specialists have often been considered by the general public, and by themselves, to have a privileged understanding of the past, one that is derived from the scholarly nature of their work. The word 'empirical' suggests that specialists develop a form of knowledge that relies on experience or experiment. Academics experience history through their education in the same way as other people, and it is only later that academic knowledge is developed more fully through university study. It is sometimes suggested that academic training means that certain specialists spend their careers developing a detailed and informed knowledge that sets them apart from others in society. At times, academics claim that they can distance themselves from their social context and the society that surrounds them as a result of their training and scholarship. This suggests that they are in some way able to stand outside the social and political concerns of the times in which they live, but this is an illusion.

It would appear to us that popular accounts and seriously researched archaeological work both engage in the creation of myths of origin. All accounts aim in some way to assess the significance of Boudica or Boadicea to modern society and provide images of her life to assess the relevance of the evidence to the present day. We all tell stories with the past, as it is not possible to describe either the past or the present without imposing our own ideas. This is not only true of popular writers. Each generation of historians and archaeologists writes a new account of the past that is more relevant to their own society than the stories they inherit. People, whether academics or not, derive ideas about the origin of their society through their education and experience. It is not, therefore, only popular writers and television producers who pick up these ideas, and 'scholars' are not immune to popular tales. The claim that a detailed understanding of the context of past events enables the academic expert to escape the concerns of the present is not realistic.

This book has set out to show that the interpretation of the archaeological evidence that we have available today is deeply influenced by

perceptions of Boadicea or Boudica's role within Roman and English
national history. Historians and archaeologists, however committed
they are to scholarly enquiry, take on the 'mythical thought' which exists
within their own societies.[16] We have seen several examples of scholars
adopting popular myths about Boadicea in this book. In fact, the playwright Howard Brenton claims that 'the academic world is as full of
bullshit as any other, including mine!'[17] He suggests that academics are
no more reliant on secure evidence and a critical assessment of this
information than knowledgeable members of the public. They often
express their ideas more forcefully, but with no greater justification.
Whether they are written by popular writers or by 'scholars', all
accounts of the past are created as stories in order to make observations
that are relevant to the time in which they are written. Positive and
negative attitudes, including fascination and fear, have influenced the
ways that evidence for Boudica and Boadicea has been collected and
interpreted.

Most of the accounts and images we have examined use information
from the past in order to create authenticity for the ideas that they project. As a final illustration, we include a reconstruction of Boudica in her
chariot that draws upon recent research (figure 44), but that also seeks
to display deliberate messages about the past to the viewer. We have
found that writers and artists throughout history have usually attempted
to pick up accurate and up to date information with which to construct
their stories and images. This is true of the sixteenth-century accounts,
although the information presented was often inaccurate, due to the
limitations of the copies of the classical texts that were available. It is
also true of many accounts published on the internet. People often want
to tell their own stories or to write their accounts in a critical and con-
structive way.

Does this mean that all accounts of the past *are* equally valid? Or, to
take a more critical view, does this make all these stories equally flawed?
The tales that we tell about the past are often intended to provide audiences with a sense of historical rootedness and those about Boudica and
Boadicea are no exception. To take an extreme point of view, it could
be argued that it does not really matter whether a story is produced by
a film dramatist, popular writer, playwright or academic. In reality,
many of those who produce images of our past aim to do comparable

things. We attempt to tell tales that will interest and enthuse our audiences, stories that are relevant to our contemporary contexts. The degree of imagination that we show in developing such images is important, as it is a fundamental element in the creation of an understanding of the past. A story also tells us a great deal about its creator.

This type of perspective leads us into ultrarelativism. Although not many would argue such an extreme position, ultrarelativism is a serious issue for academics. Relativism incorporates the idea that all accounts of the past have a value, while ultrarelativism would suggest that each account, whoever the author, has an equal value. An extreme version of ultrarelativism would suggest that attending an event such as the 'Boudica Celebrations' would provide as adequate an understanding of the ancient past of Britain as reading a detailed study of the archaeological and historical evidence. For example, it would mean that a popular television drama has the same value as this book in terms of the archaeological and historical information.

We have seen that certain authors and artists feel more of a responsibility to stay close to the available evidence than others. Plays, novels and television dramas are different from popular histories, since their producers and writers often appear to feel free to change the story or to elaborate on the evidence to dramatise the tale for a contemporary audience. After all, these accounts are created to entertain us and their popular character may, in turn, make them relevant to future historians. The plays that were produced in the seventeenth and eighteenth centuries help us to understand how people comprehended Boadicea at this period. The novels of the nineteenth and twentieth centuries are comparable sources, providing an understanding of how her image has developed. Andrew Davies's television dramatisation and other contemporary accounts of Boadicea on the internet may, in turn, become useful to future students of the twentieth and twenty-first centuries. The stories that we ourselves tell about the past will help those in the future to understand us, just as stories about Boadicea help us to think about our own history.

The critical assessment and appreciation of information is a vital part of the research that academics are trained to undertake and this does help to inform their accounts. It is important to remember, however, that this does not mean that such accounts have some form of objective

44. Reconstruction drawing of Boudica in a chariot with war trappings.

The chariot features a fighting platform with a suspension system of plaited leather 'Y'-form straps attached to fixed loop frames. The driver controls the horses with leather reins running through bronze terrets, or rings, attached to the wooden yoke. The form of the vehicle follows the reconstruction commissioned by the British Museum of a chariot excavated at Wetwang in the Yorkshire Wolds in 2001.

Boudica is equipped with a Roman sword, but she is wearing it in a non-Roman way, slung from a long strap, or baldric. Her driver wears a Roman cavalry helmet, probably a war trophy, very similar to the example that has been found at Witcham Gravel in Cambridgeshire. These items of Roman material culture have been included to show that the divisions drawn by anti- and pro-Roman images of Boudica are too simplistic.

(*Drawn by Christina Unwin*)

truth that we can all rely upon. We cannot avoid taking sides when we study the past, but we can attempt to explore whose side we are on,[18] even if there is no simple and clear answer. The stories of Boudica and Boadicea enable us to pose some questions, although we have seen that it does not provide *any* straightforward solutions; nor should it. The events of AD 60 to 61 are quite distinct from modern-day Ireland, Afghanistan or Iraq. We cannot avoid being influenced by our social contexts but we need to be aware of the possible nature of that influence upon our understanding. If we keep these issues in mind and try to comprehend the rich complexity of past events, perhaps this is an achievement in itself. The past may help us to understand the present, but we should not try to use the former as a direct analogy for the latter, or we will simply be continuing a long tradition of forcing information into inappropriate frameworks that are the result of current concerns.

One solution to this issue of relativism is to ensure that people are able to access the information that we do have for the past if they wish to. Telling an interesting but totally fictitious story may entertain but it cannot really inform us, as it is not based on a critical appreciation. Archaeological discoveries made since the 1920s and their interpretation are helping to fill in our understanding of Boudica and her rebellion. Some direct evidence has been forthcoming, such as the information for the destruction of the Roman settlements at Colchester and London. Otherwise, Boudica is difficult to relate to particular places. Archaeological research has, however, provided us with a far fuller understanding than that possessed by the Victorians, for example, of the nature of ancient British society and the impact of Rome upon the people of Britain. This means that we can place the stories of the Roman writers in context and counter some of the dismissive and biased ideas that Victorian writers held about native societies. Scholarly analysis of the classical texts referring to Boudica also have a major role in improving our understanding.[19]

We shape our own past, either to get what we need from it or to answer questions about the times we ourselves live in – we get the past we desire. Fundamental to all interpretations and representations of the past and the people in it is the recorded evidence, and it is mainly through the work of specialists that we derive our information. In order to strip away the layers of elaboration, bias and adaptation we must assess the quality of the historical and archaeological information that is available to us. We will then be able to construct stories about our past that are firmly linked to the evidence, while also enabling us to think about our own world.

Notes

Notes to Introduction

1. Webster 1978, 13.
2. Hingley 2001a.
3. Pastor Muñoz 2003
4. King 2001.
5. Hessing 2001; Struck 2001 and Wells 2003.
6. Also addressed in various sources as Caractacus, Caratach, Caradoc. For the classical sources that mention Caratacus see Braund (1996, 112–16), for early modern and modern representation see Smiles (1994).
7. Williams 1999a, 20.

Notes to Chapter 1: Iron Age and Roman Britain

1. See Cunliffe 1991; 1995; Haselgrove 1999; Hill 1995 and James and Rigby 1997 for accounts of the Iron Age.
2. Cunliffe 1995; Haselgrove 1999; Millett 1990, 12–13; Potter 2002, 12.
3. James and Rigby 1997, 51–55; Haselgrove 1999.
4. James and Rigby 1997, 27.
5. For an account of the appearance of these people and their possessions see James and Rigby 1997.
6. Hobbs 2003, 59–65.
7. James and Rigby 1997, 44.
8. Ibid.
9. James and Rigby 1997, 57; Cunliffe 1995.
10. Braund 1996, 46–48.
11. Cunliffe 1995, 94
12. J. D. Hill personal communication.
13. Cunliffe 1995, 95.
14. Dudley and Webster 1962, 18–19.
15. Braund 1996, 124–32.

16. James and Rigby 1997, 74.
17. Haselgrove 1999, 132.
18. Potter 2002, 18.
19. James and Rigby 1997, 78.
20. Ibid.
21. Braund 1996, 71
22. Creighton 2000.
23. James and Rigby 1997, 81. The term '*oppidum*' is problematic, but has been used in this book in order to avoid a lengthy discussion of terminology. An alternative that has been used by some Iron Age archaeologists is the term 'Royal Sites' (Hill 1999, 202).
24. Potter 2002, 21.
25. Crummy 1997.
26. Millett 1990, 21; Haselgrove and Millett 1997, 286.
27. Niblett 2001.
28. Cunliffe 1991.
29. James and Rigby 1997, 79–80.
30. Potter 2002, 16. A reconstruction of the grave can be seen in the British Museum's Prehistory Gallery.
31. Suetonius, *Caligula* 44.2.
32. Creighton 2000.
33. Millett 1990, 15.
34. Burnham et al. 2001.
35. Millett 1990, 20.
36. Potter 2002, 18.
37. Piggott 1975.
38. Webster 1999.
39. Webster 1978.
40. Ibid.
41. Potter 2002, 11–12.
42. Clarke 2001, 96
43. *The Conquest of Gaul* 5:12.
44. Clarke 2001.
45. Braund 1996, 12.
46. Ibid.
47. Potter 2002, 12.
48. James and Rigby 1997; see Hingley 1998 for the brochs of Scotland which are some of the most impressive buildings in prehistoric Europe ...
49. Creighton 2000.
50. See Potter 2002, 27–33.

51. Crummy 1997.

52. For the complexity of the naming of the various elements of Camulodunum, see Crummy 1997, 55–56.

53. Sealey 1997, 17.

54. Braund 1996.

55. Ibid, 112–13; James 2000, 279.

56. Potter 2002, 28.

57. Cunliffe 1998.

58. Crummy 1997, 53.

59. For a detailed discussion of the urban structure of the colony see p. x.

60. Sealey 1997, 16.

61. Crummy 1997, 23.

62. Millett 1990; Wacher 1995.

63. Millett 1990.

64. Sealey 1997, 35.

65. For a detailed discussion of early Roman Verulamium, see p. x.

66. Haselgrove and Millett 1997; Niblett 2001.

67. Wacher 1995, 27.

68. Rivet and Smith 1979, 374.

69. Ibid.

70. For additional written sources see ibid.

71. *Annals* 12.31.

72. Ibid.

73. For reviews see Ashwin 1999; Davies 1996; Davies and Williamson (eds) 1999 and Hill 1999.

74. Chadburn 1999.

75. J. D. Hill personal communication.

76. Jackson and Potter 1996, 677.

77. A total number of 6113 coins is recorded by the Celtic Coin Index in Oxford. This provides the fullest record that we have but does not to contain all the coins that have been located. It is likely that the total is well over 10,000 and probably closer to 15,000 (Philip de Jersey personal communication).

78. Davies 1999, 22.

79. Chadburn 1999

80. This area may have been incorporated into the terriotory of the Iceni at a late stage in the Iron Age. See Evans 2003, 254.

81. Philip de Jersey personal communication.

82. Ashwin 1999 and 2000; Davies 1996; Hill 1999; Martin 1999; West 1989.

83. Ashwin 1999, 119; Trevor Ashwin personal communication.

84. Davies et al. 1992; Martin 1999, 59–62.
85. Trevor Ashwin, personal communication.
86. Malim 1992.
87. Jackson and Potter 1996, 677.
88. Potter and Robinson 2000.
89. Ibid.
90. Ibid.
91. Ibid, quoting information from Rog Palmer.
92. Davies 1996, 85.
93. Hill 1999, 186–87; Trevor Ashwin personal communication.
94. Sealey 1997; Potter 2002.
95. This evidence has recently been considered in detail by Hill (2002, 157–58). Some wheel-made forms are adopted, but the range of types is very limited (ibid., 158).
96. West 1989, 109.
97. Davies 1999, 33–36; Evans 2003, 257–58; Hill 1999, 187. Further research in the territory of the Iceni may provide additional and more conclusive information for *oppida*, and perhaps for wealthy late Iron Age burials and imports, in due course. At the moment it appears, however, that this area did not undergo the same type of change that were occurring in the south east at this time. The sites shown on figure 16 appear to be very different from the *oppida* at Camulodunon and Verlamion (Trevor Ashwin personal communication).
98. Davies 1996, 1999. The Norfolk Museum Service's thirty-year liaison project with metal-detectorists has provided much of the evidence for the site (Trevor Ashwin personal communication).
99. Chadburn 1992; Evans 2003, 257; Jackson and Potter 1996.
100. Ashwin 2000, 241. Once again, much of the available information derives from the Norfolk Museum Service's liason with local metal-detectorists.
101. Gregory 1992, 197.
102. Sealey 1997, 12.
103. Martin 1999.
104. Colin Haselgrove personal communication.
105. J. D. Hill personal communication.
106. Gregory 1992.
107. Ibid., 197; Davies 1999, 34
108. *Annals* 14.31.
109. Ibid.
110. Braund 1996, 132–33.
111. Ibid., 70.

112. Ibid.
113. Ibid, 133
114. Williams 2000, 278.
115. Ibid.
116. Some coins of the tribe called the Corieltauvi have a very similar legend, suggesting links between these to areas at this time (Colin Haselgrove personal communication).
117. Creighton 1994.
118. Ibid.
119. Braund 1996, 133.
120. Ibid.
121. Finley 1973; Laurence 1998a, 2.
122. Laurence 1998a, 2.
123. Curti et al. 1996; Laurence 1998b, 103–4.
124. Braund 1996, 134.
125. See for instance, Martin 1999, 59.

Notes to Chapter 2: The Classical Sources

1. Dudley and Webster 1962, 143.
2. Ibid.
3. Webster 1978, 15.
4. Including Spence 1937; Dudley and Webster 1962; Webster 1978 and Sealey 1997.
5. Dudley and Webster 1962, 54.
6. Webster 1978, 87–102.
7. Ibid., 100.
8. Sealey 1997.
9. James and Rigby 1997, 7.
10. Farrell 2001.
11. Fantham 1996; James 2000.
12. See Clarke 2001 for attitudes to Britain and Braund 1996 for opinions about non-Roman women. Braund's work provides a more subtle interpretation of the historical accounts of Boudica than many of the previous accounts. Following his arguments, we suggest that it is not realistic to use much of the information that is provided by the classical writers as a direct account of the historical events of the rebellion without an appreciation of the backgrounds, interests and objectives of the two writers who wrote the accounts.
13. James and Rigby 1997, 7.

14. Ogilvie and Richmond 1967, 7.
15. Martin 1981, 26.
16. James 2000, 278.
17. Ogilvie and Richmond 1967, 11.
18. Webster 1978, 16.
19. Ibid.
20. Tacitus, *Agricola* 14–16.
21. Braund 1996, 145.
22. Tacitus, *Agricola* 14–15.
23. Ibid., 15.
24. Schlüter 1999; Struck 2001, Wells 2003.
25. Tacitus, *Agricola* 15.
26. Braund 1996, 145; James 2000 and Huskinson 2002.
27. Tacitus, *Agricola* 16.
28. Ibid.
29. Ibid, 31.
30. Ibid, 16.
31. Tacitus, *Annals* 14.29.
32. Carroll 1979, 197.
33. Webster 1978, Sealey 1997.
34. Tacitus, *Annals* 14.31.
35. Braund 1996, 134.
36. Ibid.
37. Tacitus, *Annals* 14.31.
38. Braund 1996.
39. Tacitus, *Annals* 14.31.
40. Ibid., 32.
41. Ibid.
42. Ibid., 33.
43. Ibid.
44. Braund 1996, 136.
45. Ibid., 34.
46. Ibid., 35.
47. Ibid., 36–37.
48. Ibid., 37.
49. Ibid., 38.
50. Webster 1978, 16; Macdonald 1987a, 44.
51. Braund 1996, 144.
52. Dio LXII, 1.1.
53. Ibid., 1.1–1.2.

54. Ibid., 2.2–2.4.

55. Ibid., 3.1–3.4.

56. Ibid., 4.2–4.3.

57. Ibid., 6.1–6.4.

58. Dio refers to this goddess with the names Andraste and Andate. This is presumably a result of a later copying error.

59. Braund 1996, 141; Williams 1999, 22.

60. Dio LXII, 7.1–7.3.

61. Macdonald 1987a, 46.

62. Dio LXII, 8.1–8.2.

63. Ibid., 8.2–8.3.

64. Ibid., 12.1–12.6.

65. Braund 1996, 2.

66. Huskinson 2002, 109.

67. Braund 1996, 118. Braund has argued that 'They occupied a special place in the torrid imaginations of the male writers whose accounts we use as sources'.

68. Braund 1996, 118.

69. Braund has argued that 'An all-powerful man was threatening enough, but an all-powerful woman was awe-inspiring' and could also be shocking to the Roman way of thinking (1996, 118).

70. For an informed account of gender in Roman society, see Montserrat 2000.

71. Braund 1996, 118.

72. Ibid., 131

73. Ibid., 7, 132.

74. Ibid., 135

75. Ibid., 136.

76. Williams 1999a, 21.

77. Ibid.

78. Ibid.

79. Braund 1996.

80. Macdonald 1987a, 44.

81. Ibid.

82. Braund 1996, 141.

83. Ibid.

84. Montserrat 2000, 156–57.

85. Williams 1999a, 22.

86. Ibid.

87. Macdonald 1987a, 44–45.

88. Williams 1999a, 22.
89. Gildas, 6.1–2.
90. Dudley and Webster 1962, 114.
91. Bede, 1, 3.
92. Dudley and Webster 1962, 114.

Notes to Chapter 3: The Archaeological Evidence

1. Wheeler 1930; Dunning 1945; Creighton 2001.
2. Fraser 1988, photograph opposite p. 144.
3. Bradley and Gordon 1988.
4. Jenkins 1842, 54–55.
5. See Spence 1937, 217.
6. Hull 1930; Crummy 1997, 50.
7. Webster 1978, 118.
8. Crummy 1997, 50.
9. Philip Crummy personal communication.
10. Crummy 1997, 50 and Philip Crummy personal communication.
11. Philip Crummy personal communication.
12. Millett 1987.
13. Johns 1971.
14. Hull 1958.
15. Hawkes and Hull 1947, 20–21; Hull 1958, xxvi.
16. Millett 1987.
17. Philip Crummy personal communication.
18. VCH 1909, 3; Wheeler 1930, 21.
19. Hull 1958, xxvi.
20. Wheeler 1930; Hull 1958; Millett 1987.
21. Crummy 1997, 79.
22. Grant 1976.
23. Dudley and Webster 1962, 107–8; Webster 1978, 123.
24. Sealey 1997, 36–37.
25. Niblett 2001, 67.
26. Tacitus, *Annals* 32.4.
27. Crummy 1997, 58.
28. Wacher 1995, 114–32; Crummy 1997.
29. Crummy 1997, 55.
30. Ibid., 56–57.
31. Ibid., 57.
32. Ibid., 55–56.

33. Ibid.
34. Wacher 1995, 117–18.
35. Crummy 1997, 58.
36. Ibid., 64
37. Phillip Crummy personal communication.
38. Hawkes and Hull 1947, 40–43.
39. Ibid., 56.
40. Ibid., 336.
41. Ibid., 93.
42. Crummy 1997, 16.
43. Hull 1958, xxvi and Crummy 1997, 79.
44. Crummy 1997, 79.
45. Sealey 1997, 22.
46. Crummy 1997, 79.
47. Ibid., 84.
48. Ibid.
49. Ibid., 79
50. Crummy 1999, 93.
51. Ibid.
52. Sealey 1997, 23.
53. Crummy 1997, 83.
54. Hull 1958, 153–4; Crummy 1997, 82–83.
55. Crummy 1997, 80.
56. Sealey 1997, 23.
57. Crummy 1997, 80.
58. Ibid.
59. Ibid., 82.
60. Ibid, 79.
61. Sealey 1997, 26.
62. Ibid.
63. Hull 1930.
64. Sealey 1997, 26.
65. Crummy 1997, 80.
66. Brunaux 1987, 17–21.
67. Woodward 1992, 79.
68. Ibid.
69. Haverfield 1914; Macdonald 1927, 3; Toynbee 1964, 46–48.
70. Toynbee 1964, 46–48.
71. Ibid., 47.
72. Lawson 1986, 333.

73. Ibid., 339.
74. Ibid., 334.
75. Toynbee 1964, 47.
76. Macdonald 1927, 6; Webster 1978, 125.
77. Webster 1978, 125.
78. Bradley 1990; James and Rigby 1997, 64–65.
79. Perring 1991, 3; Milne 1995, 41.
80. Milne 1995, 40.
81. Rowsome 2000, 18.
82. Perring 1991; Watson et al. 2001, 31; Drummond-Murray et al. 2002, 14.
83. Perring 1991.
84. Schofield and Maloney 1998, 212. We are grateful to Francis Grew for this reference.
85. Perring 1991, 6.
86. Rowsome 2000, 19.
87. Ibid., 18
88. Drummond-Murray et al. 2002, 25.
89. Rowsome 2000.
90. Milne 1995, 43.
91. Drummond-Murray et al. 2002, 41.
92. Milne 1995, 45
93. Ibid., 11–12
94. Milne 1995, 45.
95. Museum of London 2001 and information in the Museum of London's prehistory display.
96. Milne 1995, 44.
97. Perring 1991, 10.
98. Ibid., 12–13. Some of these objects are on display in the Museum of London.
99. Sealey 1997, 30.
100. Ibid., 18.
101. Grew 2000; see further p. x.
102. Sealey 1997, 33.
103. Rowsome 2000, 21.
104. Drummond-Murray et al. 2002, 41.
105. Sealey 1997.
106. Perring 1991, 18.
107. Milne 1995, 42; Sealey 1997, 32.
108. Perring 1991, 22.
109. Drummond-Murray et al. 2002, 48.

110. Milne 1995, 44.
111. Museum of London 2001.
112. Sealey 1997, 33.
113. Rowsome 2000.
114. Ibid., 22.
115. Museum of London 2001. The fragment was featured in a recent episode of the television archaeology series *Time Team*.
116. Information in the Roman gallery at the Museum of London.
117. The Museum of London display asks: 'was the golden statue desecrated during the destruction of Roman London by Queen Boudica in AD 60 to 61 ...?'
118. See Stewart 1999 for the context.
119. This is noted in the Museum of London display.
120. *Annals* 14.3.
121. Sealey 1997, 35.
122. Laurence 2001, 88.
123. For critiques of the military interpretation, see Haselgrove and Millett 1997, 249; Niblett 2001, 56–58.
124. Ibid., 59.
125. Ibid., 58.
126. Ibid., 61
127. Ros Niblett personal communication.
128. Niblett 2001, 66.
129. Ibid., 66.
130. Frere 1972.
131. Ibid., 64.
132. Niblett 2001, 65.
133. Ibid., 65, 76.
134. We are grateful to Ros Niblett for this reference.
135. Frere 1972, 26.
136. Ibid., figure 49, 160
137. Ibid.
138. Niblett 2001, 67
139. Sealey 1997, 37.
140. Niblett 2001, 67.
141. For instance, Sealey 1997, 36.
142. Niblett 2001, 67.
143. Frere 1972; Sealey 1997, 36.
144. Niblett 2001, 67.
145. Ibid., 67.

146. Sealey 1997, 36–37.

147. Sealey 1997, 37.

148. Neal et al. 1990, 37

149. Millett 1987, 94 and Niblett 2001, 67.

150. van Arsdel 1989, 24.

151. Ibid., 213.

152. Including those of Esuprastus, discussed above, p. x.

153. Creighton 1994, 329.

154. Creighton 1994; Davies 1999, 28–9; Sealey 1997.

155. Sealey 1997, 47.

156. Creighton 1994, table 1.

157. Sealey 1997, 45.

158. Ibid., 46.

159. Ibid.

160. Creighton 1994. Hill suggests that these hoards may have begun rather earlier than Creighton has argued (J. D. Hill personal communication).

161. Sealey 1997, 47; Davies 1996, 85.

162. Sealey 1997, 47.

163. Ibid., 49–50.

164. Johns has discussed the dating evidence for the objects in the Hockwold hoard (1986, 10) and there is no conclusive evidence for a Boudican date.

165. Bradley 1990; Cunliffe 1995, 100–8.

166. See the debate between Millett (1994) and Johns (1994).

167. Davies 1996, 85–86.

168. Hill 1999, 188; Hutcheson forthcoming.

169. Cunliffe 1995, 100–8; Millett 1994.

170. www.thebritishmuseum.ac.uk/compass/ixbin/print?OBJ1483. We are grateful to J. D. Hill for drawing out attention to this object.

171. Webster 1978, 97.

172. Dudley and Webster 1962; Webster 1978.

173. Webster 1978.

174. Ibid.

175. Dudley and Webster 1962, 74; Webster 1978, 97.

176. Rivet and Smith 1979, 409–10.

177. Webster 1978, 97.

178. Ibid.

179. See Bob Trubshaw's website (http://www.indigogroup.co.uk/edge/boudica6.htm).

180. Sealey 1997, 40.

181. Schlüter 1999; Wells 2003.

182. Webster 1978.

183. Booth 1996, 30.

184. Jones 2002, 119.

185. Potter and Robinson 2000.

186. Museum of London 2000. We are very grateful to Francis Grew for this reference.

187. Evidence indicates continuity of settlement at a number of places in the Fens (Evans 2003, 254).

188. Sealey 1997, 42.

189. Gregory 1992, 190.

190. Ibid.

191. In an area that also produced the important 'Thetford Treasure' (see Gregory 1992, 1–2 and figure 1). Unfortunately, this area was not studied in detail prior to its re-development for a new factory.

192. Crummy 1997, 85–86.

193. Ibid., 89.

194. For London in general see Perring 1991, 22; for the site at 1 Poultry see Rowsome 2000, 24 and for Southwark see Drummond-Murray et al. 2002, 54.

195. Fulford 2002, 42 and 48–49. The remains of this monument are now on display in the British Museum, while a full-sized replica can be viewed in the Museum of London. See Grasby and Tomlin (2002) for a recent discussion of the tomb.

196. Niblett 2001, 68.

197. Ibid., 72.

198. Wacher 1995.

199. Crummy 1997.

200. Perring 1991.

201. Niblett 2001.

Notes to Chapter 4: Finding Boadicea

1. Translated by Valentina Vulpi.

2. MacDougall 1982, 11.

3. Ibid.

4. Creighton 2000, 140–41.

5. Hay 1950, xiii.

6. For a translation see Vergil 1844.

7. Hay 1950, ix–x.

8. Ibid., xviii.

9. Ibid., xxvii.
10. Vergil 1844, 30.
11. Webster 1978, 13; see also MacDougall 1982, 18.
12. MacDougall 1982.
13. Marshall 1905, 3.
14. MacDougall 1982.
15. Dudley and Webster 1962, 115.
16. Ibid.
17. Ibid.; Martin 1981, 237–38.
18. Piggott 1975, 123.
19. Brigden 2000, xi.
20. Piggott 1989, 85; Brigden 2000, 274.
21. See Clarke (1999, 69–73) for the consequences of exploration and conquest in the ancient and the modern worlds.
22. Brigden 2000.
23. Helgerson 1992, 1.
24. Ibid., 2.
25. Mikalachki 1998.
26. Piggott 1989.
27. Moatti 1993.
28. Shepherd 1981, 150.
29. Mikalachki 1998, 8.
30. Ibid., 3.
31. Piggott 1975, 128–29; 1989, 60.
32. Helgerson 1992, 243.
33. Williams 1999a, 19.
34. Mikalachki 1998; Williams 1999a.
35. Mikalachki 1998, 4.
36. Ibid., 1998, 11.
37. Ibid.
38. Ibid., 12.
39. Macdonald 1987b, 7.
40. Mikalachki 1998, 13.
41. For the context, see Henderson and McManus 1985, 4.
42. For a brief introduction to these medieval traditions see Henderson and McManus 1985, 9–11.
43. Henderson and McManus 1985, 8.
44. Vergil 1844, 60–72.
45. Mikalachki 1998, 119.
46. Vergil 1844, 17.

47. Ibid, 70.
48. Dudley and Webster 1962, 116.
49. Vergil 1844, 65–66; see Dudley and Webster 1962, 116.
50. Vergil 1844, 71–72.
51. Dudley and Webster 1962, 117; Macdonald 1987a, 46.
52. Dudley and Webster 1962, 117.
53. Ibid., 117
54. Böece 1938,145.
55. Macdonald 1987a, 47.
56. Ibid.
57. Böece 1938, 156.
58. Macdonald 1987a, 47–48; 'durst pretend sik thingis abone pe spreitt and curage of wemen' (Böece 1938, 156).
59. Shepherd 1981, 133.
60. Ibid.
61. Macdonald 1987a, 48.
62. Dudley and Webster 1962, 118.
63. Brigden 2000, 239–73.
64. Mikalachki 1998, 117.
65. Dudley and Webster 1962, 118.
66. See Shepherd 1981 for Britomart and Elizabethan views of Amazons and warrior women.
67. Crawford 1999, 359.
68. Mikalachki 1998, 116.
69. Ibid.
70. Ibid., 126–29
71. Hackett 1995, 239.
72. Mendelson and Crawford 1998, 349.
73. Gosson 1868, 38–39.
74. Ibid.
75. Holinshed 1586, 43–45.
76. Patterson 1994, 104.
77. 'a long and very pithie oration' (Holinshed 1586, 43).
78. Holinshed 1586, 43–44; Patterson 1994, 105; see Mikalachki 1998, 116–17 for a more detailed account.
79. Holinshed 1586, 43.
80. See Piggott 1989, 85; quoting communications by Bryony Orme.
81. See Mikalachki 1998, figure 2 for an illustration of this painting.
82. Piggott 1989, 74–75 and plates 16–17.
83. But see Piggott 1989, 75.

84. Ibid.; Moser 1998, 168–76.

85. Piggott 1989, plate 16–17, 76, 82.

86. Mikalachki 1998, 13.

87. Ibid., 14.

88. Holinshed 1586, 45.

89. Ibid.

90. Mikalachki 1998, 13.

91. Dudley and Webster 1962, 119.

92. Ibid.

93. Ibid., 120. Ubaldini He also mentions that Voadicea is sometimes called 'Boadicia' (1591, 7).

94. The variations in the names of the two individual figures also appear to relate the the two classical sources that have been used.

95. Dudley and Webster 1962, 120–21.

96. Ubaldini 1591, 8. All translations of Ubaldini's work in this section are by Valentina Vulpi.

97. Ibid.

98. Ibid.

99. Ibid., 9.

100. Dudley and Webster 1962, 120–21.

101. Ibid., 11.

102. Spenser 1979, 341 and 429.

103. Mikalachki 1998, 124–25.

104. Piggott 1989.

105. Dudley and Webster 1962, 117.

106. Schnapp 1993, 139.

107. Camden 1610, 49–51.

108. Ibid., 446.

109. Ibid., 51.

110. Ibid., 50 and 61.

111. Camden 1984, 167.

112. Speed 1611.

113. Ibid., 198.

114. Ibid., 176.

115. Akerman 1849, 187 and figure facing page 190; Cunliffe 1991, 122.

116. Speed 1611, 177.

117. Piggott 1989, figures 5 and 6; see also Smiles 1994, 129–30.

118. See Piggot 1989, 62–63 and Smiles 1994, 129–31 on the contemporary context of these illustrations.

119. Speed 1611, 179.

120. Ibid., 181.
121. Ibid., 182.
122. Williams 1999b.
123. Speed 1611, 182. In support of this suggestion, Speed observes that women, when being drowned, swim with their 'foreparts' down, while men do the opposite!
124. Williams 1999b.
125. Speed 1611, 182.
126. Ibid.
127. Ibid., 198–200.
128. Ibid., 198.

Notes to Chapter 5: Subordination

1. Glover 1797, 39.
2. Henderson and McManus 1985, 113.
3. Greg 1951; Hoy 1979; Jowitt 2003, 478.
4. Smiles 1994, 153; Williams 1999a, 32; Williams 1999b, 1:29.
5. Dudley and Webster 1962, 121.
6. Ibid.
7. Piggott 1975, 131; Smiles 1994, 77.
8. Piggott 1975, 131.
9. Hoy 1979, 156.
10. Green 1982, 309.
11. Williams 1999a. 23.
12. Williams 1999a, 23; Crawford 1999.
13. Shepherd 1981, 147.
14. Crawford 1999, 357.
15. Fletcher 1979, act 1, scene 1, 16–19.
16. Williams 1999a, 23.
17. Fletcher 1979, act 3, scene 5, 125–37.
18. Crawford 1999, 363.
19. Shepherd 1981, 148; Crawford 1999, 364.
20. Macdonald 1987a, 49.
21. Williams 1999a, 24–25.
22. Crawford 1999.
23. Shepherd 1981, 149.
24. Jowett 2003, 491.
25. Braund 1996.
26. Henderson and McManus 1985, 55.

27. Orgel 1981.
28. Herford, Percy and Simpson 1950, 493.
29. Ibid.
30. Jonson 1941, 311.
31. Ibid., 310.
32. Esther and Haman were ancient characters from Jewish and Persian history (Henderson and McManus 1985, 218).
33. Henderson and McManus 1985, 11.
34. Sowernam 1985, 218.
35. Mikalachki 1998, 123.
36. Henderson and McManus 1985, 21; Macdonald 1987a, 54–55.
37. Sowernam 1985, 219.
38. Ibid.
39. Sowernam 1985, 229; also quoted in part by Mikalachki 1998, 123.
40. Henderson and McManus 1985, 4.
41. Tuvil 1616, preface.
42. Ibid., 136.
43. Quoted in the Dedication.
44. Newstead 1620, 19.
45. Heywood 1640, Dedication.
46. Ibid., 70.
47. Fraser 1988, caption to figure between pages 144 and 145.
48. Heywood 1640, 69.
49. Ibid., 72 (partly quoted by Crawford 1999, 375).
50. Shepherd 1981, 66.
51. Ibid.
52. Macdonald 1987a, 54; Mendelson and Crawford 1998, 466.
53. Henderson and McManus 1985, 11.
54. Piggott 1975, 36.
55. Heywood 1640, 91–92.
56. Piggott 1975, 36.
57. Barnard 1790, 23.
58. Milton 1677, 80; also quoted in Warner 1985, 50–51.
59. Milton 1677, 79–80.
60. Macdonald 1987a, 50–51.
61. Milton 1677, 80.
62. Mikalachki 1998, 146.
63. Piggott 1989, 63.
64. Sammes 1676, 223–29.
65. Mikalachki 1998, 181.

66. Sammes 1676, 229.
67. Ibid., 227.
68. Smiles 1994, 161.
69. Sammes 1676, 228.
70. Ibid., 229.
71. Bonduca 1696; Purcell 1906, vii; Maxwell 1928, 6.
72. Bonduca 1696, second page of the dedication.
73. Ibid., pages 2–3.
74. Bonduca 1696.
75. Holman 1999.
76. Purcell 1906, vii.
77. Ibid.
78. Bonduca 1696, 22.
79. Ibid.
80. Williams 1999b.
81. Mikalachki 1998, 147.
82. Bonduca 1696, 34.
83. Ibid., 52.
84. Howe 1992, 161, x.
85. Ibid., 161.
86. Bonduca 1696.
87. Maxwell 1928, 80, 81.
88. Hopkins 1697, act 4, scene 2, 41, quoted in Williams 1999a, 27.
89. Piggott 1975, 131; Smiles 1994, 75–112.
90. Piggott 1975.
91. This tradition comes through to the present day with Graham Webster's suggestion that Boudica's rebellion was a 'religious war'; Webster 1978, 132.
92. Ibid., 86.
93. Quoted in Maxwell 1928, 79.
94. Howe 1992, 30.
95. Williams 1999a, 26.
96. Ibid.
97. Hopkins 1697, 10.
98. Mikalachki 1998, 147–48.
99. Glover 1797.
100. Macdonald 1987a, 50; Williams 1999a, 28.
101. Dudley and Webster 1962, 123.
102. Glover 1797.
103. Williams 1999a, 29.

104. Glover 1797, 11.

105. Ibid., 9–10

106. Macdonald 1987a, 50.

107. Glover 1797, 39.

108. Ibid., 57.

109. Williams 1999a, 31.

110. Glover 1997, 65.

111. Ibid., 31.

112. For this topic, see Mikalachki 1998, 117.

113. See Williams 1999a, 31.

114. Female Revenge 1753, 1.

115. Ibid., 9.

116. Ibid., 10.

117. Ibid., 16.

118. Ibid., 19.

119. Dudley and Webster 1962, 125.

120. Ibid.

121. Ibid.

122. Horsley 1734, 26.

123. Ibid., 15.

124. Smiles 1994, 160–61.

125. Piggott 1989; Schnapp 1996, 188–98.

126. Piggott 1975, 147 and 148.

127. Smollett 1758, 60.

128. Ibid., 62.

129. Smiles 1994, 159.

130. Williams 1999a, 32.

131. Ibid.

132. Mikalachki 1998, 147.

133. Macdonald 1987b, 7.

134. Mikalachki 1998, 148–49.

135. Macdonald 1987a, 54.

136. Mikalachki 1998, 4.

137. Macdonald 1987a, 40.

Notes to Chapter 6: Imperial Icon

1. Vance 1997; Hingley 2000.

2. Stray 1998.

3. Jenkyns (ed.) 1980.

4. Jenkyns 1992; Vance 1997; Stray 1998.
5. Hingley 2000, 5; 2001b.
6. Porter 1988.
7. Ibid.
8. Hingley 2001a, 20.
9. Ibid., 21.
10. Bruce 1851, 40–41; also quoted by Smiles 1994, 144.
11. Hingley 2000, 21.
12. Vance 1997, 198; also see Smiles 1994, 148.
13. Bratton 1986, 79.
14. Locke 1878, 9.
15. Vance 1997, 198–201; Hingley 2000, 72–85.
16. Smiles 1994, 17 and 153–64; Macdonald 1987a, 51.
17. Newey 1982.
18. Macdonald 1987a, 51.
19. Smiles 1994, 137.
20. Hingley 2000, 74–75.
21. Cowper 1980, lines 25–32.
22. Ibid., lines 41–44.
23. Hingley 2000, 75.
24. Williams 1999a, 32.
25. Macdonald 1987a, 51.
26. Ibid., 51–2
27. Vance 1997, 198; Hingley 2000, 73.
28. Williams 1999a, 32.
29. Ibid.
30. Newey 1982, 168.
31. Williams 1999a, 32.
32. Williams 1999b.
33. Hingley 2000, 77.
34. Williams 1999b, 1:30.
35. Williams 1999a, 32.
36. Ibid.
37. Smiles has considered these images in some detail (1994, 160–66).
38. Ibid.
39. Ibid., 161, 163.
40. Ibid., 161.
41. Eagleton 1986, ix.
42. Ricks 1987a, 613. For the 'experimental' character of this poem see Dudley and Webster 1962, 126.

43. Macdonald 1987a, 52–53.
44. Tennyson 1905, lines 1–6.
45. Ibid., lines 64–69.
46. Macdonald 1987a, 53.
47. Tennyson 1905, lines 38–44.
48. Ibid., lines 78–86.
49. Ricks 1978a, 613.
50. Ibid.
51. See David 2002 for an account of the violent atrocities carried out by both sides in the conflict of the Indian Mutiny.
52. Ibid.
53. Ricks 1987b, 36.
54. Ibid.
55. David 1995, 167–81.
56. Ibid., 172.
57. David 1995, 172.
58. Ibid., 174
59. Eagleton 1986, 45.
60. Ricks 1987a, 613.
61. Henderson 1903, 210. This work is referred to in Dudley and Webster 1962, 129.
62. Henderson 1903, 210.
63. Ibid., 216.
64. Hingley 2000, 82.
65. Dudley and Webster 1962, 126.
66. Webster 1978, 14; Warner 1985, 49; Macdonald 1987a.
67. Barker 1859, iii.
68. Ibid., v.
69. Ibid., 167.
70. Ibid., 163–64.
71. Hingley 2000, 77.
72. Bratton 1981.
73. Bratton 1986.
74. Smiles 1994, 45.
75. Kennedy 1977; Hingley 2000, 76.
76. See Hingley 2000.
77. Henty 1893, 65.
78. Ibid.
79. Ibid.
80. Ibid.

81. Ibid., 66.
82. Ibid., 72.
83. Ibid., 76.
84. Henty 1893, 380.
85. Fletcher and Kipling 1911, 17.
86. Hingley 2000.
87. Vance 1997, 201.
88. Hingley 2000.
89. Church 1887, 109–10.
90. Macdonald 1987a, 53.
91. Smiles 1994, 163.
92. Manning 1982, 38.
93. Thornycroft 1932, 56.
94. Dudley and Webster 1962, 128.
95. Thornycroft 1932, 57.
96. Quoted by Manning 1982, 38; also quoted by Smiles 1994, 164.
97. Manning 1982, 38.
98. Ibid.
99. Thornycroft 1932, 62; Manning 1982, 40.
100. Thornycroft 1932, 62.
101. Treveylan 1900, xiii.
102. Read 1894; Thornycroft 1932, 69. See also Dudley and Webster 1962, 128; Scott 1975, 31.
103. Read 1894.
104. Ibid, 240.
105. Barnard 1790, 23.
106. Read 1894, 244–45.
107. Thornycroft 1932, 69.
108. Warner 1985, 49–50.
109. Macdonald 1987a, 53.
110. Ibid.
111. Webster 1978, 2.
112. Smiles 1994, 164.
113. Webster 1978, 2.
114. Thornycroft 1932, 69.
115. Williams 1999b, 1:32.
116. www.red4.co.uk/Folklore/trevelyan.htm
117. Trevelyan 1900, xi.
118. Ibid., x .
119. Ibid., xi.

120. See Judd's communications (1996, 154) on the crisis in January 1900 and the response of the British.
121. Trevelyan 1900, xi.
122. Ibid., xi.
123. Ibid., xi.
124. See MacDougall 1982; Smiles 1994, 113–28; and Robbins 1998, 29, for the context of this interpretation.
125. Trevelyan 1900, ix.
126. Ibid., 295.
127. Ibid., 298.
128. Ibid., xi.
129. Collins 1900, xxxiii.
130. Ibid., lxiv.
131. Hingley 2000, 80.
132. Trevelyan 1900, xii; authors' emphasis.
133. Ibid.
134. Ibid., xiii.
135. Ibid., 319.
136. Ibid., 376.
137. Ibid., 381.
138. Marshall 1905, viii.
139. Ibid.
140. Ibid., 18
141. Ibid., 19.
142. Ibid.
143. Ibid.
144. Ibid.
145. Ibid., 20.

Notes to Chapter 7: In the Modern World

1. Reynolds 1991.
2. Greene 2002.
3. Webster 1978, 13–14.
4. Dyson 1975, Mattingly (ed.) 1997, Wells 1999.
5. Dyson 1975.
6. Our account is derived from the writings of Macdonald 1987and Fraser 1988 and we have been unable to find additional relevant references to Boadicea by women at this time.
7. Quote from *The Sunday Times*, referred to by Macdonald 1987a, 55.

8. Ibid.
9. Macdonald 1987a, 55.
10. Montefiore 1927, 109.
11. Ibid., 110
12. Macdonald 1987a, 55.
13. Ibid.
14. Hamilton 1910; also referred to in Macdonald 1987a, 55 and Fraser 1988, 300.
15. Fraser 1988, 300.
16. Hamilton 1910, 41.
17. Fraser 1988, 301.
18. Hamilton 1910, 39.
19. Ibid., 43.
20. Ibid, 67. The Ranee, whose name was Laksmi Bai, held the title of 'Rani of Jhansi'. For her life, see David 2002, 350–74. She is said to have been 'the best man on the other side' (Hamilton 1910, 67).
21. Macdonald 1987b.
22. www.pmsa.courtauld.ac.uk/pmsa/AH/Region.htm
23. Ibid.
24. The artist cannot be identified; Theresa Calver personal communication.
25. VCH 1909, 3.
26. Macdonald 1927.
27. Ibid.
28. Haverfield 1914, 43.
29. Macdonald 1927, 5–6.
30. Hull 1928; Hawkes and Hull 1947, 20–21, and Hull 1958, 153.
31. Hull 1958, 154.
32. Ibid.
33. Ibid,, 198.
34. Hull 1930.
35. Spence 1937.
36. Ibid., ix.
37. Spence also wrote a number of other books on mythology.
38. Spence 1937, 251–54.
39. Ibid., 88.
40. Ibid.
41. Wheeler 1930, 21.
42. Wheeler and Wheeler 1936.
43. Niblett 2001, 18.
44. Wheeler and Wheeler 1936, 24.

45. Ibid., 25.
46. Ibid., 1.
47. Niblett 2001, 18.
48. Hull 1958, xxvi.
49. Frere 1972.
50. Frere 1972, 6.
51. Niblett 2001, 67.
52. Ibid., 24
53. Philip Crummy personal communication.
54. Webster 1978, 15.
55. Dudley and Webster 1962, 162.
56. Fraser 1988, xiii.
57. Spence 1937, 19.
58. Ibid.
59. Ibid., 269.
60. Ibid., 155.
61. Ibid. It will be noted that the final four lines are quoted from Cowper's poem.
62. Ibid., 231.
63. Abrahall 1949, 295.
64. Macdonald 1987a, 54.
65. Churchill 1956, 19.
66. Ibid.
67. Scott 1975, 10–11.
68. Ibid., 134.
69. Ibid., 133.
70. Ibid.
71. Dudley and Webster 1962, 57.
72. Webster 1978.
73. Ibid., 132
74. Ibid.
75. Ibid., 73.
76. Fincham 2001.
77. Ibid., 29
78. Ibid.
79. Webster 1978, 94,quoted by Fincham 2001, 29.
80. Webster refers to some of these; 1978, 132.
81. Ibid.
82. Fraser 1988, xiii.
83. Ibid., xiii.

84. Shepherd 1981, 133–50.
85. Warner 1985.
86. Macdonald 1987a.
87. Shepherd 1981, 133–50; Warner 1985, 51; Macdonald 1987a, 59; Fraser 1988, 4.
88. Warner 1985, 51; Fraser 1988, 314.
89. Fraser 1988, 321.
90. For some concerns about Roman archaeology in Britain and the position of women, see Scott 1998.
91. http://intraweb. stockton. edu/Roman/Results
92. Rivet 1976.
93. For instance, Sutcliff 1978, 172–73.
94. Sutcliff 1978, 114.
95. Deary 1994.
96. Ibid, 41.
97. Ibid., 45.
98. A Magazine, October/November 2002, 5 (The authors are very grateful to Ben Croxford for this reference).
99. Fraser 1988, 304.
100. Ibid.; Macdonald 1987a, 59.
101. Paul Sealey personal communication.
102. Sealey 1997, 18.
103. Paul Sealey personal communication.
104. http://www.edp24.co.uk/Content/Features/Castle/asp/010717boudica. asp
105. Ibid.
106. Ibid.
107. John Davies personal communication.
108. Grew 2001.
109. Ibid., 12.
110. Ibid., 13.
111. http://www.roman-britain.org/places/manduessedum.htm
112. http://www.indigogroup.co.uk/edge/boudica6.htm
113. http://www.indigogroup.co.uk/edge/boudica2.htm
114. Ibid.
115. http://travesti.geophys.mcgill.ca/~olivia/BOUDICA/
116. For the context of this proposal, see Fraser 1988, 100–1.
117. http://macondo.cps.unizar.es/boadicea/
118. http://www.ai.mit.edu/projects/boadicea/boadicea.html
119. http://womeninlondon.gn.apc.org/boadicea.htm
120. http://dspace.dial.pipex.com/town/estate … 1/boadicea.html

121. http://www.xenafight.com/boadicea.html
122. http://www.stevedunks.demon.co.uk/iceni/beerboad.html
123. http://www.composer.co.uk/composers/carcas.html
124. http://www.shetlandpony.com/shetlandstam/pero1075.htm
125. http://www.keough.net/category/us/0786805145.html
126. http://freepages.genealogy.rootsweb.com/~jamestow/so75/f000538.htm
127. http://www.mosaicpublicity.freeserve.co.uk/Archives/Essex%20Tourism/ 1Boadicea.htm
128. Ibid.
129. Ibid.
130. www.bbc.ci.uk/radio4/discover/archive_interviews/07.shtml
131. Ibid.
132. www.bbc.ci.uk/radio4/discover/archive_interviews/072.shtml
133. www..bbc.ci.uk/radio4/discover/archive_interviews/073.shtml

Notes to Chapter 8: A Woman of Many Faces

1. Macdonald 1987a, 41.
2. Ibid., 55.
3. Chapman et al. 1979, quoted in Branigan 1991, 104–5.
4. Ibid.
5. Brenton 1989, vii.
6. For the book *What the Romans Did for Us*, see Wilkinson 2000.
7. Hingley 2000, 2001b. See James 2001 for a recent discussion of identity in Roman Britain.
8. Williams 1999b.
9. Macdonald 1987b.
10. Macdonald 1987a, 57.
11. Trevelyan 1900.
12. Webster 1978, 17.
13. Walsh 1991, 138.
14. Ibid.
15. Ibid.
16. Samuel 1998, 14.
17. Brenton 1989, ix.
18. Beard and Henderson 1999, 47.
19. Particularly Braund 1996.

References

ANCIENT WORKS CITED

Bede (1972). *Ecclesiastical History of the English People*. Edited by B. Colgrave and R. A. B. Mynors, Oxford, Clarendon Press.

Caesar, G. J. (1951). *The Conquest of Gaul*. Translated by S. A. Handford, London, Penguin. Reprinted 1972.

Dio, Cassius (1925). *Dio's Roman History*. Edited by E. Cary, London, G. B. Putnam.

Gildas (1978). *The Ruin of Britain and Other Works*. Edited and translated by M. Winterbottom, London, Phillimore.

Suetonius, G. (1957). *The Twelve Caesars*. Translated by M. Grant, London, Penguin (1978). Reprinted 1989.

Tacitus, C. (1948). *Tacitus on Britain and Germany*. Translated by H. Mattingly, London, Penguin. Reprinted 1965.

Tacitus, C. (1958). *The Annals of Imperial Rome*. Translated by M. Grant, London, Penguin.

Tacitus, C. (1967). *De vita Agricolae*. Edited by R. M. Olgivie and I. Richmond, Oxford, Clarendon Press.

PRE-NINETEENTH-CENTURY WORKS CITED

Barnard, E. (1790). *The New, Comprehensive, Impartial and Complete History of England*, London, Alexander Hogg.

Böece, H. (1938). *The Chronicles of Scotland*. Translated into Scots by J. Bellenden, 1531. Edited by R. W. Chambers and E. C. Batho, London, William Blackwood. First produced early sixteenth century.

Bonduca (1696). *Bonduca, or The British Heroine: A Tragedy Acted at the Theatre Royal*, London, Richard Bentley. Derived from Fletcher's earlier play, but author unknown.

Camden, W. (1610). *Britannia: or A Chorographicall Description of the Most Flourishing Kingdomes, England, Scotland, and Ireland*. Translated into English by Philémon Holland, London, Georgii Bishop & Ioannis Norton. First published 1586.

Camden, W. (1984). *Remains Concerning Britain*, London, University of Toronto. Edited by R. D. Dunn. First published 1614.

Cowper, W. (1980). 'Boadicea: An Ode', in J. D. Baird and C. Ryskamp (ed.) *The Poems of William Cowper*, Oxford, Clarendon Press. 1: 1748–82, 431–32. First published 1782.

Female Revenge (1753). *Female Revenge: or The British Amazon. Exemplified in the Life of Boadicia*, London, M. Cooper, W. Reeve, C. Sympson.

Fletcher, J. (1979). 'Bonduca', in F. Bowers (ed.) *The Dramatic Works in the Beaumont and Fletcher Canon*, Cambridge, Cambridge University Press. IV, 149–259. First performed 1609–14.

Glover, R. (1797). 'Boadicea', in J. Bell (ed.) *British Theatre: Volume II*, London, British Library. First performed 1753.

Gosson, S. (1868). *The Schoole of Abuse*. Edited by E. Arber. Birmingham. First published 1579.

Heywood, T. (1640). *The Exemplarary Lives and Memorable Acts of Nine the Most Worthy Women in the World*, London, Thomas Cotes.

Holinshed, R. (1586). *The Chronicles of England, Scotland and Ireland. Newlie Augemented and Continued by John Hosker + V. Gent and Others*. Place of publication and publisher unspecified. First Published 1577.

Hopkins, C. (1697). *Boadicea Queen of Britain, a Tragedy*, London, Jacob Tonson.

Horsley, J. (1974). *Britannia Romana or the Roman Antiquities of Britain*, Ilkley, The Scholar Press. First published 1733.

Jonson, B. (1941). *Ben Jonson, Volume 7*. Edited by C. H. Herford Percy and E. Simpson, Oxford, Clarendon Press. 'The Masque of the Queens' first performed 1609.

Milton, J. (1677). *The History of Britain*, London, John Martyn.

Newstead, C. (1620). *An Apology for Women: or Womens Defence*, London, Richard Whittakers.

Purcell, H. (1906). *The Works of Henry Purcell: Volume 16*, London, Novello & Co. For words to songs first produced 1695.

Sammes, A. (1676). *Britannia Antiqua Illustrata, or the Antiquities of Ancient Britain*, London, Thomas Roycroft.

Smollett, T. (1758). *A Complete History of England from the Descent of Julius Caesar to the Treaty of Aix la Chapelle*, London, James Rivington and J. Fletcher. First published 1757.

Sowernam, E. (1985). 'Esther Hath Hanged Haman', in K. U. Henderson and B. F. McManus (eds) *Half Humankind: Context and Texts of the Controversy about Women in England 1540–1640*. Chicago, University of Illinois Press, 217–43. For Sowernam's pamphlet of 1617.

Speed, J. (1611). *The History of Great Britaine under the conquests of ye Romans, Saxons, Danes and Normans*, London, Iohn Sudbury & Georg Humble.

Spenser, E. (1979). *The Faerie Queene*, London, Penguin. First published 1590.

Tuvil, D. (1616). *Asylum Veneris, or a Sanctuary for Ladies Justly Protecting Them from the Foule Aspertions and Forged Imputations of Traducing Spirits*, London, Edward Griffin.

Ubaldini, P. (1591). *Le Vite delle donne illustri, del regno d'Inghilterra, e del regno di Scotia*, London.

Vergil, P. (1844). *Polydore Vergil's English History from an Early Translation Preserved among the MSS. of the Old Royal Library in the British Museum, Volume 1*, London, Camden Society. First published 1534.

MODERN WORKS

A Magazine (2002). *A Magazine*, Anglian Railways.

Abrahall, C. H. (1949). *Boadicea: Queen of the Iceni*, London, George G. Harrap.

Akerman, J. Y. (1849). 'On the Condition of Britain from the Decent of Caesar to the Coming of Claudius …', *Archaeologia* 33, 177–90.

Ashwin, T. (1999). 'Studying Iron Age Settlement in Norfolk', in J. Davies and T. Williamson (eds), 100–24.

Ashwin, T. (2000). 'Synthesis', in T. Ashwin and S. Bates, 230–42.

Ashwin, T. and S. Bates *Excavations on the Norwich Southern Bypass, 1989–91: Part i, Excavations at Bixley, Caistor St Edmunds, Trowse, Cringleford and Little Melton*, Ashford, East Anglian Archaeology, no. 91.

Barker, F. (1859). *Boadicea*, Norwich, Jarrold and Son.

Beard, M. and J. Henderson (1995). *Classics: A Very Short Introduction*, Oxford, Oxford University Press.

Beard, M. and J. Henderson (1999). 'Rule(d) Britannia: Displaying Roman Britain in Museums', in N. Merrieman (ed.), *Making Early History in Museums*. Leicester, Leicester University Press, 44–73.

Booth, P. (1996). 'Warwickshire in the Roman Period: A Review of Recent Work', *Transactions of the Birmingham and Warwickshire Archaeological Society*, 100, 25–58.

Bradley, R. (1990). *The Passage of Arms*, Cambridge, Cambridge University Press.

Bradley, R. and K. Gordon (1988). 'Human Skulls from the River Thames, their Dating and Significance', *Antiquity* 62, 503–9.

Branigan, K. (1991). 'Images – or Mirages – of Empire? An Archaeological Approach to the Problem', in L Alexander (ed.), *Images of Empire*, Sheffield, Sheffield Academic Press, 91–106.

Bratton, J. S. (1981). *The Impact of Victorian Children's Fiction*, London, Croom Helm.

Bratton, J. S. (1986). 'Of England, Home and Duty: The Image of England in Victorian and Edwardian Juvenile Fiction', in J. M. Mackenzie (ed.), *Imperialism and Popular Culture*. Manchester, Manchester University Press.

Braund, D. (1996). *Ruling Roman Britain: Kings, Queens, Governors and Emperors from Julius Caesar to Agricola*, London, Routledge.

Brenton, H. (1989). 'Preface', in *Plays, ii, The Romans in Britain, Thirteenth Night, The Genius, Bloody Poetry, Greenland*. London, vii–xvi.

Brigden, S. (2000). *New Worlds, Lost Worlds: The Rise of the Tudors 1485–1603*, London, Penguin.

Bruce, J. C. (1851). *The Roman Wall: A Historical, Topographical and Descriptive Account of the Barrier of the Lower Isthmus*, London, John Russell Smith.

Brunaux, J. (1987). *The Celtic Gauls: Gods, Rites and Sanctuaries*, London, Seaby.

Burnham, B., J. Collis, C. Dobinson, C. Haselgrove and M. Jones (2001). 'Themes for Urban Research: c. 100 BC to AD 200', in S. James and M. Millett (eds), 67–76.

Carroll, K. K. (1979). 'The Date of Boudicca's Rebellion', *Britannia* 10, 197–202.

Chadburn, A. (1992). 'A Preliminary Analysis of the Hoard of Icenian Coins from Field Baulk, March, Cambridgeshire', in M. Mays (ed.), *Celtic Coinage: Britain and Beyond*, Oxford, British Archaeological Reports, British, no. 222, 73–82.

Chadburn, A. (1999). 'Tasking the Iron Age: The Iceni and Minting', in J. Davies and T. Williamson (eds), 173–84.

Church, A. J. (1887). *The Count of the Saxon Shore or the Villa in Vectis: A Tale of the Departure of the Romans from Britain*, London, Seeley and Company.

Church, A. J. (1895). *Stories From English History: From Julius Caesar to the Black Prince*, London, Seeley.

Churchill, W. S. (1956). *A History of the English-Speaking People*, London, Cassell and Company.

Clarke, K. (1999). *Between Geography and History: Hellenistic Constructions of the Roman World*, Oxford, Oxford University Press.

Clarke, K. (2001). 'An Island Nation: Re-Thinking Tacitus' *Agricola*', *Journal of Roman Studies* 91, 94–112.

Collins, E. (1900). 'The Prediction Fulfilled', in M. Trevelyan *Britain's Greatness Foretold: The Story of Boadicea, the British Warrior-Queen*. John Hogg, London.

Crawford, J. (1999). 'Fletcher's *The Tragedie of Bonduca* and the Anxieties of the Masculine Government of James I', *Studies in English Literature, 1500–1900* 39, 357–81.

Creighton, J. (1994). 'A Time of Change: the Iron Age to Roman Monetary Transition in East Anglia', *Oxford Journal of Archaeology* 13, 325–34.

Creighton, J. (2000). *Coins and Power in Late Iron Age Britain*, Cambridge, Cambridge University Press.

Creighton, J. (2001). 'The Iron Age–Roman Transition', in S. James and M. Millett (eds), 4–11.

Crummy, P. (1997). *City of Victory: The Story of Colchester – Britain's First Roman Town*. Colchester, Colchester Archaeological Trust.

Crummy, P. (1999). 'Colchester: Making Towns Out of Fortresses and the First Urban Fortifications in Britain', in H. Hurst (ed.) *The Coloniae of Roman Britain: New Studies and a Review*, Portsmouth, Rhode Island, *Journal of Roman Archaeology*, Supplementary Volume 36, 88–100.

Cunliffe, B. W. (1988). *Greeks, Romans and Barbarians: Spheres of Interaction*, London, Batsford.

Cunliffe, B. W. (1991). *Iron Age Communities in Britain*, London, Routledge and Kegan Paul.

Cunliffe, B. W. (1995). *Iron Age Britain*, London, Batsford/English Heritage.

Cunliffe, B. W. (1998). *Fishbourne Roman Palace*, Stroud, Tempus.

Curti, E., E. Dench and J. Paterson. (1996). 'The Archaeology of Central and Southern Roman Italy: Recent Trends and Approaches', *Journal of Roman Studies* 86, 170–189.

David, D. (1995). *Rule Britannia: Women, Empire and Victorian Writing*, London, Cornell University Press.

David, S. (2002). *The Indian Mutiny, London*, Penguin.

Davies, J. A. (1996). 'Where Eagles Dare: The Iron Age of Norfolk', *Proceedings of the Prehistoric Society* 62, 63–92.

Davies, J. (1999). 'Pattern, Power and Political Progress in Iron Age Norfolk', in J. Davies and T. Williamson (eds), 14–44.

Davies, J. A., T. Gregory, A. Lawson, R. Rickett and A. Rogerson (1992). *The Iron Age Forts of Norfolk*, East Anglian Archaeology 54.

Davies, J. A. and T. Williamson (eds 1999). *Land of the Iceni: The Iron Age in Northern East Anglia*. Norwich, Centre for East Anglian History.

Deary, T. (1994). *The Rotten Romans*, Scholastic Publications, London.

Doughty, C. M. (1906). *The Dawn in Britain*, London, Duckworth.

Drummond-Murray, J. and P. Thompson (2002). *Settlement in Roman Southwark: Archaeological Excavations (1991–8) for the London Underground Limited Jubilee Line Extension Project, London*, Museum of London, MoLAS Monograph 12.

Dudley, D. and G. Webster (1962). *The Rebellion of Boudicca*, London, Routledge.

Dunning, G. C. (1945). 'The Two Fires of Roman London', *Antiquaries Journal* 25, 48–77.

Dyson, S. (1975). 'Native Revolt Patterns in the Roman Empire', *Aufstieg und Niedergang der Römischen Welt* II. 3, 138–75.

Eagleton, T. (1986). 'Editor's Preface', in A. Sinfield (ed.), *Alfred Tennyson*, Oxford, Blackwells.

Edwards, C. (1999). 'Introduction: Shadows and Fragments', in C. Edwards (ed.), *Roman Presences: Receptions of Rome in European Culture, 1789–1945*, Cambridge, Cambridge University Press.

Eldridge, C. C. (1996). *The Imperial Experience from Carlyle to Forster*, London, Macmillan.

Evans, C. (2003) 'Britons and Romans at Chatteris: Investigations at Langwood Farm, Cambridgeshire', *Britannia* 34, 175–264.

Fantham, E. (1996). *Roman Literary Culture: From Cicero to Apuleius*, London, John Hopkins.

Farrell, J. (2001). *Latin Language and Latin Culture*, Cambridge, Cambridge University Press.

Fincham, G. (2001). 'Writing Colonial Conflict, Acknowledging Colonial Weakness', in G. Davies, A. Gardner and K. Lockyear (eds), *TRAC 2000: Proceedings of the Tenth Annual Theoretical Roman Archaeology Conference, London 2000*, Oxford, Oxbow, 25–34.

Finley, M. (1973). *The Ancient Economy*, London.

Fletcher, C. R. L. and R. Kipling (1911). *A School History of England*, Oxford, Clarendon Press.

Fraser, A. (1988). *Boadicea's Chariot: The Warrior Queens*, London, Weidenfield and Nicholson.

Frere, S. S. (1972). *Verulamium Excavations, i, London*, Oxford University Press.

Fulford, M. (2002). 'A Second Start: From the Defeat of Boudicca to the Third Century', in P. Salway (ed.), 39–74.

Grant, M. (1976). *Cities of Vesuvius: Pompeii and Herculaneum*, New York, Harmondsworth.

Grasby, R. D. and Tomlin, R. S. O. (2002). 'The Sepulchral Monument of the Procurator C. Julius Classicianus', *Britannia* 33, 43–76.

Green, P. D. (1982). 'Theme and Structure in Fletcher's *Bonduca*', *Studies in English Literature* 22, 304–16.

Greene, K. (2002). *Archaeology: An Introduction*, Routledge, London.

Greg, W. W. (1951). *Bonduca by John Fletcher*, Oxford, Oxford University Press.

Gregory, T. (1992). *Excavations in Thetford, 1980–1982, Fison Way*, Dereham, Norfolk Museums.

Grew, F. (2001). 'Representing *Londinium*', in G. Davies, A. Gardner and K. Lockyear (ed.), *TRAC 2000: Proceedings of the Tenth Annual Theoretical Roman Archaeology Conference, London 2000*, Oxford, Oxbow, 12–24.

Hackett, H. (1995). *Virgin Mother, Maiden Queen: Elizabeth I and the Cult of the Virgin Mary*, London, Macmillan.

Hamilton, C. (1910). *A Pageant of Great Women*, London, the Suffrage Shop.

Haselgrove, C. C. (1999). 'The Iron Age', in J. Hunter and I. Ralston (eds), *The Archaeology of Britain*, London, Routledge, 114–34.

Haselgrove, C. C. and Millett, M. (1997). 'Verulamion Reconsidered', in A. Gwilt and C. C. Haselgrove (eds), *Reconstructing Iron Age Societies*, Oxford, Oxbow, 282–96.

Haverfield, F. (1914). 'Notes on the Agricola,' *Classical Review*, 28, 43–5.

Hawkes, C. F. C. and M. R. Hull (1947). *Camulodunum: First Report on the Excavations at Colchester 1930–1939*, London, OUP.

Hay, D. (1950). 'Introduction'. *The Anglica Historia of Polydore Vergil*, London, Royal Historical Society, 74, ix–lx.

Helgerson, R. (1992). *Forms of Nationhood: The Elizabethan Writing of England*, London, University of Chicago Press.

Henderson, B. W. (1903). *The Life and Principate of the Emperor Nero*, London, Methuen & Son.

Henderson, K. U. and B. F. McManus (1985). *Half Humankind: Context and Texts of the Controversy about Women in England 1540–1640*, Chicago, University of Illinois Press.

Henty, G. A. (1893). *Beric the Briton: A Story of the Roman Invasion.* Glasgow, Blackie.

Herford Percy, C. H. and E. Simpson (1950). *Ben Jonson, Volume 10*, Oxford, Clarendon Press.

Hessing, W. (2001). 'Foreign Oppressor Versus Civiliser: The Batavian Myth', in R. Hingley (ed.), 126–144.

Hill, J. D. (1995) *Rituals and Rubbish in the Iron Age of Wessex, Oxford*, British Archaeological Reports.

Hill, J. D. (1999). 'Settlement, Landscape and Regionality: Norfolk and Suffolk in the Pre-Roman Iron Age of Britain and Beyond', in J. Davies and T. Williamson (eds), 185–94.

Hill, J. D. (2002). 'Just About the Potter's Wheel? Using, Making and Depositing Middle and Later Iron Age Pots in East Anglia', in A. Woodward and J. D. Hill (eds), *Prehistoric Britain: The Ceramic Basis, Oxford*, Oxbow, 143–60.

Hingley, R. (1998). *Settlement and Sacrifice: The Later Prehistoric Peoples of Scotland*, Edinburgh, Canongate.

Hingley, R. (2000). *Roman Officers and English Gentlemen: The Imperial Origins of Roman Archaeology*, London, Routledge.

Hingley, R. (2001a). 'Images of Rome', in R. Hingley (ed.), 7–22.

Hingley, R. (2001b). 'An Imperial Legacy: The Contribution of Classical Rome to the Character of the English', in R. Hingley (ed.), 145–66.

Hingley, R. (ed. 2001) *Images of Rome: Perceptions of Ancient Rome in Europe and the United States in the Modern Age.* Journal of Roman Archaeology. Supplementary Series No. 44.

Hobbs, R. (2003). *Treasure: Finding our Past*, London, British Museum.

Holman, P. (1999). 'Introduction', in *Purcell, Henry, Ayres for the Theatre (CD)*, London, Hyperion.

Howe, E. (1992). *The First English Actresses: Women and Drama 1660–1700*, Cambridge, Cambridge University Press.

Hoy, C. (1979). 'Textural Introduction: Bonduca', in F. Bowers *The Dramatic Works in the Beaumont and Fletcher Canon*, Cambridge, Cambridge University Press. IV, 149–54.

Hull, M. R. (1928). *The Colchester and Essex Museum Annual Report 1928*, Colchester, The Essex Telegraph.

Hull, M. R. (1930). 'A Roman Tombstone Found in Colchester,' *Transactions of the Essex Archaeological Society* 19, 117–22.

Hull, M. R. (1958). *Roman Colchester*, London, Report of the Research Committee of the Society of Antiquaries of London, Oxford University Press.

Huskinson, J. (2000). 'Looking for Culture, Identity and Power', in J. Huskinson (ed.), 3–28.

Huskinson, J. (2002). 'Culture and Social Relations in the Roman province', in P. Salway (ed.), 107–40.

Huskinson, J. (ed. 2000) *Experiencing Rome: Culture, Identity and Power in the Roman Empire*, London, Routledge.

Hutcheson, N. (forthcoming). 'Torcs, Coins and Horse Equipment: Hoarding across the Landscape of Later Iron Age Norfolk', in C. Haselgrove and T. Moore (eds) *The late Iron Age in Britain and Beyond*, Oxford, Oxbow.

Jackson, R. and T. W. Potter (1996). *Excavations at Stonea, Cambridgeshire 1980–85*, London, British Museum Press.

James, P. (2000). 'The Language of Dissent', in J. Huskinson (ed.), 277–304.

James, S. (2001). '"Romanization" and the People of Britain', in S. Keay and N. Terrenato (ed.) *Italy and the West: Comparative Issues in Romanization*, Oxford, Oxbow, 187–209.

James, S. and M. Millett (eds 2001) *Britains and Romans: Advancing an Archaeological Agenda*, York, Council for British Archaeology, Research Report 125.

James, S. and V. Rigby (1997). *Britain and the Celtic Iron Age*, London, British Museum.

Jenkins, H. (1842). 'Observations on the Site of Camulodunum,' *Archaeologia* 29, 243–56.

Jenkyns, R. (1980). *The Victorians and Ancient Greece*, Oxford, Blackwell.

Jenkyns, R. (1992). 'The Legacy of Rome', in R. Jenkyns (ed.) *The Legacy of Rome: A New Appraisal*, Oxford University Press, Oxford.

Johns, C. (1971). *Arretine and Samian Pottery*, London, British Museum.

Johns, C. (1986) 'The Roman Silver Cups from Hockwold, Norfolk,' *Archaeologia* 108, 2–13.

Johns, C. (1994). 'Romano-British Precious-Metal Hoards', in S. Cottam, D. Dungworth, S. Scott and J. Taylor (eds) *TRAC 94: Proceedings of the Fourth Annual Theoretical Roman Archaeological Conference Durham 1994*, Oxford, Oxbow, 107–17.

Jones, A. (2002) *Roman Birmingham 1: Metchley Roman Forts, Excavations 1963–4, 1967–9 and 1979. Transactions of the Birmingham and Warwickshire Archaeological Society* 105.

Joshel, S. R., M. Malamud, et al. (2001). 'Introduction', in S. R. Joshel, M. Malamud and D. T. McGuire (eds), *Imperial Projections: Ancient Rome in Modern Popular Culture*, London, John Hopkins University Press, 1–22.

Jowitt, C. (2003). 'Colonialism, Politics, and Romanisation in John Fletcher's *Bonduca*,' *Studies in English Literature 1500–1900*, 43, 475–94.

Judd, D. (1996). *Empire: The British Imperial Experience from 1765 to the Present*, London, HarperCollins.

Kennedy, M. (1977). *Introduction to Elgar, E (1897–8) Caractacus*, London, EMI Records.

King, A. (2001). 'Vercingetorix, Asterix and the Gauls', in R. Hingley (ed.), 113–125.

Laurence, R. (1998a). 'Introduction', in R. Laurence and J. Berry (eds) *Cultural Identity in the Roman World*, London, Routledge, 1–9.

Laurence, R. (1998b). 'Territory, Ethnonyms and Geography: The Construction of Identity in Roman Italy', in R. Laurence and J. Berry (eds), *Cultural Identity in the Roman Empire*, London, Routledge, 95–110.

Laurence, R. (2001). 'The Creation of Geography: An Interpretation of Roman Britain', in T. Adams and R. Laurence (eds), *Travel and Geography in the Roman Empire*, London, Routledge, 67–94.

Lawson, A. K. (1986). 'A Fragment of Lifesized Bronze Equine Statuary from Ashill, Norfolk,' *Britannia* 17, 333–9.

Locke, W. (1878). *Stories of the Land We Live In: or England's History in Simple Language*, London, James Nisbit.

Macdonald, G. (1927). 'Notes on Some Fragments of Imperial Statues and of a Statue of Victory,' *Journal of Roman Studies* 14 (1926), 1–16.

Macdonald, S. (1987a). 'Boadicea: Warrior, Mother and Myth', in S. Macdonald, P. Holden and S. Ardener (eds) *Images of Women in Peace and War*, London, Macmillan, 40–61.

Macdonald, S. (1987b). 'Drawing the Lines – Gender, Peace and War: An Introduction', in S. Macdonald, P. Holden and S. Ardener (eds), *Images of Women in Peace and War*, London, Macmillan, 1–25.

MacDougall, H. A. (1982). *Racial Myths in English History*, Hanover, New Hampshire, University Press of New England.

Malim, T. (1992). 'Excavation and Site Management at Stonea Camp,' *Fenland Research* 7, 27–34.

Manning, E. (1982). *Marble and Bronze: The Art and Life of Hamo Thornycroft*, London, Tefoil.

Marshall, H. E. (1905). *Our Island Story: A History of Britain for Boys and Girls*, London, Thoman Nelson.

Martin, E. (1999). 'Suffolk in the Iron Age', in J. Davies and T. Williamson (eds), 45–99.

Martin, R. (1981). *Tacitus*, London, Batsford.

Mattingly, D. (1997). 'Dialogues in Power and Experience in the Roman Empire', in D. Mattingly (ed.) *Dialogues in Roman Imperialism: Power, Discourse and Experience in the Roman Empire.* Journal of Roman Archaeology. Supplementary Series No 23, 7–26.

Maxwell, B. (1928). 'Notes on Charles Hopkins' *Boadicea.*' *Review of English Studies* 4, 79–83.

Mendelson, S. and P. Crawford (1998). *Women in Early Modern England*, Oxford, Oxford University Press.

Merivale, C. (1877). *School History of Rome*, London, Longmans.

Mikalachki, J. (1998). *The Legacy of Boadicea: Gender and Nation in Early Modern England*, London, Routledge.

Millett, M. (1987). 'Boudicca: the First Colchester Pottery Shop and the Dating of Neronian Samian,' *Britannia* 18, 93–124.

Millett, M. (1990). *The Romanization of Britain*, Cambridge, Cambridge University Press.

Millett, M. (1994). 'Treasure: Interpreting Roman hoards', in S. Cottam, D. Dungworth, S. Scott and J. Taylor (eds), *TRAC 94: Proceedings of the Fourth Annual Theoretical Roman Archaeological Conference Durham 1994*, Oxford, Oxbow, 99–106.

Milne, G. (1995). *Roman London*, London, Batsford and English Heritage.

Moatti, C. (1993). *The Search for Ancient Rome*, London, Thames & Hudson.

Montefiore, D. B. (1927). *From a Victorian to a Modern*, London, E. Archer.

Montserrat, D. (2000). 'Reading Gender in the Roman world', in J. Huskinson (ed.), 153–82.

Moser, S. (1998). *Ancestral Images: The Iconography of Human Origins.* Stroud, Sutton.

Museum of London (2000). *Archaeology Matters, 12 (December 2000)*, London, Museum of London.

Museum of London (2001). *Archaeology Matters, 14 (May 2001)*, London, Museum of London.

Neal, D., A. Wardle and J. Hunn (1990). *Excavation of the Iron Age, Roman and Medieval Settlement at Gorhambury, St Albans*, London, English Heritage.

Newey, V. (1982). *Cowper's Poetry: A Critical Study and Reassessment*, Liverpool, Liverpool University Press.

Niblett, R. (1999). *The Excavation of a Ceremonial Site at Folly Lane, Verulamium*, London, Society for the Promotion of Roman Studies.

Niblett, R. (2001). *Verulamium: The Roman City of St Albans*, Stroud, Tempus.

O'Neil, E. (1912). *A Nursery History of England*, London, Nelson.

Ogilvie, R. M. and I. Richmond (1967). 'Introduction', in C. Tacitus *De vita Agricolae*, Oxford, Clarendon Press.

Orgel, S. (1981). *The Jonsonian Masque*, New York, Columbia University Press.

Pastor-Muñoz, M. (2003). *Viriato: A Luta pela Liberdade*, Lisbon, Ésquilo.

Patterson, A. (1994). *Reading Holinshed's Chronicles*, Oxford, University of Chicago Press.

Perring, D. (1991). *Roman London*, London, Seaby.

Piggott, S. (1975). *The Druids*, London, Thames and Hudson.

Piggott, S. (1989). *Ancient Britons and the Antiquarian Imagination*, London, Thames and Hudson.

Porter, R. (1988). *Gibbon, Making History*, London, Phoenix.

Potter, T. W. (2002). 'The Transformation of Britain from 55 BC to AD 61', in P. Salway (ed.), 11–37.

Potter, T. W. and B. Robinson (2000). 'New Roman and Prehistoric Aerial Discoveries at Gradford, Cambridgeshire,' *Antiquity* 74, 31–2.

Read, C. H. (1894). '... the Opening of the Tumulus on Parliament Hill, Hampstead, Known as "Boadicea's Grave"', *Proceedings of the Society of Antiquaries* 15 (1893–1895), 240–5.

Reynolds, D. (1991). *Britannia Overruled: British Policy and World Power in the 20th Century*, Harlow, Longmans.

Ricks, C. (1987a). *The Poems of Tennyson in Three Volumes: Volume II*, London, Longman.

Ricks, C. (1987b). *The Poems of Tennyson in Three Volumes: Volume III*, London, Longman.

Rivet, A. L. F. (1976). *Rudyard Kipling's Roman Britain: Fact or fiction*, Keele, Keele University Library.

Rivet, A. L. F. and C. Smith (1979). *The Place Names of Roman Britain*, London, Routledge.

Robbins, K. (1998). *Great Britain: Identities, Institutions and the Idea of Britishness*, London, Longmans.

Rowsome, P. (2000). *Heart of the City: Roman, Medieval and Modern London Revealed by Archaeology at 1 Poultry*, London, Museum of London.

Salway, P. (ed. 2001) *Short Oxford History of the British Isles: The Roman Era*, Oxford, Oxford University Press.

Samson, J. (ed.) (2001). *The British Empire*, Oxford, Oxford University Press.

Samuel, R. (1998). *Island Stories, Unravelling Britain*, London, Verso.

Schlüter, W. (1999). 'The Battle of the Teutoburg Forest', in J. Creighton and R. J. A. Wilson (eds), *Roman Germany: Studies in Cultural Interaction. Journal of Roman Archaeology*. Supplementary Volume No. 32, 125–59.

Schnapp, A. (1996). *The Discovery of the Past: The Origins of Archaeology*, London, British Museum.

Schofield, J. and Maloney, C. (1998). *Archaeology in the City of London 1907–1991: A Guide to the Records of Excavations by the Museum of London and its Predecessors*, London, Museum of London.

Scott, E. (1998). 'Tales from a Romanist: A Personal View of Archaeology and Equal Opportunities', in C. Forcey, J. Hawthone and R. Witcher (eds), *TRAC 97: Proceedings of the Seventh Annual Theoretical Roman Archaeology Conference, Nottingham 1997*, Oxford, Oxbow, 138–47.

Scott, J. M. (1975). *Boadicea*, London, Constable.

Sealey, P. (1997). *The Boudican Revolt against Rome*, Princes Risborough, Shire.

Seller, W. C. and R. J. Yeatman (1930). *1066 and All That*, London, Arrow.

Sharples, N. *Maiden Castle*, London, Batsford.

Shepherd, S. (1981). *Amazons and Warrior Women: Varieties of Feminism in Seventeenth-Century Drama*. Brighton, Harvester.

Sinfield, A. (1986). *Alfred Tennyson*, Oxford, Blackwells.

Smiles, S. (1994). *The Image of Antiquity: Britain and the Romantic Imagination*, London, Yale University Press.

Spence, L. (1937). *Boadicea: Warrior Queen of the British*, London, Robert Hale.

Stewart, P. (1999). 'The Destruction of Statues in Late Antiquity', in R. Miles (ed.) *Constructing Identities in Late Antiquity*, London, Routledge, 159–89.

Stray, C. (1998). *Classics Transformed: Schools, Universities, and Society in England, 1830–1960*, Oxford, Clarendon Press.

Struck, M. (2001). 'The *Heilige Romische Reich Deutscher Nation* and Herman the German', in R. Hingley (ed.), 91–112.

Sutcliff, R. (1978). *Song for a Dark Queen*, London, Pelham.

Taylor, J. (2000). 'Stonea in its Fenland Context: Moving Beyond an Imperial Estate,' *Journal of Roman Archaeology* 13, 648–58.

Tennyson, A. L. (1905). *Poetical Works of Alfred Lord Tennyson*, London, Macmillian and Co.

Thornycroft, E. (1932). *Bronze and Steel: The Life of Thomas Thornycroft*, Long Compton, 'King's Stone' Press.

Toynbee, J. (1964). *Art in Britain under the Romans*, Oxford, Clarendon Press.

Trevelyan, M. (1900). *Britain's Greatness Foretold: the story of Boadicea, the British Warrior-Queen*, London, John Hogg.

Van Arsdell, R. D. (1989). *Celtic Coinage of Britain*, London, Spink.

Vance, N. (1997). *The Victorians and Ancient Rome*, Oxford, Blackwell.

VCH (1909). *The Victoria History of London*, London, Constable.

Wacher, J. (1995). *The Towns of Roman Britain*, London, Batsford.

Walsh, K. (1992). *The Representation of the Past: Museums and Heritage in the Post-Modern World*, London, Routledge.

Warner, M. (1985). *Monuments and Maidens: The Allegory of the Female Form*, London, Weidenfield and Nicolson.

Watson, B., T. Brigham and T. Dyson (2001), London *Bridge: 2000 Years of a River Crossing. London, Museum of London*, MoLAS Monograph 8.

Webster, G. (1978). *Boudica: The British Revolt Against Rome AD 60*, London, Batsford.

Webster, J. (1999). 'At the End of the World: Druidic and Other Revitalization Movements in Post-Conquest Gaul and Britain,' *Britannia* 30, 1–20.

Wells, P. (1999). *The Barbarian Speaks: How the Conquered Peoples Shaped Roman Europe*, Princeton, Princeton University Press.

Wells, P. (2003). *The Battle that Stopped Rome: Emperor Augustus, Arminius, and the Slaughter of the Legions in the Teutoburg Forest*, London, W. W. Norton.

West, S. (1989). *West Stow, Suffolk: The Prehistoric and Romano-British Occupations*, Bury St Edmunds.

Wheeler, R. E. M. (1930). *London in Roman Times*, London, London Museum.

Wheeler, R. E. M. and T. V. Wheeler (1936). *Verulamium: A Belgic and Two Roman Cities*, London, Report of the Research Committee of the Society of Antiquaries of London, Oxford University Press.

Wilkinson, P. (2000). *What the Romans Did for Us*, London, Boxtree.

Williams, C. (1999a). '"This Frantic Woman": Boadicea and English Neo-Classical Embarrassment', in M. Wyke and M. Biddiss (eds) *The Uses and Abuses of Antiquity*, Bern, Peter Lang, 19–36.

Williams, C. (1999b). The Boadicea Phenomenon: An interview with Carolyn Williams, in *Roman Britain*, Open University Videotape, BBC.

Williams, J. (2000). 'The Silver Coins from East Anglia Attributed to King Prasutagus of the Iceni: A New Reading of the Obverse Inscription,' *Numismatics Chronicle* 160, 276–81.

Woodward, A. (1992). *Shrines and Sacrifices*, London, Batsford.

Index